The Madwoman Can't Speak

A volume in the series

Reading Women Writing

edited by Shari Benstock
Celeste Schenck

The Madwoman Can't Speak

OR WHY INSANITY IS NOT SUBVERSIVE

Marta Caminero-Santangelo

Cornell University Press

ITHACA AND LONDON

First published 1998 by Cornell University Press
First printing, Cornell Paperbacks, 1998

Printed in the United States of America

Librarians: Library of Congress cataloging information appears on the last page of the book.

Cornell University Press strives to use environmentally responsible suppliers and materials to the fullest extent possible in the publishing of its books. Such materials include vegetable-based, low-VOC inks and acid-free papers that are recycled, totally chlorine-free, or partly composed of nonwood fibers.

Cloth printing 10 9 8 7 6 5 4 3 2 1

Paperback printing 10 9 8 7 6 5 4 3 2 1

To Byron,
the partner of my life, work, and words

Contents

Illustrations   ix

Acknowledgments   xi

Introduction: Emerging from the Attic   1

1. Hearing Voices: Authority of Experience and the Asylum
   Accounts   18

2. Manless Women and Psychology in Postwar Culture:
   Three Short Stories   52

3. Multiple Personality and the Postmodern Subject:
   Theorizing Agency   95

4. Out-Hurting the Hurter: Morrison, Madness,
   and the Moynihan Report   126

5. Seeing Difference: Murdering Mothers in Morrison,
   Garcia, and Viramontes   159

Conclusion: Toward Transformation   180

Works Cited   183

Index   191

Illustrations

Figure 1. "The Lunatic Wept" 7

Figure 2. "I Never Knew a Woman Like You" 97

Figure 3. "This Is Your Wife" 99

Acknowledgments

I am indebted to John Carlos Rowe for his guidance at every step in the writing and publication of this manuscript. Thanks also to Brook Thomas and Michael Clark, invariably challenging readers whose comments forced me to test, expand upon, and sometimes rethink the limits of my arguments. My deepest gratitude goes to Jerry Mulderig, for his unflagging faith and encouragement.

Earlier versions of portions of this book appeared in other publications. I thank the editors for permission to include these articles in revised form: "The Madwoman Can't Speak: Post-War Culture, Feminist Criticism, and Welty's 'June Recital,'" in *Tulsa Studies in Women's Literature* 15.1 (Spring 1996): 123–46; "Multiple Personality and the Postmodern Subject: Theorizing Agency," in *Lit: Literature/Interpretation/Theory* 7.3 (April 1996): 63–86, © 1996 OPA (Overseas Publishers Association) Amsterdam B.V.; and "Beyond Otherness: Negotiated Identities and Viramontes' 'The Cariboo Cafe,'" in *Journal of the Short Story in English* (Fall 1996).

Thanks also to AT&T Archives for permission to reproduce the 1957 Bell Telephone advertisement "This Is Your Wife," and to the Advertising Council for permission to reproduce the U.S. Savings Bonds advertisement "The Lunatic Wept."

Special thanks are due to the University of California at Irvine Graduate and Professional Opportunities Program and to Dorothy and Donald Strauss, who funded the writing of this manuscript in its original form; to the DePaul University Research Council and the College of Liberal Arts and Sciences, which funded the revisions to the manuscript and research for Chapter 5; and to Cedric Stines, my dedicated research assistant.

Finally, thanks and love to family and friends—Mom, Dad, Mary Ann, Ralph, Beth, Jerry, Sarah, Jen, and Laura, my long-distance community and support system; and most important, to Byron, whose support is not just closer to home—it *is* home.

M.C.-S.

The Madwoman Can't Speak

Introduction:

Emerging from the Attic

The madwoman has come to stand all but universally in feminist criticism for the elements of subversion and resistance in women's writing. Sandra Gilbert and Susan Gubar's famous reading of Charlotte Brontë's Bertha Rochester as "the *author's* double, an image of her own anxiety and rage" against patriachy (88), popularized the reading of the madwoman as closet (or attic) feminist: madness signified anger and therefore, by extension, protest. The treatment of female madness by feminist literary theorists and critics has been largely unchanged ever since. In its most extreme form, this interpretive model reads madness, whenever it appears in women's texts, as a willed choice and a preferable alternative to sanity for women, "a brave, even noble reaction to [female protagonists'] presence in a world they never made—and do not accept" (Oppenheimer 164). The same fundamental assumption about madness, derived through a different route, has also informed the most influential of French feminist theory. Observing that men, who have historically controlled most of the production of (written) language, have privileged the language of rationality, French feminist theorists such as Hélène Cixous have advocated a language of non-reason for its disruption of oppressive patriarchal thinking and, thus, its enactment of a peculiarly feminine power.[1] The persistence—indeed, the ubiquitousness—of such assumptions in feminist theory prompted the National Women's Studies Association (NWSA) to ask in a 1995 call for papers: "How and why have feminist theorists and artists embraced chaos, madness, and the non-rational as a resistance strategy?" As some critics have begun to observe, however, such a strategy does little to dismantle the dichotomous thinking so criticized

[1] See Baym 203 for a discussion of this point.

by Cixous in *The Newly Born Woman* (*La Jeune Née*); rather, it simply reverses the poles, while apparently duplicating the essentialist thinking
that identifies women with irrationality in the first place.[2] The de facto
result of such a theory is that "women are resigning themselves to silence, and to nonspeech. The speech of the other will then swallow
them up, will speak *for* them, and *instead* of them" (Makward 100).

Surprisingly, however, even feminist thinkers committed to the importance of making women's voices heard continue to fall back on the
madwoman metaphor. Scholars such as Mae Gwendolyn Henderson
and Harryette Mullen, particularly attentive to the ways that African
American women's voices have historically been silenced, have returned again and again to Julia Kristeva's notion of a prelinguistic,
"semiotic" realm to argue for the subversiveness of women's silences,
moans, and howls. Patricia Yaeger, for whom women's speech is a crucial issue, weighs in against the proposition that women's writing is socially or politically radical only if it departs from norms of reasoned
discourse (30). Yet in "choosing new symbols" rather than those of the
French feminists for women's relation to language, Yaeger settles on the
"honey-mad woman," thus continuing to rely on madness as a subversive metaphor, this time for the "vision and liberation [of] the woman
writer" rather than for Gilbert and Gubar's authorial rage (15, 7).

Given that these critics are vitally aware of the importance for
women of making themselves heard within society, not just "outside"
it in some state of pure rejection, we must ask ourselves why "madness" in their formulations? That is to say, what do we gain (or lose) by
yoking utopian conceptions of women's subversive speech to notions
of madness? In order to use madness as a metaphor for the liberatory
potentials of language, feminist critics must utterly unmoor it from its
associations with mental illness as understood and constructed by discourses and practices both medical and popular. But if the connotations carried by the notion of madness must be completely suppressed
in order for such a metaphor to work—if the word must be emptied of
its meanings and provided with an entirely new set of significations (in
fact, an impossibility)—then why use it at all? The figure of the madwoman has become a focal point for perhaps *the* central question of
feminist debate: How can transformation of the sex-gender system and
of ideologies of gender (rather than just "resistance" to them) take
place? Can the symbolic resolution of the madwoman in fictional texts
contribute to such transformations in any way?

It it this set of problems that the NWSA seemed to be hinting at

[2] See, for example, Baym, Jones.

when it followed its question with another: "How does this strategy hold up in the face of the chaos of violence, abuse, battering, rape, political unrest, and discrimination that affects real women's lives?" The juxtaposition of the two questions is provocative, sounding a note of skepticism about the idea of madness as an antidote to violence, abuse, battering, and rape. Yet the characterization of all of these as examples of "chaos" is troubling, neglecting as it does the postmodern insight that battering, rape, and so on are more accurately seen as means of maintaining particular types of "order." Discrimination, as well as all sorts of sexist and racist representation, invariably plays a part in the stabilization of a conservatively organized, hierarchical society. Abuse and battering are means for men to assert power over women, to "keep them in their place," just as racial violence can be seen as a reaction to and defense against the continuing struggle for a more egalitarian, and thus less hierarchically "ordered," society.

The theory that madness is related in some way to the violence of particular types of social order has received much attention from feminists, and while the predominant critical use of the category of madness in readings of literary texts has gone virtually unchallenged, the nature of the relationship between "real-life" madness and social order has been the subject of substantial debate within feminist theoretical circles. Critics such as Hélène Cixous and Carroll Smith-Rosenberg, for example, have suggested that the nineteenth-century hysteric was in fact enacting a protest against the traditional feminine role, while others, including Elaine Showalter and Catherine Clément, counter that such protest was fundamentally ineffective and cost the protester much more than she gained. In a related discussion, Susan Bordo has grouped anorexia nervosa together with hysteria as "pathologies of female 'protest.' " Like hysteria, Bordo observes, anorexia might provide a sense of control for the woman over her appetite and her body, although both conditions are ultimately marked by absolute powerlessness. Thus, female maladies such as hysteria and anorexia "actually function as if in collusion with the cultural conditions that produced them" ("Anorexia Nervosa" 100, 105).

Bordo's comments on anorexia can shed some light on the appeal of female madness in general for much feminist theory and criticism. Perhaps the reason why the madwoman continues to be such an enticing figure is that she offers the illusion of power, although she in fact provides a symbolic resolution whose only outcome must be greater powerlessness. My theoretical starting point is the suggestion that a search for the subversive madwoman in literature not only involves some violent repressions of its own (the lesson of *Jane Eyre* is, after all, that to achieve happiness, Jane must learn to separate herself in all ways from Bertha, to stifle and finally kill the Bertha in her) but also is fundamentally misguided, since the symbolic resolution of the madwoman as an alternative to patriarchy ultimately traps the woman in silence. In other words, the NWSA is right to suggest an underlying similarity between madness and violence; but the similarity lies not in their "chaos" but in their contributions to a dominant order. Madness is ultimately complicit with what Teresa de Lauretis calls "technologies of gender," and provides the illusion of power while locating the mad (non)subject outside any sphere where power can be exerted. Rather than attempting to "rescue" texts by claiming a secretly subversive power, I propose that an ultimately more productive move in feminist literary criticism might be to trace the symbolic rejection of hopelessly disempowering solutions in fictional and nonfictional narratives of madness by women. For although the NWSA has grouped feminist theorists and artists together in its questioning of madness as a resistance strategy, the prioritizing of madness is actually much more common in current feminist theory than in the works of women artists.

This book deals primarily with works by American women in the second half of the twentieth century, since the emergence of madness as a central image and issue in women's literature is a relatively recent phenomenon—a point obscured by critical studies dealing generally with the theme of madness over broad periods of time. Aside from firsthand, autobiographical asylum accounts, of which there are several, one can point to at most a handful of works of this nature in America from the end of the nineteenth century to World War II, including Charlotte Perkins Gilman's short story "The Yellow Wallpaper" and H.D.'s autobiographical novel *HERmione*. But the period after 1945 marked a startling and unprecedented flurry of writing by American women (as, indeed, by women of other English-speaking nations) which focused on this subject—a shift that has persisted. Even *HERmione*, treating the psychological breakdown of the protagonist and written in 1927, was not published until 1981, timing which suggests that its appearance on the market was following a larger trend. Perhaps this current has been for the most part overlooked because, unlike the works of Sylvia Plath or, more recently, Toni Morrison, many of these texts are not recognized as "literary." Or possibly, "forgotten" narratives about women's madness have received virtually no critical attention because they do not fit easily with the theories of feminist critics who would otherwise recover them.

But ignoring noncanonical texts in a thematic study can result in a failure to recognize the specific historical circumstances in which even canonical texts are written, or the particular issues to which they can be seen as responding. For example, Gilbert and Gubar's reading of *Jane Eyre* pays no attention to the way in which Brontë drew on the dominant social conceptions of madness of her own time. Brontë's portrayal of Bertha as subhuman surely offered no critique of the contemporary view of "lunatics . . . as unfeeling brutes, ferocious animals that needed to be kept in check with chains, whips, strait-waistcoats, barred windows, and locked cells" (Showalter 8).[3] And while feminist critics have pointed out the associations of Bertha with female sexuality as a means of arguing for covert protest on Brontë's part, the image of the madwoman as a "voracious, sexualized monster" was a common (not a subversive) one, propagated by influential male doctors: Henry Maudsley described the madwoman as "a raging fury of lust" (82). By treating "madness" as simply another version of the archetype of the "female monster," Gilbert and Gubar ignored *Jane Eyre*'s historical placement and its particular use of contemporary discourses about madness.[4] An understanding of post–World War II women's narratives of madness, then, demands that these texts be dealt with not only thematically but also within a particular historical context. We are forced to seek explanations, first of all, for why madness became and then remained such a compelling image for women writers at precisely this point in time.

The years after World War II marked a dramatic nationwide increase in attention to issues of mental illness. In the decades leading up to the war, the assumption that insanity was incurable had determined approaches to the treatment of the mentally ill; permanent institutionalization was typical (Levine 28). But shortly after the end of the war, the horror of asylum conditions became a cause célèbre. In an "exposé" titled *The Shame of the States*, Albert Deutsch drew on the rhetorical power of the recent images of the Holocaust to make the case that mental hospitals rivaled the Nazi concentration camps, describing "buildings swarming with naked humans herded like cattle and treated with less concern, pervaded by a fetid odor so heavy, so nauseating, that the stench seemed to have almost a physical existence of its own" (42). A 1957 advertisement for U.S. Savings Bonds suggests the far-reaching scope of such representations; the advertisement, captioned "The Lu-

---

[3] This view was, according to Elaine Showalter, undergoing some transformation to a more benign conception of the mad in Brontë's time.

[4] For some further examples of ahistorical readings of madness, see works by Feder, Rigney, and Yalom.

natic Wept," displays an illustration of a sympathetic woman bending over an unkempt, emaciated, chained "lunatic," while copy suggests that mental health reform efforts were prototypically American: "Americans are seldom self-satisfied: they long to do right. That urge has helped them build a strong, stable nation in a troubled world" (Fig. 1). By the mid-1960s, in the company of a growing civil rights movement, the renewed attention to mental illness had launched a wave of impassioned psychiatric reform.[5]

What had happened to spur such a change? Murray Levine argues persuasively that mental health institutions undertook a major reevaluation of their theories and practices because of a specific problem: the potential psychiatric disturbance of the returning veteran (35, 38). But such a point of origin, Levine points out, could not fail to condition many of the questions posed by the reform movement, as well as the answers: "Because so much was concentrated on the returning veteran, largely young and middle-aged males, the development of programs for care and for training of personnel to service other populations (e.g., women, children, the aged) was neglected. The emphasis on the returning veteran led to a whole generation of mental health workers without training or encouragement to service other populations. It was the war and its requirements that defined the mental health problem" (35). The ways in which the issue of "mental health reform" was framed precluded institutional questions about female madness, even though women statistically predominated as patients in virtually all areas of mental health care.[6]

Interest in psychology was not limited to mental health reform circles. Popular culture in the years after the war posited psychiatry and psychology as a new religion, making the doctor into a god with the power to "convert" individuals as well as to redesign the world through manipulation of minds. In the 1950s, psychological methods and theories were applied to everything from the "motivational research" used in advertising to the "psychological warfare" of the cold war (Havemann, "Psychologist's Service" 100–102). In one popular magazine, Ernest Havemann described how "public health officials and organizations like the National Association for Mental Health are helping spread the gospel" of psychiatry ("Where Does Psychology Go

[5] Ironically, by identifying mental health reforms exclusively with Dorothea Dix (1802–87), whose efforts helped to shift treatment of the mentally ill from prisons to mental institutions, the advertisement placed in a safely distant past the need for the very reforms that were currently under way. The caption, "Safe as America—U.S. Savings Bonds," suggests that current treatment of the mentally ill was already completely "safe" and beyond reproach.

[6] See, for example, Warren 25, Ussher 71, Chesler 312.

The Lunatic Wept

ABRAHAM SIMMONS couldn't feel the frost that lined his cage, or taste the swill they fed him, or chafe at his iron chains—so his keepers said. He was a madman.

Then when his visitor, little Miss Dix, spoke softly to him, why did he weep?

Dorothea Lynde Dix knew why. And her knowledge kept her fighting all her life to get the mentally ill away from pits and cages, whips and chains, and into hospitals.

In nearly 40 years, she paused only once —to render heroic service as superintendent of nurses in the Civil War. Then again she began investigating, writing, fundraising, politicking, until this frail. ex-school teacher had pushed a whole country into one of the finest reforms in its history: the sane treatment of the insane.

Dorothea Dix was fortunate in having one powerful ally: the American people. For as history will show, Americans are seldom self-satisfied; they long to do right. That urge has helped them build a strong, stable nation in a troubled world—and it has helped make their country's Savings Bonds a rock-ribbed assurance of security.

The will and purpose of 168 million Americans back U.S. Savings Bonds, back them ·with the best guarantee you could possibly have. Your principal guaranteed safe to any amount—your interest guaranteed sure—by the greatest nation on earth. If you want *real* security, buy U.S. Savings Bonds. And hold on to them.

Safe as America—U. S. Savings Bonds

from Here?" 86). In another, a writer identified only as "one of England's distinguished psychiatrists" compared the treatment of mental illness with methods of religious conversion, suggesting that both ideally resulted in "sudden submission and quite uncritical acceptance of the new beliefs desired by those in charge." Through psychiatry, as through religion, "converts were reindoctrinated . . . and unsatisfactory persons discovered and weeded out after their initial conversion experience" ("Psychiatry and Spiritual Healing" 42–43). The proliferation of psychiatric discourse in the social arena, as a means of social regulation, continued apace in the following decades (Henriques et al. 4–5).

Resisting the ever-widening reach of psychiatry, a host of new, "radical" theories of madness emerged in the 1960s. The antipsychiatry movement was characterized by the work of R. D. Laing, who argued that madness was not the result of an inherited weakness (as the evolutionists had claimed) or of faulty or incomplete development (as Freud had suggested), but rather a "special strategy that a person invents in order to live in an unlivable situation" (*Politics* 115).[7] Focus was thus shifted to the "unlivable situation": the social contexts that determined madness. Labeling theory, a major influence on the antipsychiatry movement, held that a diagnosis of mental illness was simply one possible response to behaviors that violated social expectations. It was the "societal reaction" to the behaviors, rather than any actual medical condition, that was considered to be the determining factor (Scheff 54–55).

Like the mental health reform movement, the antipsychiatry movement failed to consider women explicitly, despite the obvious significance for women of a theory that defined madness in terms of deviation from social expectations. Indeed, those who extolled psychology as a means of socialization (a position antithetical to that of the antipsychiatrists) may well have had women in mind as the subjects most in need of indoctrination. Psychiatric methods, the public was told uncritically, worked best on those "easily molded to current beliefs and behavior," who would grant "final submission" to psychiatry's demands ("Psychiatry and Spiritual Healing" 42). These descriptive tags fit perfectly with conventional images of women as "easily molded" and submissive. Thus, as Barbara Deckard observes, in the 1950s "Freudian psychology, stated in a sophisticated fashion in university classrooms and in crude ways in the popular media, was

---

[7] Although the leading figures identified with this movement were British, the movement itself was, as Elaine Showalter notes (221–22) of international scope and had much influence in America.

used as a major weapon to keep women in their traditional place" (311). Although the leaders of the antipsychiatry movement remained mute on this aspect of psychiatric coercion, they had nonetheless laid the groundwork for an understanding of the connections between psychology as a means of social control and the regulation of gender roles. It remained for women writers to make the connections explicit—and they did, in ever increasing numbers.

While the reform movement ignored the implications of gender for the production, classification, and treatment of madness, then, American women writers in the decades after World War II appropriated the wave of reformist attention to psychiatric practices for their own feminist interests, often producing markedly different results from those offered by the most famous figures of psychiatric reform. The reexamination of the treatment of mental illness and of asylum conditions opened the door for women writers to address, with some degree of popular success, the implications for gender of the discourses and practices surrounding the identification and treatment of madness, and the diffusion of such discourses into everyday assumptions and behaviors on the part of non-"experts"—a significant factor in the period I am examining.

This book asks the question: What have women been saying when they write about madness? I answer it by focusing on narratives that deal explicitly with the issue of female madness, since one of my central concerns is to interrogate the value of madness itself as a metaphor for resistance. For the sake of historical specificity, I have limited myself to texts by American women in the decades since the end of World War II. In unearthing often forgotten and neglected texts that focus on the figure of the madwoman, I discovered that these texts clustered around particular issues—"angles" on madness, we might say—and that these shared foci reflected specific historical concerns that women were responding to through their writing. The texts selected for discussion in this book are representative of those foci, and demonstrate some of the various ways in which women from the mid-1940s to the present have chosen to write about madness.

The fact that so many women authors have written about female madness might suggest that these texts actually participate in the popularized representations of madwomen of their specific historical moments, but such is not the case. I argue that women's texts have strategically occupied the space of existing literary, medical, and popular models of madness—those models offered by popularized psychoanalysis, antipsychiatry, and the sociology of "the black family," to name just a few examples—in order to enact what Teresa de Lauretis calls "a movement from the space represented by/in a representation, by/in a discourse, by/in a sex-gender system, to the space not represented yet implied (unseen) in them." De Lauretis calls the latter space the "space-off," a metaphor drawn from film theory which refers to "the space not visible in the frame but inferable from what the frame makes visible" (26). A crucial component of my discussion is to show how the various texts I am examining have taken up the discursive space produced by dominant medical and psychological as well as literary representations of madness in order to reconfigure that space from within—to reveal the "space-off." For example, Eudora Welty's "June Recital" from her collection *The Golden Apples* (1949), Hortense Calisher's "The Scream on Fifty-Seventh Street" (1962), and Jean Stafford's "Beatrice Trueblood's Story" (1955) all foreground a connection between a female protagonist's madness and her manlessness (through spinsterhood, widowhood, or divorce), at precisely a period when female manlessness was a serious cultural issue sometimes linked explicitly with madness in popular discourse. This period, marked by the feverish postwar pursuit of domesticity and the "traditional" nuclear family, also served as the context for another set of cultural "texts": Shirley Jackson's novel *The Bird's Nest* (1954) was part of a flurry of interest in multiple personality in the 1950s (the film *The Three Faces of Eve* is the most memorable product of this trend) arising just when the idea of multiple feminine roles, such as wife, mother, and professional, had become socially threatening. Autobiographical asylum narratives have been around for almost as long as the asylum itself; but women's "firsthand" accounts of institutionalization after World War II (sometimes autobiographical, sometimes fictional but informed by personal experience) appropriated the renewed attention to mental health reform and the language of radical psychiatry to interrogate the implications of both for women. "Popular" novels such as Mary Jane Ward's *The Snake Pit* (1946) and Joanne Greenberg's *I Never Promised You a Rose Garden* (1964), "literary" novels such as Sylvia Plath's *The Bell Jar* (1963), and explicitly autobiographical testimonies (some popular, some utterly faded into obscurity) such as Ellen Wolfe's *Aftershock: The Story of a Psychotic Episode* (1969), Lara Jefferson's *These Are My Sisters* (1947), Kate Millett's *The Loony-Bin Trip* (1990), Susanna Kaysen's *Girl Interrupted* (1993), and—riding on the wave of interest in Prozac and other personality-altering medications—Elizabeth Wurtzel's *Prozac Nation* (1994) all constitute variations on the genre. Finally, a somewhat more recent trend is suggested by the connection of madness with categories of race and ethnicity in texts by African

American and Latina women. Addressing themselves to persistent stereotypes reflected in popular discourses about "pathology" and other irrational aberrance in marginalized groups, these writers have used the African American or Latina madwoman to suggest the dangers of complicity with an oppressive dominant culture. Toni Morrison is the founding figure of this trend; invoking madness to a degree surpassing that of any other twentieth-century American woman writer, in novels such as The Bluest Eye (1970), Sula (1973), and Beloved (1987), Morrison portrays madness as the ultimate manifestation of cultural self-sabotage. In Morrison's novels, as in Cristina Garcia's Dreaming in Cuban (1992) and Helena María Viramontes's short story "The Cariboo Cafe" (1985), the problems of not being able to recognize and deal with difference are symbolically represented through mothers who, in acts of "madness," attempt to kill their children.

In all of the narratives I examine, the association of madness with femininity is represented as the product of an entire set of discursive practices amounting to what Teresa de Lauretis (following Foucault) would call "technologies" engaged in the production of gendered (as well as racial and/or ethnic) subjectivity. For example, in Welty's "June Recital," the women who are "normal" feminine subjects find that they "never knew what happened to . . . [their] protest" (236), whereas the figure of the female artist—apparently an oxymoron—is expunged from the community through madness. Stafford's community conspires to send Beatrice Trueblood to a "good man" (that is, a psychiatrist) not only for her hysterical deafness but also for her radical repudiation of her engagement when her betrothed will not shut up. The doctor of Jackson's novel The Bird's Nest hopes to "cure" his female patient not by integrating her multiple personalities but by choosing the one that seems to him the most perfectly feminine—that is, the one most perfectly compliant with his own opinions.

Far from embracing the space of madness offered to aberrant women by dominant discourses, however, the women writers I examine generally share the premise that insanity is the final surrender to such discourses, precisely because it is characterized by the (dis)ability to produce meaning—that is, to produce representations recognizable as meaningful within society. (Whereas the authors I discuss counter representation with representation, their madwomen retreat into silence.) Even those authors who write autobiographically of experiences of madness make sharp distinctions between moments of madness and of meaning-making in their lives. Furthermore, the texts for the most part seem to share an interpretation of madness as an illusory self-representation of power that offers an *imaginary* solution to the impasse. As an illusion of power that masks powerlessness, madness is thus the final removal of the madwoman from any field of agency.

Nowhere, perhaps, is there a more vivid example of the strategic occupation of representation in order to reveal its "space-off" than in Jean Rhys's *Wide Sargasso Sea*, which addresses itself to what has turned out to be the paradigmatic image of feminine madness for literary studies: Brontë's Bertha Mason. Although Rhys is not an American author—indeed, it would be difficult to associate her with any national body of literature (she is today most often discussed under the rubric of "postcolonial" writing)—I would be remiss if I did not mention her in this study, given her appropriateness (one might say her examplariness) to my thesis. Missing from the story Brontë's Rochester tells of his first, ill-fated marriage is virtually any hint of historical context; Rhys's revision of *Jane Eyre* makes the scars of colonialism and of slavery in the West Indies central to her narrative, forcing us to attend to what it means for Bertha Mason to have been a white West Indian Creole in the immediate post-emancipation period.

The figure of the madwoman in *Jane Eyre* marks the point of intersection for discourses, implicit in Rochester's account of her, which form around binary poles: reason/madness, civilized/savage, masculine/feminine. Although these binaries seem to capture universal, timeless dichotomies, Rhys's narrative reveals their embeddedness, within Brontë's text, in a particular historical situation: British imperialism. The Algerian-born Cixous—a product, like Rhys, of colonialism—has emphasized the operations of binary thinking in all sorts of oppressive relations:

> I saw how the white (French), superior, plutocratic, civilized world founded its power on the repression of populations who had suddenly become "invisible," like proletarians, immigrant workers, minorities who are not the right "color." Women. Invisible as humans. . . . Thanks to some annihilating dialectical magic. I saw that the great, noble, "advanced" countries established themselves by expelling what was "strange"; excluding it but not dismissing it; enslaving it. A commonplace gesture of History: there have to be *two* races—the masters and the slaves. (Cixous and Clément 70)

If power is relational, then the continued production and maintenance of a single binary relation, through a plethora of discourses that reinscribe the binary, ensure a fairly stable maintanance of power. What Cixous's own observation points out, however, is that this "History" is founded on a fiction, a reduction of all possible positions (proletarians, immigrants, minorities, women) to only two: master or slave, Subject or Other.

This dynamic certainly seems to be operative in *Jane Eyre*. Rochester's peremptory condemnation of his wife, Bertha Mason, is that he "found her nature wholly alien to mine" (291). The term Rochester uses implies much more than a simple matter of incompatible personalities; it is an absolute judgment of moral difference, and marks the first step in his realization that Bertha is, quite straightforwardly, not human. For those things in Bertha's "nature" that are "alien" to Rochester are also the "excesses [that] had prematurely developed the germs of insanity" (292), and so the madwoman loses her title to humanity. From here on Rochester refers to Bertha in nonhuman terms—"monster," "wild beast," "goblin," "thing," "fury" (294–95)—and insists that she has no real claim to the name of "wife": "To tell me that I had already a wife is empty mockery: you know now that I had but a hideous demon" (300). Bertha is presented as subhuman, a beast, invoking a model of madness that had dominated until the end of the eighteenth century; simultaneously she is represented as "uncontrolled sexuality," possibly the "defining symptom of insanity in women" in the nineteenth century (Showalter 8, 74).

Furthermore, while Jane refuses to go as far as Rochester in invalidating his marriage to Bertha, her response embraces his moral distinctions. For her own impulse to be Rochester's wife is corrected by the recognition that she is momentarily, like Bertha, mad: "I will hold to the principles received by me when I was sane, and not mad—as I am now. . . . They have a worth—so I have always believed; and if I cannot believe it now, it is because I am insane—quite insane, with my veins running fire" (302). Insanity and moral principles are antithetical, an idea implied by Victorian descriptions of moral insanity as "a morbid perversion of the . . . moral dispositions" (Prichard, quoted in Carlson and Dain 131). In addition, moral principles are represented as absolutes which cannot be questioned on the basis of a contextual (or cultural) understanding.

Rhys' re-vision of Brontë's text reveals that Rochester's ability to label his wife mad is supported by discourses that construct a binary between Subject and Other, while it underscores this binary's colonialist nature. At the same time, as we shall see, *Wide Sargasso Sea* calls attention to the inescapable contradictions that such a polarity necessarily suppresses, thus destabilizing the grounds on which it is based. The Rochester figure of *Wide Sargasso Sea*, here an unnamed male narrator, regards the West Indian home of his new bride, Antoinette

Cosway, as "a beautiful place—wild, untouched, above all untouched, with an alien, disturbing, secret loveliness" (87). Implicit in his description is the assumption that what is "alien" is by its very nature "disturbing"; his surroundings, while beautiful, are "wild" and "untouched" as opposed to civilized. The narrator's sense of the "alien" is also projected onto Antoinette herself, who has "long, sad, dark alien eyes. Creole of pure English descent she may be, but they are not English or European either" (67). What such musings reveal is that the primary basis of the category "alien" is not moral inferiority on some absolute scale but rather cultural difference: Antoinette strikes her husband as being "not English or European either." Yet for this narrator, as for Brontë's Rochester, that which is alien (both "this place" and Antoinette herself) is an absolute Other; it is everything that he is not. Moreover it is essentially opposed to him: "The feeling of something unknown and hostile was very strong. 'I feel very much a stranger here,' I said. 'I feel that this place is my enemy and on your side' " (129). Antoinette corrects him: "[This place] is not for you and not for me. It has nothing to do with either of us" (130).

If the Rochester figure of Rhys's novel admits his own lack of knowledge about the Other, it is only to justify a project of exploitation and violation, that is, a colonial project: "[The land] kept its secret. I'd find myself thinking, 'What I see is nothing—I want what it hides—that is not nothing' " (87). The narrator's desire to extract meaning from the West Indies is highly conditional. Whatever signification he might discover in his surroundings (or impose upon them) must support his own construction of the world or be destroyed: "I passed an orchid with long sprays of golden-brown flowers. . . . 'They are like you,' I told her. Now I stopped, broke a spray off and trampled it into the mud. This brought me to my senses" (99). The place of the rational subject—he who is "brought to his senses"—is ensured only by the complete subordination of the Other.

While Rhys's Rochester postulates a position of undifferentiated Otherness for all that which is "not English or European either," Antoinette's identity suggests an alternative model of subjectivity, as constituted by a multitude of discourses and practices that position her differentially: "white cockroach. That's me. That's what they call all of us who were here before their own people in Africa sold them to the slave traders. And I've heard English women call us white niggers. So between you I often wonder who I am and where is my country and where do I belong" (102). As Antoinette's childhood nurse, Christophine, tries to explain to the Rochester figure, "She is not *béké* [white] like you, but she is *béké* and not like us either" (155). It is the possibility of an unstable, shifting subject that is so threatening to the Rochester figure. To insist on his own supremacy as a subject and an agent is to insist simultaneously on a simple, stable, and absolute polarity between "Self" and "Other." But the male narrator's construction of reality is exposed as insufficient to account for "the experience of contradictions in subjective positionings" (Henriques et al. 118). There are "blanks in [his] mind that cannot be filled up" (76)—at least, not by him.

The male narrator's inability to comprehend subject positions outside of the dichotomy European/alien converts his own relationship with Antoinette into a colonizing one—ironically so, given that she is herself the descendant of European colonizers and even identifies at times with a European worldview. Again, Christophine's commentary is telling: "She don't come to your house in this place England they tell me about, she don't come to your beautiful house to beg you to marry with her. No, it's you come all the long way to her house—it's you beg her to marry . . . and she give you all she have" (158). And though the male narrator attempts to legitimate his colonial conception of the world by negating the validity of any reality outside his own (the West Indies are "unreal and like a dream"), his perspective is challenged by Antoinette, for whom it is "London [that] is like a cold dark dream" (80–81).

The male narrator-as-colonizer would seem to be a stranger to Brontë's Rochester, but he is not; rather he is what is "not represented yet implied" in the original. For Brontë's Rochester, like his counterpart, insists on his claim to superior culture even as he appears to be repudiating forms of exploitation: "Hiring a mistress is the next worse thing to buying a slave: both are often by nature, and always by position, inferior, and to live familiarly with inferiors is degrading" (296–97). Rochester's rejection of slavery is based not on a condemnation of its legitimizing arguments (e.g., the enslaved are inferior) but on a fear of contamination by those "inferiors." The discourse by which the alien is constructed as culturally and morally inferior can thus be wielded by Brontë's Rochester simultaneously to condemn slavery and to justify his incarceration of his West Indian wife: "I repudiated the contamination of her crimes. . . . Still . . . something of her breath (faugh!) mixed with the air I breathed" (292). Bertha is confined, in other words, in a sort of moral quarantine: Rochester does not wish to be contaminated. This justification, I might add, is not at all problematized within the text; the presumption of corrupt morality, as in the case of moral insanity, is sufficient warrant for incarceration. Thus Rochester explains away his actions with a single, unchallenged, parenthetical statement: "(since the medical men had pronounced her mad, she had, of course, been shut up)" (292). She is "shut up" in another way as well. As Nina Baym observes, "Bertha will never get to tell her own story" (202), and thus Rochester's narrative is presented as a stable, uncontested set of signifiers, reinforcing his own position as rational Western Subject.

Rochester's desire to shut Bertha up is understood by Rhys for what it implies but does not represent: his desire to rob her of the power to represent herself through speech:

> "We won't talk about it now," I said. "Rest tonight."
> "But we must talk about it." Her voice was high and shrill.
> "Only if you promise to be reasonable." (Rhys 129)

The process of Antoinette's silencing is, once again, implicit in the structure of the Brontë text, in which Bertha has been silenced once and for all, not only by Rochester but also by Brontë herself. Rhys's male narrator uses his assumptions about rationality to stop Antoinette's voice; she represents for him the irrational, and as such has no authority to represent herself. The ironic commentary on this position is provided near the end of the novel, when the male narrator demands angrily of his wife, "What right have you to make promises in my name? Or to speak for me at all?" Antoinette replies, "No, I had no right, I am sorry. I don't understand you. I know nothing about you, and I cannot speak for you" (171). While Antoinette acknowledges that she cannot speak for those she does not understand, the male narrator shows no such compunctions. Indeed, his colonizing strategy is to render Antoinette incapable of speaking in her own name: he renames her Bertha.

For readers of *Wide Sargasso Sea* who know *Jane Eyre*, the name Bertha comes highly charged: it is the name of female madness. Madness in *Wide Sargasso Sea* thus marks the woman's capitulation to the narratives of others. The beginning of Antoinette's surrender is marked by her dawning belief that "words are no use, I know that now" (135). Giving up words, she gives up the battlefield to the Rochester figure's representations, which will come to stand as universal. When Antoinette comes, madly, to participate fully in her renaming as Bertha by carrying out the expected ending in which she burns her husband's ancestral home, we cannot help but think of the parrot on fire at the beginning of the novel who falls from the rooftop of another burning house, Antoinette's childhood home, crying in mimicry the words "Qui est là?" (41). For the Antoinette who has been replaced by Bertha, the answer to the question is "nobody." As the Rochester figure recollects, "I saw the hate go out of her eyes. I forced it out. And with the hate her beauty. She was only a ghost. . . . Nothing left but hopelessness" (170). Madness is not rage or even hate but hopelessness—not a challenge to constraining representations but a complete capitulation to them.

As I have tried to argue, Rhys takes up the representational space of *Jane Eyre* in order to expose and critique particular and interrelated historical discourses embedded within that text but disguised by it—discourses of madness and of colonialization. As we shall see, the American narratives of women's madness take up more fully contemporary discourses for similar purposes. Accordingly, in the chapters that follow, my methodology first involves locating these texts in their discursive contexts. I then "read" madness for what it signifies in the narratives, using the analytical framework provided by feminist theory as it elaborates on theories of subjectivity and of ideological production, while grounding this theory in the historical realities of the texts and in the lived experiences of women. (I should add that, as the texts I examine were so often responding to and located within a culture of psychoanalysis, I will at times be invoking psychoanalytic theory as a way of understanding the possible assumptions under which the narratives worked out their symbolic engagements with their social contexts.) I argue that postwar American women's narratives of madness (like *Wide Sargasso Sea*) reject the stance, characteristic of radical psychiatric discourses, that madness is to be celebrated as a complete rupture with constraining traditions and stale conventions. They also mark a distance from the way antipsychiatric thought has been inherited by much recent feminist criticism, from the Gilbert and Gubar school, in which madwomen are subversive rebels expressing their rage, to the feminist version of labeling theory, in which madness is entirely explicable as a category imposed on women in punishment for unfeminine behaviors. Though always sympathetic to the causes that render their female protagonists speechless, the writers, like Brontë, finally must separate themselves from their madwomen, even when those madwomen are their own former selves, although with decidedly different implications from those suggested by Brontë's text.

1

Hearing Voices
Authority of Experience and the Asylum Accounts

I once attended a women's studies conference at which a participant spoke powerfully about her experience of being diagnosed with mental illness and of moving in and out of mental institutions. A self-declared feminist with a strong interest in the continuing antipsychiatry movement, the woman nevertheless had encountered at some level a tension, if not a contradiction, between her political beliefs and commitments and her personal experience with "madness." She described how friends who shared her own feminist and antipsychiatric allegiances criticized her for continuing to take antidepressant medication; such drugs, they told her, signaled complicity with a patriarchal psychiatric establishment which functioned purely in the interests of social normalization and control. These were criticisms she seemed tacitly to understand, if not to accept, and which she answered in terms not theoretical but personal and pragmatic; she noted that when she was depressed, she could not work, write, or—often—even get out of bed.[1]

Although I contend throughout this book that the madwoman cannot speak, women who have been viewed as "mad," and been institutionalized for it, have spoken—if not at the time, then certainly after the fact. And, given the premise that women's voices have historically been silenced in a male-dominated society which has defined madness in particular ideologically oppressive ways, it is surely of the utmost importance from a feminist point of view to listen to what women who have experienced madness have to say about it. How, in other words,

[1] "Feminist Dialogues across Disciplines: Students and Teachers Learning Together," Fourth Annual Southern California Women's Studies Conference, Irvine, Calif., April 30, 1994.

are feminist critics and scholars to respond to the testimony of women—like the speaker at the conference—who tell us that they are helped by antidepressants to be functioning human beings? Is it "all in their heads"?

Not all testimony, of course, comes in such direct form. While some women, particularly in recent years, have written autobiographies of madness and institutionalization (a fact possibly indicative of a growing social tolerance for episodes of "madness"), others have chosen to write fictional narratives on this nexus of experiences, or at least in some cases to present them as fictional, even though—or perhaps because—they themselves had personally confronted that nexus. The different generic choices made by women who have been institutionalized and then have written about it forces us to attend to what the *form* of the madness narrative might be telling us. It is possible, for example, that "fictional" texts such as *The Snake Pit* by Mary Jane Ward, *The Bell Jar* by Sylvia Plath, and *I Never Promised You a Rose Garden* by Joanne Greenberg, all of which at some point have been called "autobiographical novels," grant the authors a greater distance from their mad protagonists. After all, the distinguishing feature of autobiography is arguably not, as has been traditionally asserted, that it is more "accurate" in terms of some externally verifiable set of "facts"—a position that has been increasingly discredited—but rather that it is an act of self-presentation, however "accurate" or "verifiable" its "facts," in a way that a novel, even an "autobiographical" one, is not.[2] Thus authors who choose to write narratives closely corresponding to their personal lives but to present those narratives as fiction have chosen not to present *themselves* as the former madwomen of their narratives. And the more "fictional" an account seems—the more it does not correspond to the verifiable "facts" of the author's own life—the greater that distance becomes.

Yet distancing maneuvers are hardly absent even from the more explicitly "autobiographical" narratives of madness. Ellen Wolfe's *Aftershock* focuses entirely on the recovery period after the author's "psychotic episode." In *These Are My Sisters*, Lara Jefferson defines the act of writing her narrative as a strategy to stave off madness: so long as she is writing, she is not fully mad. Both Susanna Kaysen's *Girl, Interrupted* and Elizabeth Wurtzel's *Prozac Nation* end with the protago-

[2] On the "traditional" standard of objective (verifiable) truthtelling in autobiography, as well as on the discrediting of this claim, see works by Gilmore, Wong, Adams, and Eakin. On the subject of autobiography as self-presentation, Eakin writes: "One could conflate autobiography with other forms of fiction only by willfully ignoring the autobiographer's explicit posture *as autobiographer* in the text" (4).

nist "cured." (The last page of *Girl, Interrupted* is a reproduced medical record with the word "recovered" stamped under the line "Outcome with Regard to Mental Disorder" [169].) Kate Millett denies her madness altogether in *The Loony-Bin Trip*.

Although generic form does matter in this discussion as an artistic and/or personal choice that these women have made, the broader issue of factuality and verifiability that has traditionally differentiated autobiography from fiction is less pertinent here. In neither the discussion of autobiographies nor the treatment of novels that follows in this chapter am I concerned with whether the events depicted "actually happened" to the authors. We can now take as a given that even the narrators of autobiographies are creatively constructed personas, the products of deliberate artistic choices.[3] Since all artistic choices—both "fictional" and "autobiographical" ones—are conditioned by the author's own social and historical experiences, and thus by her own perspective, I posit a potential commonality between "fictional" and "autobiographical" narratives of madness and institutionalization by authors who have behind them the "authority" of personal experience in these matters. In all cases the authors are presenting perspectives on these issues which must of necessity be heavily informed by their own experiences. It is precisely their perspectives, as revealed through their artistic choices, that I wish to make the focus of this chapter. What, in other words, do these women have to say about madness and incarceration, having been through the experience themselves? I propose that we attempt to listen to these "madwomen's" voices so that we may keep them in mind when we theorize about madness.

The prominent Marxist critic Richard Ohmann has suggested that the "illness story" proliferated in American literature from 1960 to 1975, and that this genre, focusing as it did on a single individual's psychological "illness," was profoundly apolitical: "For the people who wrote, read, promoted, and preserved fiction, social contradictions were easily displaced into images of personal illness.... Through the story of mental disorientation or derangement, then, these novels transform deep social contradictions into a dynamic of personal crisis, a sense of there being no comfortable place in the world for the private self" (212, 217). Ohmann's explanation for the outpouring of personal accounts of mental illness in the second half of the twentieth century is a compelling one. He suggests that these stories reflected a shifting national perspective which, some have hypothesized, had its origins in

---

[3] See, for example, Eakin 3.

the post-World War II period. In her 1963 bestseller *The Feminine Mystique*, Betty Friedan proposed that "after the war, Freudian psychology became much more than a science of human behavior. . . . It provided a convenient escape from the atom bomb, McCarthy. . . . It gave us permission to suppress the troubling questions of the larger world" (115). (I will return to this claim in later chapters.) Marilyn Yalom agrees with Ohmann that later twentieth-century accounts of mental illness, specifically by women, are primarily personal rather than political: "The 'dischords' of poverty and deprivation, the wounds of class and race, the brutalities of war and violence. . . . However true and however horrible, these are not the dominant chords one hears when listening to the combined voices of women writing about madness in the second half of the twentieth century" (105). And according to the editors of *Women of the Asylum*, women who wrote about their experiences of institutionalization were increasingly concerned, as the century progressed, "with their personal experiences of asylum care and not with the broader issues of reform" (Geller and Harris 263).

Yet the asylum narratives have also been read as part of the larger movement of mental health care reform which I discussed in my introduction, and thus as decidedly political, raising questions about the reasons for this widely diverging reception. Phyllis Chesler, author of *Women and Madness*, a pioneering study that examined mental health diagnoses and treatment specifically with an eye to gender issues, writes in her foreword to *Women of the Asylum* that the defining characteristic of this collection is the power of the narratives to speak on issues beyond the purely personal: "They [the women's accounts] bear witness to what was done to them—and to those less fortunate than themselves, who did not survive the brutal beatings, near drownings, and force-feedings, the body restraints, the long periods in their own filth and in solitary confinement, the absence of kindness or reason, which passed for 'treatment'" (Geller and Harris xiii). Mary Jane Ward's bestselling novel *The Snake Pit* (which is excerpted in *Women of the Asylum*) was converted into a film precisely on the basis of its "exposé of dehumanizing and overcrowded conditions in the nation's mental hospitals"; connections were drawn to Albert Deutsch's *Shame of the States*, which compared mental institutions to concentration camps (Fishbein 136–37). A reading of *The Snake Pit* confirms the novel's concern with asylum reform. The protagonist, Virginia, imagines writing a book about her asylum experiences (an analogue, perhaps, to Ward's writing of *The Snake Pit*), and then projects the response of a skeptical reader regarding the institutionalized "mad": "They have a good roof over their heads and they don't have to worry about where the next meal is coming from or who's going to pay the gas bill. I'd say it is an ideal existence and here you've gone and made it sound perfectly icky. Why, I've always said if anything ever happened to one of my family . . . I would put him into an institution right off the bat and my heavens if I believed your book I'd hesitate" (105). Embedded in the imaginary reader's obtuseness lies a glaring metafictional signpost: Ward's novel, like Virginia's projected autobiography, is meant to be a critique of asylum conditions which will actually change public perceptions.

But even further, *The Snake Pit* and subsequent autobiographically informed accounts of madness indict institutionalized forms of treatment of mental illness in general, rather than just localized asylum conditions, viewing such treatments within a much larger system of social control—one that includes, for example, public executions. In this sense, the accounts are clearly located within, and are an active part of, a growing international trend toward understanding psychiatric practices as an encoder and enforcer of social norms, a view that would become widely popularized with the advent of antipsychiatry in the 1960s and would become prominent in critical discourse on madness with the publication of Michel Foucault's *Madness and Civilization* (Showalter 221–22).

In *The Snake Pit* a vague understanding of the connection between social control and electroshock treatment slowly dawns on Virginia: "They were going to electrocute her. . . . What had you done? You wouldn't have killed anyone and what other crime is there which exacts so severe a penalty? Could they electrocute you for having voted for Norman Thomas? Many people had said the country was going to come to that sort of dictatorship but you hadn't believed it would ever reach this extreme. . . . If I say I demand a lawyer they have to do something. It has to do with habeas corpus, something in the Constitution" (43). Virginia's imagined scenario—in which aberrant behavior is equated to unpopular political beliefs, and both are punishable by electrocution—is presented as ludicrous; it is clearly a caricature, with features exaggerated to make a point. By the 1950s, the perceived threat posed to American society by those with unpopular political positions, such as communist leanings, had taken on ever-greater proportions. The opening sentence of *The Bell Jar* establishes the time of the novel's setting as "the summer they electrocuted the Rosenbergs" (1). Plath's protagonist, Esther, recalls that after her first experience with electroshock, "I wondered what terrible thing it was that I had done" (118). The comparison, no longer presented as a caricature, marks Plath's critique of electroshock as a means of ideological control on a par with political execution.

Electroshock has had gendered political implications as well, as Elaine Showalter (citing Peter Breggin) observes: "Women more often receive this treatment because they 'are judged to have less need of their brains.' Much psychiatric literature on ECT, [Breggin] maintains, recommends it for the less-skilled persons whose livelihoods are not dependent on the use of memory and intellect; housewives can be seen as excellent candidates on these terms" (207).[4] In Ellen Wolfe's *Aftershock*, electroshock is portrayed as a punishment for a particularly gendered "crime," that of abortion:

> I used a knife during a storm. I stretched out on a table and parted my legs and said to the doctor, "Cut!"
> He cut, and two minutes or two months later—what does it matter?—lightning struck.
> Another man fastened electrodes to my forehead: cold metal plates. Lightning struck: my body twitched with convulsions. (195–96)

For "killing" her unborn child, Wolfe herself has been metaphorically executed; as Showalter comments in her discussion of *The Bell Jar*, "political dissidence and sexual dissidence both will be punished electrically" (218).

Repeatedly the asylum narratives respond to coercive medical, social, and political practices in terms not of a "private self" but of a more collective protest: the "I" turns into a "we." Virginia emerges from shock treatment wanting to make a speech: "Ladies! Now is our chance to organize. Unless we organize we are lost. Are we going to continue to accept this oppression? United we have great strength. . . . [D]o we not owe it to those who will come after us" (Ward 48). In *The Bell Jar*, when Esther realizes, after losing her virginity, that she is bleeding, "the stories of blood-stained bridal sheets and capsules of red ink bestowed on already deflowered brides floated back to me. . . . I smiled into the dark. I felt part of a great tradition" (187). Esther's sense of physical vulnerability impels her to recognize her connection to women throughout history who have been similarly vulnerable, and to conceive of a solidarity based on an undercover resistance: "capsules of red ink" are a stratagem meant to disguise a woman's violation of the social requirement of virginity. Kate Millett, forcibly incar-

---

[4] Showalter cites Peter R. Breggin, *Electroshock: Its Brain-Disabling Effects* (New York: Springer Publishing, 1979), 8, 126–27.

cerated in a mental institution in Ireland and heavily medicated against her will, responds with a hallucinatory sense of "the pull to be solid with the oppressed, the moral imperative toward solidarity" (238). She writes: "And you dream of witches by the fire, uprisings, the whole gang of us building the fire high and higher and defying the doctors and nurses and the nuns, even the Pope. An insurrection of the mad, the wretched of the earth in an incendiary fervor" (235).

Significantly, when real hope finally comes for Millett, in the form of a friend who has managed to enter the asylum illegally to find her (amazingly, Millett has "disappeared" to the outside world; her location is concealed and lied about even by her own lawyer), Millett's immediate, dazed response is to continue spinning out a fantasy of witchlike resistance: "We are all witches here, D'arcy. . . . You should meet the others, the rest of us—they'd love you. We could build the fire high; you could spend the night" (235). The reason why such passages in both *The Snake Pit* and *The Loony-Bin Trip* are after all comical is that the "mad" cannot organize. Millett muses, "If they could talk, their stories of how they got here . . . " (247), implicitly recognizing that most of them cannot talk, and that she will thus need to speak for them: "If you get out, what of the others? How do you help them, how do you change these places? [T]hose who slide through . . . never want to discuss it, even to think about it. . . . So—when you leave them all behind—then what? I'll tell, somehow I'll tell about it" (247–48). While all the asylum narratives describe alliances, friendships, and sacrifices for others among inmates, they also all ultimately point toward the impossibility of political solidarity among the mad. The civil rights of the mentally ill require, more than any other civil rights movement, representation of those who cannot speak for themselves by those who remember what such speechlessness was like. This point goes a long way toward explaining why texts with such a clear political agenda are repeatedly criticized as being "too personal."

Something more is at stake, however, in the debate over the "personal" versus the "political" content of madness narratives: the politics of silencing the woman's voice in the name of objective reason. Much of the asylum literature of the late twentieth century constitutes a protest against "objective" dismissals of the "madwoman's" perspective. *The Snake Pit* opens with an exchange between doctor and patient:

> "Do you hear voices?" he asked.
> You think I am deaf? "Of course," she said. "I hear yours."
> . . . Now he was explaining that she misunderstood. . . . He was speak-

ing, he said, of voices that were not real and yet they were voices he expected her to hear. He seemed determined that she should hear them. (3)

In the process of projecting expected symptoms onto Virginia which he can then "read" as psychosis, the doctor makes irrelevant Virginia's subjective experience of her illness and thus renders Virginia herself mute; as she comments later, "He [is] always talking about hearing voices and never hearing mine" (43).

In this early interview Virginia attempts to establish the legitimacy of her viewpoint by turning the tables on the doctor, so that it is he who is made to seem irrational. Virginia is not supposed to "count" the empirical evidence of the sound of his own voice in answering his question, and yet he expects her to hear sounds that are not there. In her response to the doctor's questions, then, Virginia invokes the standard of rationality (the empirical evidence of our senses) even as she mocks its representative. But the critique of authorized perspectives on mental illness in *The Snake Pit* is inscribed in Virginia's less fully "rational" moments as well. Having temporarily forgotten the circumstances of her confinement, Virginia fantasizes that she is doing research for a novel: "Virginia knew where she was. It was some sort of training school for underprivileged and delinquent girls and she had come to study Conditions. I must be doing a novel with Social Significance. All these new friends of ours always pestering me about why don't I write something that has Social Significance" (24–25). Shortly she modifies her supposed subject matter: "Criminals? That is it. The key. The locked door. . . . One of our friends has roped me into doing a prison novel. . . . But I will not go through with it. . . . There will be a special notation after my name: writer, here to observe" (26–27). Virginia's elaborately constructed explanation for her surroundings is of course a means of gaining a psychological distance from them, as represented by the distance of the objective, outside observer from her subject matter. Her obvious reluctance to write the novel of "Social Significance" comes not from her unwillingness to take up this expected stance but from the pain of her underlying recognition that she bears a more personal relationship to her surroundings. The ironic, metafictional commentary, however, is precisely on a notion of "objectivity" that would exclude and even silence the perspective of personal experience.

In fact, we learn that Virginia has previously taken up the objective stance of the researcher:

Once Virginia wrote a short novel about a man who had a nervous breakdown and after she had finished the book she thought it might be a good idea to read up on the subject. She really hadn't thought of this herself. Someone had said how in the world would you know anything about such a subject and did you do an awful lot of research. . . . She read maybe a dozen books on the subject. . . . Her hero's breakdown was artistic and private . . . and of course, broken-down, [he] was a far more attractive person than he had been before. It was a romantic book. She knew this when she was writing it. What she did not know until she came to Juniper Hill was that the dozen scholarly volumes she had read on the subject were also very romantic. (69–70)

Neither Virginia nor the authors of "scholarly volumes" apparently bothered to ask the inhabitants of asylums or the mentally ill about their experiences. Similarly, critics of *The Bell Jar* have often assumed that a personal perspective on madness is not valuable because it is not trustworthy in terms of facts. How, after all, can we take a madwoman's explanation of her experience at face value? Thus, one early critic laments, "As Esther Greenwood breaks down, the tone becomes more personal, and I don't think these later sections are completely successful" (Wall 100). More recently, Linda Wagner-Martin has suggested that "the reader . . . is asked to create what a more objective telling of the experiences might be. . . . Plath's text shows clearly . . . that the reader does not need to accept Esther's view of her experience" (74). Ironically, Wagner-Martin herself observes in another context that "no one will listen to Esther, no matter how clearly she speaks. Various doctors, her mother, and friends persist in translating what she is literally saying . . . into words acceptable to them" (42). *The Bell Jar*, like *The Snake Pit*, suggests that we must listen attentively to the madwoman's account for what it tells us about self and world. The personal *is* political, and its silencing by whatever means—including through theory and criticism which obscure the personal point of view—is a political act.

In *The Bell Jar*, Esther (like Virginia) tells of repeated attempts to adopt the clearly privileged stance of the distanced and detached observer. She explains in those terms her desire to tag along with her friend Doreen and Doreen's newly acquired (and quite sleazy) "date" to his apartment:

I wanted to see as much as I could.
I liked looking on at other people in crucial situations. If there was a road accident or a street fight or a baby pickled in a laboratory jar for me to look at, I'd stop and look so hard I never forgot it.
I certainly learned a lot of things I never would have learned otherwise

this way, and even when they surprised me or made me sick I never let
on, but pretended that's the way I knew things were all the time. (10–11)

Subsequently she says of Doreen herself that "I decided I would watch
her and listen to what she said, but deep down I would have nothing
at all to do with her" (19). Stan Smith has astutely observed, however,
that Plath "subvert[s] the whole disinterested stance" in the novel, and
that such detachment in fact signals a "schizoid" distancing from experience, reflecting "a world that dismisses that experience as mere delu-
sion" (36–37). This reading suggests that insistence on a "disinterested
stance" not only silences Esther's perspective, but is in fact one cause
of Esther's illness. Buddy Willard, Esther's onetime boyfriend, is
clearly the representative of a world that places a premium on objectivity and is contemptuous of other forms of experience. Esther tells us: "I
spent a lot of time having imaginary conversations with Buddy
Willard. He was . . . very scientific, so he could always prove things.
When I was with him I had to work to keep my head above water"
(46). In those imagined conversations, Esther does not adopt the distanced position she maintains elsewhere; she insists, after the fact, on
the validity of her own point of view, so that when Buddy calls a poem
a "piece of dust," she answers him in her mind: "So are the cadavers
you cut up. So are the people you think you're curing. They're dust as
dust as dust. I reckon a good poem lasts a whole lot longer than a hundred of those people put together" (46).

Susanna Kaysen, in her autobiography *Girl, Interrupted*, is particularly determined to establish for readers the legitimacy of her personal
perspective over seemingly "objective" criteria. Kaysen claims that she
was admitted to a mental institution by a doctor she had never seen
before, after a twenty-minute interview. But the doctor maintains, in a
memo to the hospital (photographically reproduced in the text), that
the interview lasted more than three hours. Despite "hard evidence"—
a nurse's report listing time of admission—which seems to support the
doctor's memo, Kaysen insists: "I still think I'm right. I'm right about
what counts. But now you believe him." Kaysen recognizes that what
"counts" for her (the doctor did not talk to her sufficiently to make an
informed judgment about her state of mind) might not "count" in the
same way for a reader for whom she has already been stigmatized by
the label of insanity and condemned by "official" admitting docu-
ments. For that reader, the vast discrepancy between her account and
the doctor's will only serve as proof of the diagnosis by which she was
admitted to the hospital to begin with. But Kaysen insists on making
her point of view "count" with us, too: "Don't be so quick. I have more

evidence," she says, and produces an admission note written by another doctor, before the nurse's admitting report. From a revised recon-
struction based on the new, earlier time of admission, she "proves" her
claim correct after all. Recognizing that only such "objective" criteria
will allow us to be convinced of the "truth" of the perspective she herself trusted all along, she notes cynically, "Now you believe me"
(71–72). For Kaysen, as for Ward and Plath, part of the political project
is to insist on the authority of the personal and subjective, even while
at times strategically employing institutionally and socially sanctioned
criteria of objectivity to make us, as readers, listen to her voice.

Women's asylum accounts are centrally located within a feminist politics which attempts to rescue the hitherto unheard voice of the woman
and restore it to view in the larger debates about mental health care.
Yet, ironically, these voices have occasionally continued to be silenced
by exactly those people with the greatest commitment to hearing them.
For in telling their own stories, asylum authors often present challenges to positions in which feminist critics—in many cases strongly
influenced by the antipsychiatry movement and its critique—are heavily invested. For example, it has been generally accepted among recent
feminist theorists of madness that lesbianism, as one of the behaviors
that deviate from the socially acceptable feminine role, will often be labeled madness. Indeed, in *The Loony-Bin Trip*, Kate Millett cites two
separate incidents in which lesbianism earns the "diagnosis" of mental
illness. But in *The Bell Jar*, Joan's lesbianism is hardly provocation for a
psychiatric label of madness; indeed, in Esther's discussion with Dr.
Nolan on the subject, Nolan seems to accept lesbianism. It is, in other
words, virtually impossible to read Joan's lesbianism in connection
with society's condemnation of a woman's sexual difference. In order
to link Joan's lesbianism with feminist imperatives, critics must reach a
bit further; consequently Elaine Showalter argues that, because "Joan,
the lesbian who is Esther's alter ego in the novel, kills herself[,]
Esther's graduation from the asylum . . . comes at the price of her feminist double's death" (218). But the equation of lesbianism with feminism in this reading is again problematic; Joan certainly poses no very
strong challenge to the social organization of gender. Her role model is
Mrs. Willard (178), who is characterized by sayings such as "What a
man wants is a mate and what a woman wants is infinite security," and
"What a man is is an arrow into the future and what a woman is is the
place the arrow shoots off from" (58).

Joan is, in this sense, more nearly Esther's double than Showalter acknowledges. Esther rejects the conventional role for women when it conflicts with her ambition to be an artist; so does Joan, but for different reasons. Yet Esther continues to be attracted to traditional conceptions of femininity; and Joan, too, finds herself longing for the idealized 1950s image of family, which she projects onto the Willards: "I loved them. They were so nice, so happy, nothing like my parents" (178). Joan's suicide represents not the killing off of the feminist "part" of Esther, but a reflection of the death that Esther herself has sought as a possible escape from the paralyzing tensions of these conflicting imperatives. Perhaps we can read Joan's eventual suicide as a signal that those tensions were even greater for the woman who dared to stray from the only permissible model of female sexual desire at the time, but we need not read it as a commentary on Esther's feminism. Nor ought we to view Esther as somehow "unfeminist" because she manages to shake off madness and live, while Joan dies.

An even more recalcitrant textual detail in The Bell Jar for several feminist critics has to do with the eventual role of electroshock in alleviating Esther's suffering. Both Phyllis Chesler and Elaine Showalter, in their landmark studies on gender and madness (Women and Madness and The Female Malady, respectively), regard electroshock as inherently patriarchal. Thus, in her overview of The Bell Jar, Chesler cites Esther's first response to electroshock at the hands of the male Dr. Gordon—"I wondered what terrible thing it was that I had done" (Plath 118)—and observes that this punishment metaphor is "Plath's description of this treatment of choice for 'manic-depressives,' most of whom are women" (Chesler 14). But Chesler does not discuss the electroshock treatment subsequently administered by the female Dr. Nolan, or its beneficial effects for Esther. Showalter attempts to argue for an extended symbolic linkage of electroshock with male oppression: "ECT has the trappings of a powerful religious ritual, conducted by a priestly masculine figure. . . . [Electroshock is] painful and controlled by men. . . . When a man first touches Esther's hair, 'a little electric shock' flares through her" (217–18).[5] A feminism informed by Foucauldian and antipsychiatric analyses of the treatment of madness often tends to understand electroshock as part of the larger technologies of gender, and certainly at least some of the asylum accounts support this view. But to accept this model as a given preempts any discussion of other possible functions of electroshock suggested by the asylum accounts. Esther's more positive representations of elec-

[5] For another feminist reading of electroshock in The Bell Jar, see Wagner-Martin 60.

troshock, as we shall see, do not fit so comfortably with Showalter's thesis that "women's accounts of institutionalization and treatment reflect their powerlessness in patriarchal institutions" (219).

Far from severing Esther from her feminist consciousness, as Showalter claims, electroshock seems to enable her to act out her resistance to expectations of "appropriate" feminine roles such as virginity and motherhood. Esther recalls preparing to receive ECT: "Miss Huey *helped me climb up* and lie down on my back" (175; emphasis added); at the end of the next chapter, Esther is being fitted for a diaphragm: "I *climbed up* on the examination table, thinking: 'I am climbing to freedom, freedom from fear, freedom from marrying the wrong person, like Buddy Willard, just because of sex, freedom from the Florence Crittenden Homes where all the poor girls go who should have been fitted out like me' " (182; emphasis added). The climbing up in the first scene in some sense makes possible the more active, and more overtly feminist, climbing up in the second; Esther has not rejected her womanhood but has somehow laid claim to control over it through electroshock: "I was my own woman" (182).

Esther's description of her state of mind after the successful electroshock treatment immediately reveals why feminist critics almost universally avoid any mention of these scenes: "All the heat and fear purged itself. I felt surprisingly at peace. The bell jar hung, suspended, a few feet above my head. I was open to the circulating air. . . . I tried to think what I had loved knives for, but my mind slipped from the noose of the thought" (176). The "bell jar" is of course the image through which Plath conveys the heart of madness, as experienced by the madwoman herself: "To the person in the bell jar, blank and stopped as a dead baby, the world itself is the bad dream" (193). The madwoman is "stopped," has become an object rather than a subject and agent. And though the passive voice suggests that the stopping has been achieved through some external force, the "noose" of Esther's suicidal thoughts suggests the degree to which the madwoman has come to participate in her own "stopping." The passage describing Esther's reaction to electroshock suggests recovery—at least of a sort—according to this internal (as opposed to social or medical) assessment of madness.

There is nevertheless something about electroshock that remains troubling. The terms in which Plath describes the actual experience of ECT, even the second time around, are unsettling: "Darkness wiped me out like chalk on a blackboard" (175). Chalk here recalls snow, as in Esther's portrait of Valerie, a lobotomized fellow patient with a "calm, snow-maiden face behind which so little, bad or good, could happen" (196). Remembering unhappy moments from her own history, Esther thinks to herself: "Maybe forgetfulness, like a kind of snow, should numb and cover them. But they were part of me. They were my landscape" (194). Perhaps electroshock can lift the bell jar only by "wiping out" a part of Esther herself, her memories; perhaps electroshock provides peace in exchange for "forgetfulness." These connections are tenuous at best in *The Bell Jar*, however, and the tension they produce is never overtly resolved. Esther seems to have reached the point, by the end of the novel, at which she can lay claim to the uglier aspects of her landscape while holding off the bell jar's descent. She never renounces the second set of electroshock treatments, and their position in the text strongly suggests a contribution to her ultimate recovery. We might prefer Esther to reject the respite of even a temporary numbness; we might wish her to go down fighting to her death, like McMurphy in Ken Kesey's *One Flew Over the Cuckoo's Nest*, a novel strongly influenced by antipsychiatry's equation of psychiatric treatment with social control and regulation.[6] How can a treatment with such ominous implications—even within the totality of Esther's own telling—aid in her recovery? The temptation to dismiss such a recovery as unacceptable to a radical politics is great.

As it turns out, we repeatedly find in the autobiographical narratives—even those that are most overtly "exposés" of asylum conditions and care—examples of highly questionable "treatments" which nevertheless offer the madwoman some relief. In *I Never Promised You a Rose Garden*, the cold-sheet pack is depicted as a form of torture: Deborah, the protagonist, finds herself "lying on a bed with an icy wet sheet stretched under her bare body. . . . Then came restraints, tightening, forcing her breath out, and punching her deep into the bed. She did not stay for the completion of whatever was being done" (57). And yet, facing a breaking wave of terror and madness, Deborah actually requests such treatment: "It's going to hit harder than I can stand up under. I should be in a pack when it hits" (133). In *These Are My Sisters*, after elaborating a long list of the asylum's contrivances "to torture maniacs" (33), Lara Jefferson pauses at the straitjacket: "Though it looks like an implement of torture designed in the Dark Ages, there are times when it looks like God's protecting arm round you. To feel yourself going berserk is a terrible sensation . . . [you] know that when your frail thong of self-control breaks you will be a maniac—raging, charging, and bent on destruction. At such a time, a strait-jacket looks like

---

[6] Remarkably, in *Cuckoo's Nest* the figure for coercive psychiatry is an emasculating woman, Nurse Ratched, who serves the function in this novel of legitimating misogyny and sexual violence on the part of the male protagonist.

God's angel sent to protect you. The very loveliest thing ever made" (35). Indeed, the restraint of the straitjacket turns out to be curative for Jefferson, who—like Deborah in *Rose Garden*—requests it for herself. Afterwards she says: "I looked back at the immense expanse of the jacket. . . . A perspiration soaked, evil smelling coffin for my madness. Truly I wanted to bury it with great ceremony but without regrets" (221).

Such forms of treatment seem highly distasteful when viewed through the lens of feminist theory. Are these women asking to be rendered inactive—immobilized, as it were, so that they may resume the proper feminine stance of submission? Certainly, it would be more comforting from an ideological point of view if these women could achieve health through the dramatic ripping and tearing of the bonds that bind them, rather than by meekly accepting, and even requesting, those bonds. It is perhaps understandable, then, that there is virtually no discussion of such passages in any of the feminist studies of madness in literature. Nevertheless, the demand for ideological purity inevitably leads to an impasse of effective action—as was brought home to me powerfully in the case of a politics that would proscribe medication at the cost of a woman's capacity to be an effective, fully functioning agent of change. Recall the anecdote that opens this chapter. According to such imperatives, if abusive medical treatments such as lobotomy and clitoridectomy have been associated with biological and hereditary models of madness, then no connection between biology and mental illness must be recognized, and all treatments invested in this medical model are inevitably complicit and abusive. I am reminded of another conference, where a woman concluded a presentation on nineteenth-century notions of hereditary madness in literature with a warning that so long as mental disorders are treated with drugs, we are still operating on a dangerous model of madness as biological taint. (Is this the equivalent of saying that women should not take birth control pills because they imply that our subordinate social status has a biological origin?) It seems highly risky to pin all arguments about the social and regulatory aspects of technologies of madness, including their production of gender ideology, on the premise that mental illness must be completely severed from biology; any scientific evidence to the contrary will then inevitably undermine the cause. There must be room in feminist theories for the possibility of recovery based on forms of treatment supported by women's testimony, even if these forms have a "biological" or physical basis.

A provocative starting point in conceptualizing such a model comes from an unlikely source: Peter Kramer's *Listening to Prozac*. Kramer hypothesizes that a variety of "adaptive" behaviors can develop out of similar physiologically grounded characteristics. Thus, for example, the "constellation of behaviors amounting to a caricature of femininity" once understood as hysteria might be a product of adaptive behavior in someone who is "physiologically wired to be deeply sensitive to rejection" (74, 71). While both men and women can be rejection-sensitive, only women would respond with behaviors that appear to be "a caricature of femininity," since only women would experience social rejection as a result of not being feminine. Furthermore, the physiological basis for "rejection sensitivity" might itself be an effect of what we call environment. Kramer notes that it is possible for "psychological trauma" to produce "physiological consequences"—in the form, for instance, of a "biologically encoded personality trait" such as rejection sensitivity (107). Kramer concludes that "pain, isolation, confinement, and lack of control," all situations with a high level of relevance for studies of gender, "can lead to structural changes in the brain" (117). His model is valuable to feminist theories of madness in that it allows us to see how we might account for social constructions of gender while granting the potential effectiveness of certain biological forms of treatment such as drugs. The goal in both cases is to enable women to act as agents.

Perhaps an even more significant area in which asylum accounts coexist uneasily with the feminist and antipsychiatric framework deployed to understand them lies in the contrasting definitions of madness itself. In the context of late 1960s radicalism and pacifism, R. D. Laing wrote in *The Politics of Experience* (1967): "In order to rationalize our industrial-military complex, we have to destroy our capacity to see clearly. . . . Long before a thermonuclear war can come about, we have had to lay waste our own sanity. We begin with the children. . . . By the time the new human being is fifteen or so, we are left with . . . a half-crazed creature more or less adjusted to a mad world. This is normality in our present age. . . . The texture of the fabric of [our] socially shared hallucinations is what we call reality, and our collusive madness is what we call sanity" (57–58, 73). The "mad" person, in this view, was one who did not accept, could not adjust to, or indeed "protested" the mad conditions of the supposedly "sane" world. Late antipsychiatry rendered quite arbitrary the distinctions between madness and sanity and often privileged the former over the latter. Chesler made explicit the gendered implications of this philosophy in *Women and Madness*, commenting that women such as Plath "were desperately and defiantly at odds with the female role . . . [and] attempted to escape its half-life by 'going crazy.' . . . [In the asylum] they were superficially freed from their female roles as private social losers, as wives and mothers" (15). Although Chesler acknowledges that the symbolic rejection of "female powerlessness" in madness was ultimately "unsuccessful" (16), there nevertheless seems a certain grudging admiration in such an account. After all, if the "sane" female and the "mad" one are equally power- less, then the attempt to "reject and overcome" (16) that state, unsuc- cessful or no, is at least something; for isn't it better to be even "superficially" freed from constraining roles than never to be freed from them at all? It is not difficult to find, lurking behind this position, the persistence of late Laingian antipsychiatric thought: the "protest" of madness is the only "sane" response to a society that so thoroughly disempowers women, and it follows that a society which would so stunt the growth of half its members is "insane."[7]

Admittedly, the asylum accounts seem to give considerable support to the antipsychiatric framework; the narrators are fond of undermin- ing or even at times overtuning the dichotomy between the sick and the well. *The Snake Pit* is full of characters who "embody the blurred distinction between normality and disease": a patient whom Virginia mistakes for a nurse (147), a head nurse "who is not all there, not en- tirely normal" (111), a new nurse who exhibits more "instability" than some patients (266), and a former nurse who has become a patient (260). The ironic commentary on the degree to which distinctions are preserved by means of sheer power is provided near the novel's con- clusion, by a nurse: "When there's more sick ones than well ones, by golly the sick ones will lock the well ones up" (278). *I Never Promised You a Rose Garden* rehearses in a more solemn tone the blurring of boundaries between sick patients and healthy caretakers: a handful of nursing students run "in terror from the whip of subtle similarity be- tween the mad-women's uttered thoughts and their own unuttered ones" (100), and one hospital attendant in particular "wanted people [in the asylum] to be crazier and more bizarre than they really were so that he could see the line which separated him . . . from the full- bloomed, exploded madness of the patients" (66). Deborah provides her own answer to the attendant's implied question: "The only thing

---

[7] For some additional examples of antipsychiatry's influence on feminist theory and criticism, see Showalter, who acknowledges her debt to Laing in conceiving of "schizo- phrenia . . . as a form of protest against the female role" (222); Garry Leonard, who inter- prets Esther's madness in *The Bell Jar* as a feminist-Marxist resistance (67); and Linda Leonard, who variously interprets madness as "repressed rage," "feminine creative en- ergy," a label for "unconventional" or "creative" behavior, and a "metamorphosis" on the road to further growth (xvi–xviii).

that separated him from us was three inches of metal key he used to fondle for assurance" (94).

Nevertheless, the interrogation of boundaries between the sane and the insane in these examples still assumes a distinction between the two by focusing on specific problematic characters. Both *The Snake Pit* and *I Never Promised You a Rose Garden* juxtapose troublingly disturbed caretakers with clearly healthy ones, thus merely reinscribing the boundaries in these cases so that they do not fall quite so predictably. Other asylum novels press further in pointing out the difficulty of any assessment of sanity. At the end of *The Bell Jar*, Esther muses: "What was there about us, in Belsize, so different from the girls playing bridge and gossiping and studying in the college to which I would return? Those girls, too, sat under bell jars of a sort" (194). And for Susanna Kaysen in *Girl, Interrupted*, the compulsion to determine where the boundaries lie is not simply the self-preserving instinct of one secretly disturbed individual but a general tendency of the "healthy." The question we all ask, she says, is: "Could that happen to me? The less likely the terrible thing is to happen, the less frightening it is to look at or imagine. A person who doesn't talk to herself or stare off into nothingness is therefore more alarming than a person who does. Someone who acts 'normal' raises the uncomfortable question, What's the difference between that person and me? which leads to the question, What's keeping me out of the loony bin?" (124). If there is no discernible, self-evident difference between the sane and the insane, then "craziness" would seem to be little more than an unstable signifier, and institutionalization in the "loony bin" a means of artificially restabilizing the categories of madness and health.

In *The Snake Pit*, Virginia mirrors, within the asylum walls, the attempts of the supposedly "sane" to stabilize identity by differentiating themselves from the "really" crazy. The "snake pit" metaphor, invoked when Virginia is moved to a ward for very serious cases, is meant to suggest not only the "exposé" of abusive asylum treatment but also, more important here, a claim to sanity through contrast with those who are less sane: "When you realize you aren't the sickest in your ward, it does something for you.... Long ago they lowered insane persons into snake pits; they thought that an experience that might drive a sane person out of his wits might send an insane person back into sanity.... [A] more modern 'they' had given V. Cunningham a far more drastic shock treatment now.... They had thrown her into a snake pit and she had been shocked into knowing that she would get well" (216–17). The "shock" Virginia receives is that of being "thrown" in with patients whose sickness she judges incommensurate with her own, and against whom she must violently assert her difference. Yet repeatedly in the novel Virginia's efforts to comfort herself about her comparative sanity are utterly undermined. When a man accuses her of biting him, she treats him in the careful and condescending manner with which one approaches a dangerous psychopath: " 'No one would want to bite you,' she said. 'You are a very nice person, I'm sure.' Get his mind off violence" (156). But in fact the man is a doctor, not a patient, and Virginia *has* bitten him. At another moment Virginia overhears two patients talking about a woman whose condition has seriously deteriorated and who has been "sent to pack." "That's silly," Virginia thinks. "You wouldn't be sent home when you were worse." The incident reassures her that "at least she knew she was not so sick as [the two patients]" (68). (Virginia's error results from a misrecognition of the referent for the phrase "sent to pack," which in this context means not "to be sent packing" but to undergo wet-pack therapy.) It would appear that the comfort to be derived through a contrast with the "crazy" other is a precarious one at best.

In *Girl, Interrupted* only the asylum walls seem at times to keep the occupants from blending seamlessly with the "outside world" of the 1960s, which the madwomen keep tabs on through television. Kaysen reflects, "People were doing the kinds of things we had fantasies of doing: taking over universities and abolishing classes; making houses out of cardboard boxes and putting them in people's way; sticking their tongues out at policemen. . . . We thought eventually they'd get around to 'liberating' us too. 'Right on!' we'd yell at them" (92). Even as the merging of madwomen's fantasy and external reality suggests the lack of essential difference between madness and sanity, however, some distinctions are being made—between real and imagined protest, for example. Kaysen continues:

> When we saw Bobby Seale bound and gagged in a Chicago courtroom, . . . Cynthia was particularly upset. "They do that to me!" she cried. It was true that they did tie you down and put something in your mouth when you had shock, to stop you from biting your tongue during the convulsion.
> Lisa was angry too, but for another reason. "Don't you see the difference?" she snarled at Cynthia. "They have to gag him, because they're afraid people will believe what he says." (93)

Here the correlation we have encountered in *The Bell Jar* and *The Snake Pit* between punishment for political dissidence and the treatment of the insane is brought up only to be self-consciously deflated. There are, after all, different kinds of "silencing": some carry a recognizable symbolic weight in society—so that "silencing" can become martyrdom, with a certain power of its own—while others do not. The women in the asylum wish to imagine themselves as part of a larger revolution, but the symbolic function of the asylum in society is to strip them of "credibility" (Kaysen 93), to ensure that all forms of protest within its walls are rendered socially meaningless. Kaysen suggests that she has had to learn this harsh lesson, recounting retrospectively the reasons why she participated in her own "voluntary" admittance as a teenager: "The opportunity to be incarcerated was just too good to resist. It was a very big No—the biggest No this side of suicide. Perverse reasoning. But back of that perversity, I knew I wasn't mad and that they wouldn't keep me there, locked up in a loony bin" (42).

Despite the recognition of ineffective forms of protest, however, these passages still seem to suggest that it is only social labeling (see Introduction) and public perception which distinguish between the "No" of the political protest and the "No" of the madwoman: society completely withholds credibility from the "mad," thus rendering their protests powerless. That implication in Kaysen's text places her very close indeed to the ideas of late Laingian antipsychiatry. In contrast, *I Never Promised You a Rose Garden* intimates something quite different about why the "mad" cannot engage in effective protest. The "world gone mad" in this novel is not the occasionally amusing world of the 1960s counterculture but the unbearable world of Nazism and the Holocaust—a world hardly preferable to the asylum. Deborah's German-born doctor remembers one particularly sick patient who recovered from his madness only to die in Dachau at the hands of the Nazis (42), and another who "[broke] out of the hospital in Nuremburg, disappearing into the swastika-city, and coming back laughing that hard, rasping parody of laughter.' Sholom Aleichem, Doctor, they are crazier than I am!' " (106). Acknowledging the horror of a world in which people are exterminated for their difference, Dr. Fried tells Deborah: "My help is so that you can be free to fight for all of these things. The only reality I offer is challenge, and being well is being free to accept it" (106). Freedom is, in this novel, not freedom from confining asylum walls or from the social stigma of being crazy (though the narrative acknowledges both), but freedom from a "madness" that prevents one from challenging the larger "madness" of the world.

Given that the means by which a narrator differentiates between those of greater and lesser sanity can open a window onto her most pressing concerns about her own psychic condition, it is notable that the strategies of differentiation found in these texts are rarely based on the standard of rationality in the sense of being able somehow to grasp and represent "objective" reality—though this is quite often the standard used by representatives of the medical establishment in the texts. In *The Snake Pit*, for instance, Virginia is grilled during a staff interview—meant to determine whether she is "sane" enough to leave the hospital—about whether she remembers how often she is permitted visitors, where her husband works, and what his home address is. One doctor asks accusatorially, "How do you explain the fact that you remember a rather involved and lengthy prescription when you can't remember your home address? . . . You are certain that [your husband] is residing in your former apartment?" and Virginia replies, "I was. . . . Of course now you have made it obvious that he isn't" (141–42). To the doctor, Virginia's failure to remember her husband's move to a different address is a sign of her continued madness. But careful readers might notice an entirely different textual detail: Virginia's scrupulous attention and responsiveness to language. She registers the fact that the doctor says "former," not "current." As it turns out, her husband, Robert, neither works nor lives where Virginia says he does, but this is because he "didn't think to tell" her about the changes (159). As it further turns out, electroshock causes loss of memory (231). What we as readers, occupying the same "objective" stance as the doctors, have been taking as a sign of Virginia's madness is actually a product of her "treatment."[8] Wherein, then, does her madness lie?

In *Listening to Prozac*, Peter Kramer speculates on what it means to say that one is "feeling [or not feeling] like myself." He writes, "Ordinarily, if we ask a person why she holds back socially, she may say, 'That's just who I am,' meaning shy or hesitant or melancholy or overly cautious" (19). In this case, regardless of how others might regard such qualities—whether as shortcomings or difference or even signs of mental illness—the person herself identifies them with what defines her as a self, a subject. Compare such a perspective to one in which the same traits might be regarded by the self as "not-me . . . alien . . . defect . . . ilness" (Kramer 19). For example, in *These Are My Sisters*, Lara Jefferson describes her mad self as "a creature . . . [who] is a stranger to me" (14). And Esther's looming madness in *The Bell Jar* takes the figurative form of strangers, often described as non-Western Others, who stare back at her from mirrors: a "smudgy-eyed Chinese woman" (15), a "sick Indian" (92), and someone so foreign that Esther thinks, "It wasn't a mirror at all, but a picture" (142). Perhaps we can approach these images

---

[8] Ellen Wolfe treats the implications of electroshock-induced memory loss in much greater detail in *Aftershock*.

of madness by way of Kramer's distinction between a subject's "understanding of what [is] essential to her and what [is] intrusive and pathological" (19).[9] Whether something can "objectively" be "essential" to someone is irrelevant here. I am speaking of the subjective experience of self, and of madness understood not as difference from others (the supposedly "mad" subject often accepts such differences without difficulty) but as difference from "self." Indeed, what this argument implies is the possibility of being able to conceive of a self that does not necessarily correspond with social constructions of the gendered subject and yet is a subject (i.e., not "crazy").

In *The Snake Pit*, Virginia recalls that she "had always heard that crazy people think themselves sane. Does it follow then that if you think you are crazy, you are sane?" (136). The answer the text provides is clearly no. When Virginia's self-evaluation as crazy is set against her doctor's evaluation of her as increasingly "sane," it is his evaluation, not hers, that is found wanting: "Dr. Kik, when she saw him, went on at great rate about how much better she was; like Robert, he talked too fast for her. He never seemed disturbed by her answers and so they must have fitted. How long could she continue the pretense?" (136). *The Snake Pit* lays claim to something that would please neither "labeling" theorists nor proponents of "objective" psychology: the right to define for oneself—in a way not necessarily "objective" but with enormous implications for the treatment of the mentally ill—the experience of madness. Contrary to psychiatry's claim that the mad person "lacks insight into the fact that anything is wrong" (Claridge, Pryor, and Watkins 28)—a claim on the basis of which all sorts of societal difference and deviance have been "punished" with institutionalization—Virginia is indeed fully aware that something is wrong. She describes her state of mind: "You never had a conscious moment in which you were not aware of being sick. You could no more, while conscious, forget your sickness than you could forget to breathe. Asked your greatest

---

[9] Kramer actually demonstrates a degree of discomfort with this distinction, since it can be affected by medication. Prozac, for example, can change a quality such as depression or timidity, which an individual might always have understood as "just part of who I am," into an unnecessary quality experienced as being "not myself." But Kramer's discussion is nevertheless stimulating precisely because it offers the possibility that, given the opportunity to experience the "self" differently, an individual might see that self as a construct that can be reformulated, redefined, whereas previously it was perceived as "given," to be accepted. To suppose that the act of remaking the self—which is, after all, the goal of much psychotherapy—is somehow illegitimate because it is made possible by a drug seems odd, given Kramer's own argument that what may begin as social "causes" for particular personality traits can become biologically inscribed. The assumption, then, that only nonbiological attempts to change or "control" such traits are legitimate seems, in this context, anachronistic.

wish in life you would have replied at once—sanity" (188). But her narrative suggests that "wrong" is defined by subjective experience, not behavioral "symptoms."

In *The Bell Jar*, as in *The Snake Pit*, what is "wrong" is again measured by subjective experience. When Dr. Gordon asks Esther what she thinks is wrong, she reacts with fury: "What did I *think* was wrong? That made it sound as if nothing was *really* wrong, I only *thought* it was wrong" (106). Esther rejects the distinction between "real" and subjective and insists on the "reality" of her own illness against the doctor's tendency to dismiss it. There is clearly a distinction in the novel between madness used as a category of social deviation—as when Buddy calls Esther "crazy" after she declares that she's "never going to get married" (76)—and Esther's own perception of madness within herself.

Let us glance for a moment at one writer's model of madness as experienced from within. In *Girl, Interrupted*, Kaysen proposes figuratively that "mental illness seems to be a communication problem between interpreters one and two" within the mind:

> INTERPRETER ONE: There's a tiger in the corner.
> INTERPRETER TWO: No, that's not a tiger—that's a bureau.
> INTERPRETER ONE: It's a tiger, it's a tiger!
> INTERPRETER TWO: Don't be ridiculous. Let's go look at it. (139)

What is striking about this description is that it is not the hallucination which constitutes madness in and of itself for Kaysen but rather the figurative failure in communication. To return again to *The Snake Pit*, Virginia's persistent preoccupation in evaluating the madness both of herself and of those around her is the effectiveness of communication. It is surely telling that she reads Robert's failure in communication (his neglecting to inform her about his move and job change) as a sign of her own illness, in a way in which she never did during the confusion of the staff meeting. It is only at this point that Virginia thinks, "Of course when you are ill you don't expect to understand what well people say" (159).

Furthermore, there seems to be a qualitative difference between perceptions of madness based on the criterion of effective communication and the more frivolous judgments that are a product of Virginia's memory loss. In the incidents cited earlier which undermine Virginia's assertions of her superior sanity, her erroneous judgments are, as we eventually learn, a function of electroshock-induced disorientation: she misunderstands the meaning of being "sent to pack" because she cannot remember what a "pack" is; similarly, she forgets having bitten the doctor and thus assumes that he is a "dangerous male patient" when he accuses her of having done so. These scenes stand in contrast to one in which Virginia is faced with a patient who simply cannot understand the meaning of a sentence:

> "You are my sister, aren't you?" she whispered anxiously. "You said so."
> ... "No," [Virginia] said as kindly as she could. "I said my sister's name is Margaret. You and my sister have the same name."
> "You said," whimpered Margaret. "You said."
> "Well," said Virginia, "perhaps for the time being we are sisters of a sort. Yes, there is a sort of relationship."
> Margaret perked up. "I knew," she said. "I recognized you right away even though you have been dead so many years."
> It was no use to talk to these women; they were crazy. (76)

Although Virginia judges Margaret "crazy," Virginia's superior health here is established not by the judgment itself but by her greater flexibility with language. Whereas Margaret is an extreme literalist, permitting only the narrowest possible meaning of the word "sister," Virginia allows for the possibility of meaning on a level other than the purely literal one. That is, she permits the possibility that Margaret's claim does in fact make "sense." The firsthand experience of madness connects her and Margaret in a metaphorical kinship. The title of *These Are My Sisters* points, similarly, to the connection between Jefferson and a fellow patient who imagines her illness in terms of the literal loss of speech: "My throat has been cut, my tongue is cut out, my lips are cut off!! I cannot swallow—I can't even speak—(she makes guttural noises to prove it)" (73–74).

In *The Snake Pit* it is precisely in terms of linguistic failure that Virginia experiences her madness; what is "wrong" is defined by the inability to speak or to understand the speech of others. When Robert comes to visit her during a period of delirium, Virginia "tried to talk to him, to tell him how cold she was, but all she could do was cry. She wept while Robert talked quietly to her. She liked to hear his voice, but she never knew what he was saying" (181). As her own powers of meaning making deteriorate, she becomes increasingly aware of the (in)capacity for meaning in those around her: "Virginia watched the women with whom she ate her meals. These women never talked to each other. Now and then one of them would speak, but she was not speaking to anyone in the room" (181). Like herself and Robert, whose lines of communication have been severed as though by a soundproof wall, these women produce words directed at no audience. Indeed,

Virginia notes the early progress of her own madness with the recognition that she has begun to disregard the imperative of a listening other for speech: "I spoke aloud and not to anyone within hearing. I am one of them" (54).

As a more healthy Virginia, by her own standards, prepares to leave the hospital at the end of the novel, she cracks to a nurse, "Sent to pack," to which the nurse responds, "You slay me" (276). The exchange represents a very subtle change in Virginia's ability to grasp meaning. She is still using the phrase "sent to pack" in the same sense as before; but whereas before it was an indication of her own confusion, it is now a self-conscious joke, remarkable for the required attunement to shades of meaning. Virginia holds both senses of "pack" in her mind simultaneously and uses the hospital context to produce the clashing expectations that mark a pun. In *These Are My Sisters*, linguistic facility is also connected to the return to health. Jefferson, writing from within the asylum, postulates that "anything that can be whittled down to fit words—is not all madness" (25). Thus she hopes to use writing to ward off her own mental deterioration: "Once you have . . . seen the very force of yourself flow out in a stream of insanity you get a pencil and sit down and write; anything—anything to try and forestall a repetition of your experience" (45). This conclusion leads to some striking passages of prose, seemingly written in the very heat of an onset of madness: "Write faster—you fool—if you do not want to disintegrate into a jittering idiot. . . . [It is] the only thing keeping you from becoming another howling maniac. . . . Keep on with your writing" (194). Jefferson's strategy works, for at the end of her narrative she is being moved to the "best" ward, not because of extensive therapy or psychoanalysis but because she has "built a barrier—a breakwater of small black words around me" (236).

Likewise in *The Bell Jar*, the most striking characteristic of Esther's madness in her own understanding of it is an impasse in written language: "I told Doctor Gordon about not sleeping and not eating and not reading. I didn't tell him about the handwriting, which bothered me most of all. . . . [W]hen I took up my pen, my hand made big, jerky letters like those of a child, and the lines sloped down the page from left to right almost diagonally, as if they were loops of string lying on the paper, and someone had come along and blown them askew" (106). Showalter argues that the crux of Esther's problem is that "motherhood and writing" are "incompatible," but in fact it is Esther's "schizophrenia" that is absolutely incompatible with her writing; the central division suggested by the novel is between *madness* and *creativity*. Sometimes Esther seems to include motherhood as one of her goals

(180), sometimes not (96, 182); certainly she expresses a desire to be permitted to be both mother and writer, though she is aware of society's sanctions against such multiple roles for women. (In the often-cited fig tree metaphor, one of the figs represents "a husband and a happy home and children," while another is "a famous poet." Esther fears that she will starve because "choosing one meant losing all the rest" [62–63].) In contrast, the moment of Esther's madness is marked by an inability to read or write—the death of literary creativity. Whatever obstacles the traditional roles of womanhood have placed in the path of Esther's authorial ambitions, they pale against the insurmountable barriers placed there by her madness. Significantly, as Esther recovers, she keeps watch over a patient, Miss Norris, and "brood[s] over the pale, speechless circlet of her lips," hoping to induce her to speech: "But in all my hours of vigil Miss Norris hadn't said a word" (158).

Thus we reach the paradox that to listen to (former) madwomen speak about their own experiences with madness is to recognize, precisely, that madwomen can't speak. Whatever the liberatory potential of madness in theory, these women who have experienced madness and then written about it have found it to be nothing less than a total silencing. Their autobiographical narrators and fictional protagonists alike have struggled first and foremost to recover their voices. When we treat madness as a theoretical construct without regard to how it is experienced from the inside, we relegate protagonists' (and authors') recovery of self-expression to a status of secondary importance.

The Loony-Bin Trip, by Kate Millett, is perhaps the most remarkable literary testament to the tension between experience and theory, between the urge to bear witness and the temptation not to listen. Unlike the other authors I have discussed so far, Millett persistently asserts that she was not mad at any time leading up to or during her institutionalization. Indeed, a major focus of the early part of her narrative is on how the presumption of madness prescribes the way in which those around her interpret her every behavior: "If only no one had told them I was mad. Then I wouldn't be. They wouldn't imagine it and act accordingly" (143). Yet, while Millett criticizes others for not attending to her perspective, she herself has difficulty in attending to the implications of her own story.

Kate Millett is both a "woman of the asylum" and a recognized theorist of gender relations, and she brings both roles to bear on her writing about her experience. They do not seem to coexist easily, and they produce striking gaps in the text. Explaining her perspective on lithium,

Millett could be one of the feminist friends of the woman whose story opens this chapter, except that she is speaking of her own situation rather than someone else's: "Stopping the lithium . . . stopped the shame, the compliance. . . . Hypothetically, I could still be taking lithium and . . . validate the past. But lithium represented collusion; when I stopped I was no longer cooperating in some social and emotional way" (95). Millett's narrative goes on to recount her forced institutionalization (which resulted from friends' and family members' unwillingness to accept her decision to stop taking lithium), her eventual release, and her subsequent plunge into suicidal depression. And it is here that Millett, in contradistinction to well-meaning family, friends, and doctors, defines madness for herself—once again, strikingly, in terms of a failure in the production of language: "Now, only now, are you crazy to yourself. . . . During depression the world disappears. Language itself. One has nothing to say. Nothing. No small talk, no anecdotes. . . . [N]ot even to have words to protect one from the vacuum. To grow mute as well as helpless" (257, 283–84).

It is against this loss of the ability to represent and reconstruct that Millett finally agrees to take lithium, the "medicine that might prevent this pit, this hollow valley, from becoming my life" (257). From the theoretical standpoint by which Millett is informed, this decision represents capitulation, failure. Thinking of a feminist friend, she writes: "How disgusted Monika would be by my coming here: head-shrinkers and drug therapy are mind control, she would say. But she doesn't have my disease. I do." (257). Like Ward and Plath, Millett is suggesting a distinction between a judgment of madness based on internal standards—a perceived loss of agency—and a judgment based on external social ones. Simultaneously, she is insisting that feminist theory account for and listen to the personal experience of the "madwoman." ("She doesn't have my disease. I do.") But Millett herself subsequently recants, telling us in the conclusion to her account that "the last section," that is, the one in which she describes taking lithium for depression, "was written first, in a hangover of penitence and self-renunciation. . . . Now, when I reread it, I find something in it rings false" (309). Depression has become a "false consciousness"; madness, Millett declares against her previous statements, "doesn't exist" (315). Millett the author of Sexual Politics, the feminist, antipsychiatric theoretician (she makes explicit references to Laing, Szasz, and Cooper [248]), wins out over Millett the woman who has had a personal encounter with madness, defined not as social deviance but as loss of agency. She herself is ultimately unwilling to listen to the authority of her experience.

Although all the asylum narratives I have discussed frequently blur the boundaries between the sane and the insane, Millett's is, strikingly, the only one to suggest at any point that madness simply does not exist. And yet it is possible that Millett can make this assertion because she has not encountered madness to the same degree as others who have written about their experiences. Millett herself proposes the notion of a mild form of madness, saying of those responsible for her first hospitalization that they "would never see a middle ground of being a little crazy (flipped out, upset, frazzled), or see crazy as a mixed state, an ambivalent affair" (86). She implicitly assumes here the existence of degrees of sanity; yet she later asserts in absolute terms that what we call "madness" is simply a "certain speed of thought, certain wonderful flights of ideas" or "states of perception" (315).

Nevertheless, Millett's narrative points strongly toward a difference (even as she elides it) between herself and some of the other asylum occupants, who "after a certain time . . . agree to be crazy; they surrender. And withdraw. And as time goes by, they cannot or finally will not return; it is too far, it is too unrewarding, it is too dubious—they have forgotten" (218). Even granting hypothetically Millett's insinuation that no one has arrived at the asylum this way—that all have been reduced to the state of surrender and withdrawal by institutionalization itself rather than anything that came before it—there is an obvious differentiation between the retreat into "some carefully wrought fantasy" without possibility of return and Millett's own situation. It is worth noting that Millett herself regards her fantasies of being Joan of Arc as potentially dangerous, not because others will condemn her for them but because they threaten her ability to wage any effective resistance: "Cut this out, stop wandering in history, stop following the metaphor. Concentrate, for God's sake, go in there and make some more lists, bring some toilet paper and write another letter" (243).

Millett textually inscribes her responsibility to the women who will never find their way out of madness, telling herself, "If you are to be any use, you will have to stop equating madness with captivity; that is, stop proving you aren't crazy, since this assumes that if you were, you might deserve to be locked up: you're only innocent if you're sane. . . . Not till you permit madness, coming apart into smithereens, can you really stand against the bin as prison and punishment. Then you have a case—not otherwise" (248). Only by ceasing to distinguish between those deserving and those not deserving of institutionalization can Millett speak, not only of the injustice of her personal situation but also, more significantly, to the larger issue of the treatment of mental illness. But the slippage by which we move from one erasure (deserving/not deserving) to the next (crazy/not crazy) is troubling precisely because it undercuts the very point that Millett most wishes to emphasize through her moment of revelation: that is, her responsibility to speak on this matter (248). If no one is crazy after all, then all can resist. Millett need not take on the burden of speaking for the madwomen she has left behind, because they can speak for themselves.

I have noted in passing how Millett deflects attention from the possibility that anything other than the asylum itself could make anyone crazy enough to withdraw beyond the point of no return. Millett's primary political point in writing her narrative is to confront the issue of forced institutionalization, and so it makes some degree of sense that madness, when she allows it to exist, does so only as a direct function of the asylum. We might even say that madness is a signifier in Millett's text for the despair of incarceration in a "mental hospital." A similar dynamic is at work in the writing of many other theorists as well. Madness is treated to a remarkable extent as a signifier for socially constructed femininity and/or for protest against it. This assumption, accurate though it may be at times, marks the point where asylum narratives and feminist critiques part company. For whatever social explanations for mental illness are put forth by the autobiographical texts, the experience of madness ultimately exceeds those explanations and can no longer be contained by them.

The Bell Jar serves as perhaps the most powerful and pertinent portrayal of a madness that comes to outgrow its causes. Early reviewers were quick to observe the dramatic contrast between the first and second parts of the narrative. As Melvin Maddocks noted on the appearance of the American edition, the second half of the novel is "less a contrast than a discontinuity" (11). J. D. O'Hara remarked that when "the New York adventures end . . . a strange new book begins. The funny incidents are funny in a different way, and suddenly Esther is undergoing psychiatric treatment, and suddenly she's in an asylum" (102). And Geoffrey Wolff pointed out that "the heroine leaps from a life of customary troubles to a far world of madness all at once" (113). That sense of radical disjunction tells us something important: ultimately, none of the contributing factors of madness are commensurate with the described experience of breakdown itself. (I am not proposing that the causes described in *The Bell Jar* are not sufficient for a breakdown; I am, rather, arguing that the experience of madness to some degree defies rational explanations. Thus, in the moment when Esther's breakdown occurs, the causal narrative is abruptly abandoned for an entirely new set of textual functions.) More than simply a shift in tone or subject matter, the split that severs the narrative in two leaves a gap that cannot fully be bridged by critical explanations, much as these try.

Numerous readers have attempted to connect the "bell jar" metaphor to the roots of Esther's madness, suggesting in various ways that it represents the social expectations of femininity which surround Esther.[10] Perhaps Esther is referring to the social coercion of feminine roles when she says that she feels, near the onset of her madness, "as if I were being stuffed farther and farther into a black, airless sack with no way out" (105). We can easily read this forerunner of the bell jar image as representing Esther's sense that society is pushing her into an unpleasantly confining condition—wifehood and motherhood—and will not allow alternatives, such as a career as an artist, to coexist in that narrow space. But it is only by dint of force that we can continue to read these concerns in the fully extended metaphor of the bell jar, manifested in Esther's realization that "if Mrs. Guinea had given me a ticket to Europe, or a round-the-world cruise, it wouldn't have made one scrap of difference to me, because wherever I sat—on the deck of a ship or at a street café in Paris or Bangkok—I would be sitting under the same glass bell jar, stewing in my own sour air. . . . The air of the bell jar wadded round me and I couldn't stir" (152). In no way is motherhood evoked by "sitting on the deck of a ship or at a street café in Paris or Bangkok." Whatever specific social conditions Esther has experienced as a young woman in 1950s America, what she is telling us at this moment is that she would continue to feel their effects anywhere. Not only does she carry those effects with her, but also she recreates them; far from being "stuffed" into an "airless sack," she is now the producer of her "own sour air."

Esther's illness, in other words, has surpassed its social causes and can no longer be fully accounted for by them. As Ellen Wolfe writes, a bit more straightforwardly, of her own breakdown, "I can say yes, these were the causes" (214); and yet something is inevitably felt to be wanting in such an approach. Elizabeth Wurtzel, poignantly aware of a gap between causal explanations and the experience of depression, declares point-blank that she "can't equate the amount of pain and misery and despair I have suffered . . . with the events of my life" (30); it would actually be a relief to "have my life circumstances match the oppressiveness I feel internally" (44). To say that madness comes to seem incommensurate with its roots, however, is decidedly not to reduce madness yet again to "personal pathology"—the age-old strategy of depositing blame at the feet of the individual's fundamentally

---

[10] See, for example, Garry Leonard 62, Yalom 22, Wagner-Martin 79.

"flawed" (i.e., inferior) biology or character. It is rather to recognize that madness takes on a life of its own, quite apart from whatever causes, social or otherwise, we may be able to identify in its beginnings.

Once again I find Peter Kramer useful here. Presenting the case of a patient whose enormous sensitivity to even the smallest rejections caused her great emotional distress (although this was far from qualifying as "madness"), Kramer reviews the widely varying interpretations that might be attached to such a "symptom": "Father hunger, mother hunger, adolescent rebellion, repetition compulsion, or a delayed grief reaction. Each of these very different frames is historical: to 'understand' Lucy's behavior is to place it in relation to her traumatic past. . . . Lucy understands this sensitivity, too, as originating in the apprehension that she will lose anyone she loves. But she cannot shake it—*it has a life of its own*" (68–69; emphasis added). Lucy, that is, understands her own pain historically, much like the narrators of asylum accounts; and yet that understanding does not eliminate the pain, which is after all her prime concern at the moment when she comes to Kramer for help. Lucy's case prompts Kramer to elaborate on a debate regarding the status of causes:

> To a psychoanalyst, every hysterical symptom has hidden within it, in secret code, its cause—both the historical cause (early emotional trauma) and the ongoing, active cause (unconscious conflict . . .). . . . For psychoanalysis, the route to recovery is bringing the unconscious struggle into consciousness. Psychoanalysis . . . revolves around an appealing, humane view of symptoms and the people who carry them: that the truth can set men free. Functional autonomy implies that symptoms become unmoored from their origins, so there is no longer any special reason to imagine that truth will have the power to heal. (75–76)

Kramer's analysis implies that historical explanations for madness (whether offered by psychoanalysis or social critics), while important, might not ultimately help the person in the immediacy of her suffering. It also offers yet another perspective on why madness narratives have so often been read as "personal" rather than "political": we might say that, in the moment of madness, the individual cannot move beyond her own personal pain. To attend only to the causes of a mental "disorder," then, becomes another way of shutting our ears to the felt experience of madness in the present. As Wurtzel puts it, "The particulars of what has driven this or that person to Zoloft, Paxil, or Prozac, or the reasons that some other person believes herself to be suffering from a major depression, seem less significant than the simple fact of it." Everything the therapist tells her about the possible roots of her depression "seems perfectly plausible, but it's all one big *so what?* as far as I'm concerned. I know all this stuff already. For me the problem is what to do about it" (30, 38).

It is remarkable how rarely the narratives of madness that I discuss in this book work on a "mystery" model of madness, with a therapist-as-detective and a climactic revelation of origins. *The Bell Jar* presents such a notion of treatment as an absurdly simplistic fantasy: "Then [the doctor] would lean back in his chair and match the tips of his fingers together in a little steeple and tell me why I couldn't sleep and why I couldn't read and why I couldn't eat and why everything people did seemed so silly, because they only died in the end" (105). And in *I Never Promised You a Rose Garden*, Joanne Greenberg treats with derision the idea that madness might be accounted for through a mere explication of its origins. The male therapist, Dr. Royson, who takes the place of Dr. Fried (Deborah's regular—and female—doctor) seeks only to get at the roots of the secret language of Deborah's hallucinated world:

> He worked hard to convince her that Yri was a language formulated by herself. . . . He had taken the first words she gave him and shown her the roots of them from scraps of Latin, French, and German that a nine- or ten-year-old could pick up if she tried. He analyzed the structure of the sentences and demanded that she see that they were, with very few exceptions, patterned on the English structure by which she, herself, was bound. . . . [T]he more profound he was the more profound was the silence which enveloped her. She could never . . . tell him that . . . his proofs were utterly and singularly irrelevant. At the end she marshaled all of her strength, and with as good a clarity as she could give him, she said, "Please, Doctor, my difference is not my sickness." It was a last cry and it went unheard. (160)

On some level Deborah understands already that Yri is a world of her own creation, but it will take far more than this truth to set her free.

The same holds true for the social origins of Deborah's illness. Certainly, much of *Rose Garden* is in fact about those of Deborah's "differences" that offer partial explanations for her madness. As a child she was made vividly aware of her gender difference, and of the cultural shame attached to it, by an early operation to remove a tumor: "She had been five, old enough to be ashamed when the doctors shook their heads about the wrongness inside her, in the feminine, secret part. They had gone in with their probes and needles as if the entire reality of her body were concentrated in the secret evil inside that forbidden place" (44). And her difference from a dominant Anglo-Saxon culture is also advanced as a possible source: " 'Jew, Jew, dirty Jew; my grand-mother hated your grandmother, my mother hates your mother and I hate you!' Three generations. . . . The instincts of these hating children were shared, for Deborah heard sometimes that a man named Hitler was in Germany and was killing Jews with the same kind of evil joy" (50). Indeed, gender and ethnic differences connect and collapse in Deborah's mind: "In the camp a riding instructor mentioned acidly that Hitler was doing one good thing at least, and that was getting rid of the 'garbage people.' She wondered idly if they all had tumors" (50).

Yet despite the obvious importance of these incidents as explana-tions for Deborah's madness, what is remarkable about the novel's form is that they are all provided within its first fifty pages, rather than presented near the end as the climactic "solution" to her illness. Debo-rah tries to explain that her difference—the possible beginnings of her madness—is not the madness itself. As Dr. Fried tells Deborah's par-ents: "It was as if she had her head down . . . waiting for the blows. . . . And then there came a time, later—a time when she began to arrange for the blows to fall" (42). Such a description points to the ways in which Deborah, like Esther, has become her own victimizer through her madness, unmoored as it has become from its causes.

To address the ending of madness is similarly problematic; as Esther asks at the conclusion of The Bell Jar: "How did I know that someday—at college, in Europe, somewhere, anywhere—the bell jar, with its stifling distortions, wouldn't descend again?" (197). In her autobiogra-phy, Susanna Kaysen conveys the same sense of bewilderment at the lack of explanations: "I got better and Daisy didn't and I can't explain why" (158). We might say that madness is "over-determined"; no mat-ter how much critics long to fit female protagonists' madness into a theoretical framework, it will always escape us to some degree. The very chasm in The Bell Jar between the reasons that Esther herself pro-poses for the onset of her madness and her description of its experi-ence serves to underscore the fact that it has taken on a life of its own—and can thus experience a mysterious death of its own as well. To listen to Esther's story is, finally, to hear not only her explanations but also her silences.

In this chapter I have shown how personally informed accounts of madness and institutionalization problematize some of the claims made by feminist theory. Scores of women in modern history have in-deed been pronounced mad for reasons of social difference, for "un-feminine" behavior, for ambition; we will see this pattern played out in some of the texts I discuss in the following chapters. Yet even though many of the narrators of asylum accounts recognized their aberration from a "proper" feminine model, they also all experienced madness as something more than a label attached to difference. Many women have assuredly been "driven crazy" by their lack of options, and their madness can be understood as a last protest against the world—even if it is stuck, as it were, in the woman's throat. For many of the authors discussed in this chapter, gender roles clearly contributed in their own minds to their very real madness; some even conceived of madness in its initial stages as protest—what Kaysen calls "the biggest No this side of suicide." And yet it inevitably surpassed its causes, overshadowed them, and rendered helpless the women in its grasp. All the narrators certainly decry the conditions in mental hospitals and asylums, and especially condemn forced institutionalization by others. But it is also true that some managed to gain health from the treatments they received there—a circumstance that, as we have seen, causes no end of trouble for critics who continue to wish for "pure" and "untainted" forms of resistance. Finally, in no case does a narrator who has returned to health long for the protest, the creativity, the rage of madness. Unlike theorists who have only read of madness in books (like *The Snake Pit*'s naive Virginia before her own encounter with madness), the authors of these texts have been there, they have crossed whatever boundary separates the mad from the sane, and, as Kaysen writes, they "do not want to cross it again" (159). We literary critics, like the doctor in *The Snake Pit*, talk interminably about hearing voices. But is it the voices of the mad that we really wish to hear, or only our own?

2

Manless Women and Psychology in Postwar Culture
Three Short Stories

Michel Foucault has become, in literary and theoretical circles, the leading figure associated with the notion that madness is not a stable category and that its representations have served varying purposes in different historical moments. (As we have seen, radical psychology was arriving at similar insights at the same time.) "In the modern world," Foucault wrote, madness came to be represented as "the secret thrust of instincts against the solidity of the family institution and against its most archaic symbols" (254). Furthermore, he noted, the methods supposedly in place to "treat" madness actually functioned as guarantors of the bourgeois family and the moral system built up around it: "In one sense, confinement and the entire police system which surrounds it are used to control a certain order in the family structure. . . . The familial institution traces the circle of reason; beyond it threaten all the perils of insanity."[1] Anything that attacked the institution of the family thus came to be a sure sign of madness.

While the complicity of psychiatry (and its dissemination in popular culture) with the institution of the bourgeois family was by no means new to the postwar years, there were new developments that made Foucault's analysis of modern madness particularly pertinent. One was the rush of World War II veterans into the security of family life, as noted by Betty Friedan in *The Feminine Mystique*: "All of us went back into the warm brightness of home. . . . [We] shrugged off the bomb, forgot the concentration camps, . . . [and] avoided the complex larger problems of the postwar world . . . in a catch-all commitment to 'home'

---

[1] This passage is from "Le Monde correctionnaire" (trans. Byron Caminero-Santangelo), a chapter of Foucault's *Histoire de la folie à l'âge classique* that was not included in the Vintage Books translation, *Madness and Civilization*.

and 'family' " (178).[2] The reality of American family structures was certainly not quite as monolithic as Friedan pictured it. Since "traditional" family arrangements in which women did not need to work were not available to large segments of the population, Friedan's inclusive "all of us" actually meant primarily white middle-class and upper-middle-class men and women. Yet the image of the middle-class family consisting of working husband, homemaker, and children nevertheless operated as a powerful ideal within the dominant American culture.

At the same time, Americans began a feverish investigation of the psychology of the individual. Friedan saw this trend, too, as its own form of retreat: "After the war, Freudian psychology became much more than a science of human behavior. . . . It provided a convenient escape from the atom bomb, McCarthy. . . . It gave us permission to suppress the troubling questions of the larger world" (115). Thomas Szasz, a leading figure in the antipsychiatry movement, seemed to agree, condemning the tendency to explain incomprehensible events such as the Holocaust in terms of the "madness" of the culprits, thus diminishing the significance of those crimes with a vocabulary of individual psychology (*Manufacture* 81).[3] Writers as dissimilar in other ways as Friedan and Szasz both saw the pursuit of psychology, in its postwar forms, as an escape from the responsibilities imposed by the horrific burdens of the "outside" world. Szasz noted that it was at this time that mental illness became a legal means to avoid criminal responsibility (*Manufacture* 317).[4] Concurrently, the absence of responsibility in the insane became a rallying cry for advocates of mental health reform such as Albert Deutsch, who noted that the mentally ill "cannot be held responsible for their acts" and are thus victims in need of assistance (27).

Not everyone, however, escaped responsibility through the new obsession with psychology. Predictably in the postwar climate, explanations of madness looked to family structures; and it is no far stretch to conclude that women, as those primarily responsible for home, family, and domesticity, would receive the brunt of this shifting emphasis. In fact, the popular and influential *Modern Woman: The Lost Sex*

---

[2] See also O'Neill 33.

[3] "Psychiatrists declare that the Nazis were mad. I insist that [such] . . . interpretations are worse than false; by interposing mental illness . . . they conceal, excuse, and explain away the terrifyingly simple but all-important fact of man's inhumanity to man" (Szasz, *Manufacture* 81).

[4] In 1954, *Durham v. United States* set the legal precedent known as the Durham rule: "The rule we now hold . . . is simply that an accused is not criminally responsible if his unlawful act was the product of mental disease or mental defect." *Durham v. United States*, 214 F. 2d 862 (D.C. Circ. 1954), 874–75, cited in Szasz, *Manufacture* 317.

(1947) by Ferdinand Lundberg and Marynia F. Farnham held women responsible not only for their own mental illness but also for the mental instability which, according to them, was spreading like a disease throughout the country. Lundberg and Farnham warned, in near-apocalyptic terms, of a "crisis" that was "fundamentally psychic in original cause and in present effect. . . . [W]omen are the principal transmitting media of the disordered emotions that today are so widely spread throughout the world and are reflected in the statistics of social disorder. . . . The spawning ground of most neurosis in Western civilization is the home. The basis for it is laid in childhood, . . . [and] the principal agent in laying the groundwork for it is the mother" (23, 303). The source of women's deep-seated neurosis was their dissatisfaction with their natural domestic role. The authors' prescription was that women should "recapture those functions in which they have demonstrated superior capacity[:] . . . women should obtain status and prestige through motherhood" (368, 370). We might easily guess what would befall manless women in such a climate. Lundberg and Farnham were not subtle in their suggestion that the unmarried woman posed an enormous psychic threat to the social fabric: "What would happen to the spinsters? They would, perhaps, be encouraged to marry. . . . A great many children have unquestionably been damaged psychologically by the spinster teacher, who cannot be an adequate model of a complete woman either for boys or girls" (365). For women who were "sick" because they were not, according to the common wisdom, being women, there was no escape from responsibility.

It is perhaps not surprising, then, that when women wrote about madness during this period, it was connected with manlessness. The female protagonists' psychological descent in three short stories—Eudora Welty's "June Recital" (1949), Jean Stafford's "Beatrice Trueblood's Story" (1955), and Hortense Calisher's "The Scream on Fifty-Seventh Street" (1962)—is linked thematically with their "condition" as spinster, divorcée, or widow. That junction might suggest an underlying conservatism on the part of these writers—a complicity with postwar gender ideology. I will argue, however, that this was emphatically not the case. The writers were actually writing about ideology itself, about how social definitions of gender could draw lines of inclusion and exclusion that had a share in en-gendering madness. For just as representations of madness help to produce and regulate "normal," "healthy" femininity, so too do our notions of the "normal" feminine subject require, and even determine, the boundaries of a negative position that marks abnormality, deviance, and sickness. I read these stories by Welty, Stafford, and Calisher as a powerful countertext to

Lundberg and Farnham; taking up the representative space of the "manless madwoman," these women writers reveal it to be a social production.[5]

Yet the stories also offer a counternarrative to the dominant strain of feminist criticism which likes to read madness (along with manlessness) as resistance. Aberrance from the feminine role may well indicate resistance to it, but these writers depict madness as the *end* of any such resistance and as the signal that society has successfully reinscribed its definitions of femininity. I suggest that current feminist criticism tends to ignore—when it does not actively misread—narratives such as these that link madness explicitly with an absolute surrender to cultural conservatism. It becomes essential, then, to restore these texts to view so that we may make a more representative argument about what madness means in women's texts.

Peter Schmidt has accurately observed that myth criticism has dominated approaches to Eudora Welty's short story cycle *The Golden Apples*, particularly in the 1960s and 1970s. Such readings of Welty attempt to interpret her "allusions to classical myth, folktales, and Celtic and northern European legend" (Phillips 56), as well as to discover a mythological "structure" to the cycle of tales.[6] They thus assume an uncritical view of myth and miss Welty's commentary on its *functions*. In *The Golden Apples*, classical as well as contemporary myths are the images and narratives that support the community's system of beliefs.

King MacLain, the wanderer most mythologized in *The Golden Apples*, is clearly the primary representative for the "Wandering Aengus" figure of the poem by Yeats which gives Welty's collection its title. He seeks "a glimmering girl of some sort," an image perfectly in keeping with his amorous wanderings as celebrated by the residents of Morgana, Mississippi (Bryant, "Seeing Double" 144–145). It has been well documented that King is also a figure for Zeus in *The Golden Apples*; this allusion is usually taken to indicate King's own poetic stature. King's prototypical wanderings have been interpreted as freedom, as power, and as escape from the closed community that would keep him in confinement.[7] Such readings, however, gloss over the nature of

---

[5] In "June Recital," Welty critiques postwar ideology through a much earlier moment of representation; retrospective flashbacks recount the story of a spinster piano teacher from the perspective of the 1920s, itself a highly paradoxical period for gender ideology, marked by a sense of political and sexual liberation for women which, as historians have pointed out, was largely illusory. See, for example, Deckard 298.

[6] See, for example, works by Phillips, Pitavy-Souques, and McHaney.

[7] See, for example, McHaney, Demmin and Curley.

King's adventures, which are hardly portrayed as transcendent or insightful; rather, they more often seem to be images of seduction and rape. Characterized throughout the stories by a certain careless destructiveness with regard to women, King is hardly an exemplar of some triumphant response to social limitations.

Instead, we must understand the mythology surrounding King, and depicting him as Zeus, as revealing something about the residents of Morgana who *create* that mythology, beginning with Katie Rainey, who in "Shower of Gold" tells the story of King's godlike visitation to his wife. Katie Rainey is no impartial narrator; she is one of the most entrenched members of the Morgana community, with a particular investment in representing King MacLain as a pseudo-divinity while simultaneously casting his wife, Snowdie, as an object of pity. By the time we reach the third story in the collection, "Sir Rabbit," the legend of King MacLain has become Morgana lore: Mattie Will wants "to show him she'd heard all about King MacLain and his way" (98). And in the last story, "The Wanderers," King's son Ran, who has acquired a similar reputation, has been likewise glorified by the community: "They had voted for him for that—for his glamour and his story, for being a MacLain and the bad twin, for marrying a Stark and then for ruining a girl and the thing she did [i.e., committing suicide]" (238). Peter Schmidt correctly observes that "conventionalism in Morgana . . . is often disguised as mythological experience. Far from being exempt from historical prejudices, for example, the tales of King's Zeus-like 'heroism' in 'Shower of Gold' and elsewhere embody his society's most ingrained stereotypes about proper male and female behavior" (62). The members of the Morgana community are committed to and invested in the myth of the bad boy King MacLain and his progeny—a myth that they themselves have constructed.

Contrary to the critics who would like to claim a redemptive power for King MacLain and the story's other wanderers, I prefer to focus attention on what I see as a countertrend in the narrative which suggests that what characterizes wanderers is their uneasiness, if not their suffering, in the position constructed for them by Morgana's stories—a position always strongly conditioned by considerations of gender. For stories (that is to say, representations) are necessarily always engaged in ideological production. In *The Golden Apples* it is stories that make people what they are. As a result, Welty attributes a certain amount of responsibility to the community of Morgana for what King MacLain has become. More significant for our purposes—and much more self-evident—is the responsibility it holds for the fate of the unmarried piano teacher Miss Eckhart in "June Recital." King MacLain and Miss

Eckhart are clearly meant to be figures of each other in some sense. Young Cassie Morrison, who provides the narrative perspective for a good portion of this story, seems to recognize the connection in a limited way; as Miss Eckhart is finally dragged away to a mental hospital in full view of the town of Morgana, Cassie thinks: "People saw things like this as they saw Mr. MacLain come and go. They only hoped to place them, in their hour or their street or the name of their mothers' people. Then Morgana could hold them, and at last they were this and they were that. And when ruin was predicted all along, even if people had forgotten it was on the way, even if they mightn't have missed it if it hadn't appeared, still they were never surprised when it came" (90). Cassie is momentarily shocked by the lack of surprise in Morgana at Miss Eckhart's madness. But her own meditation suggests not only that predicted ruin is met with a lack of surprise, but also that *predicted ruin*—as a story about a person which can "place" and "hold" that person—has a share in making that person what she or he is ("At last they were this and they were that"). Welty's characters, in other words, can be read as dramatizing the process of becoming subjects within ideology.

Much of *The Golden Apples* takes its shape from the ways in which various characters are constrained by "mythical gates and barriers" (247)—a reference, perhaps, not to myths about barriers but to barriers consisting of myths: the myths the community constructs around its members in the process of constructing them as particular subjects. That is to say, the stories that the community of Morgana tells and retells about its members become ideological barriers prohibiting the possibility of re-vision. King and other wanderers are condemned by myth to "roaming on the face of the earth . . . like lost beasts" (96)— only in King's case that wandering is literal. For Miss Eckhart, a fellow "lost beast" constrained by stories, the "wandering" into which she is thrust is not geographical but a wandering of the mind: madness.

But if Welty's characters often do become the stories told about them, this process is not conflict-free. What remains after a person's death, we learn in "The Wanderers," is "not the dead's story, but the living's" (238). This formulation suggests that the dead person, now silenced forever, once told a story, and that story may or may not have coincided completely with the story told by the living. In *The Golden Apples* (as in "The Scream on Fifty-Seventh Street" and "Beatrice Trueblood's Story"), the battle that takes place on the field of representation is crucial. And as Teresa de Lauretis has suggested, "the construction of gender is also effected by its deconstruction; that is to say, by any discourse, feminist or otherwise, that would discard it as ideological misrepresentation" (3). Just as inherited stories can participate in the production of constraining ideological barriers, so do alternative stories (and, in Welty's text, art in general) have the potential to "deconstruct" the barriers, providing ideological representation of a more transformational sort.

King, I have suggested, is constructed (and constrained) by the heroizing stories about him, which keep him chasing the image of the beautiful young girl of Yeats's poem. The feminine version of this myth, however, is not heroic but horrible: the archetype of the monstrous woman, in various manifestations, surrounds Miss Eckhart as representation. She is associated—and to some degree associates herself—with Medusa (in "The Wanderers" 275–76) and with the Sibyl (in "Music from Spain" 203), who, as Thomas McHaney observes, "requested and received the gift of long life, but . . . forgot to ask for enduring youth, and so she grew ugly" (122). But we also cannot encounter the spinster piano teacher without calling to mind Lundberg and Farnham's caution about the psychological ills that could be wrought on innocent children by the "spinster teacher" who is not a "complete woman" (Lundberg and Farnham 365).

The community's images of Miss Eckhart are filtered through the perspective of Cassie Morrison, who, at the threshold of womanhood, seems poised to take up this position unproblematically. Her chance of gaining insight from Miss Eckhart's experiences is hampered by her own acceptance of the community's representations of both femininity and aberrance. It is through Cassie that we learn "the town's view of [Miss Eckhart] . . . for Cassie has been much influenced by the town's (and her own parents') judgment of her former music teacher" (Schmidt 88). The images from Cassie's memory seem culled directly from Morgana's fearful and suspicious regard of the spinster: "Tireless as a spider, Miss Eckhart waited so unbudgingly for her pupils that from the back she appeared asleep in her studio. . . . [S]he hated flies. She held a swatter in her down-inclined lap. . . . All at once as you played your piece, making errors or going perfectly it did not matter, smack down would come the fly swatter on the back of your hand" (38–39). We might extrapolate, from Cassie's perspective, Morgana's view of Miss Eckhart as the deceptively still spider waiting to trap and strike her (mostly female) students. This representation also has its classical allusion, reminding us of Arachne, yet another woman whose beauty has become distorted in the monstrous form of a spider.

Miss Eckhart is also figured as Circe, the enchantress who lured Ulysses' men with exquisite food and wine and then turned them into swine: "[Miss Eckhart's] hair was as low on her forehead as Circe's, on

the fourth-grade wall feeding her swine" (75). This image, too, suggests a dangerous entrapment: "It was known from Mr. Wiley Bowles,
the grocer, that Miss Eckhart and her mother . . . ate pigs' brains. . . .
Cassie yearned—she did want to taste the cabbage—that was really the
insurmountable thing, and even the brains of a pig she would have put
in her mouth that day. . . . But when Miss Eckhart said, 'Please—
please, will you stay to dinner?' Virgie and Cassie twined arms and
said 'No' together" (62–63). The classical myth is reconfigured so that
the apparent threat is, once again, to children—specifically to young
girls. Virgie and Cassie are tempted by the food which has become the
swine.

Circe, of course, is a highly sexualized enchantress, and in point of
fact there seems to be a strong sexual undercurrent to Miss Eckhart's
relationship with Virgie, her star pupil: "Virgie carried in the magnolia
bloom like a hot tureen, and offered it to Miss Eckhart, neither of them
knowing any better: magnolias smelled too sweet and heavy for right
after breakfast. . . . At the exact moment of the hour . . . [Miss Eckhart]
would dismiss Cassie and incline her head toward Virgie, as though
she was recognizing her only now, when she was ready for her; yet all
this time she had held the strong magnolia flower in her hand, and its
scent was filling the room" (41). The heady scent of the flower gives a
suppressed sensuality to this scene, in which Miss Eckhart appears to
be playing the part of coy woman to Virgie's "suitor," who woos her
with flowers. Peter Schmidt is right, I believe, in suggesting that for
Morgana, Miss Eckhart's "close contact with her female pupils becomes vaguely ominous—as much an affront to proper womanhood as
the sexual scandals surrounding her" (92). But Morgana's figuring of
Miss Eckhart as Circe/sexual temptress elides and suppresses the potentially threatening issue of young Virgie's own sexuality. In fact it is
Virgie who seems to be seducing Miss Eckhart, particularly in a scene
that clearly renders the girl as a foil for Mr. Sissum, Miss Eckhart's supposed lover:

> Virgie put a loop of clover chain down over Miss Eckhart's head. . . . She
> hung Miss Eckhart with flowers, while Mr. Sissum plucked the strings up
> above her. Miss Eckhart sat on, perfectly still and submissive. She gave no
> sign. She let the clover chain come down and lie on her breast.
>   Virgie laughed delightedly and with her long chain in her hand ran
> around and around her, binding her up with clovers. Miss Eckhart let her
> head roll back. (52)

Though Cassie seems to recognize here that Miss Eckhart is under
Virgie's spell rather than the reverse, this insight does not keep her

from regarding the teacher as a menacing enchantress at other times. Indeed, Virgie seems to share this view.

The more contemporary version of the Circe story is provided by Cassie's mother, who tells her that Miss Eckhart's "studio was in some ways like the witch's house in Hansel and Gretel . . . including the witch" (39). Virgie, the figure of conquest over Miss Eckhart, "often took the very pose of that inventive and persecuted little heroine who coped with people she thought were witches and ogres" (44). The imagery of the fairy-tale witch is clearly part of Cassie's instruction in womanhood; her brother Loch derides her "miserable girls' books and fairy tales" (22), suggesting the interrelatedness of the two. (Both kinds of texts share in the construction of gender.) Miss Eckhart, as witch and spider, is regarded as possessing a certain suspicious moral taint: the spider sitting in wait for flies and the witch luring children with candy for evil purposes are both stylized versions of Lundberg and Farnham's mentally deranged old spinster, insidiously distorting the developing psyches of young children.

At the same time, the community's derisive descriptions of Miss Eckhart as a fairy-tale witch play out a mock version of the denunciations of historical "witches" by their communities; and indeed the final outcome for Miss Eckhart—she is carted off to a mental institution by the representatives of "law and order" (78)—can be read as a version of execution. Within her community Miss Eckhart seems to serve the same social function that Jane Ussher has argued was served by historical witches: "The witch provided a powerful depository for the unknown or feared phenomena besetting the closed village community. Confidence in the evil of witchcraft was more acceptable than uncertainty or self-blame" (47). Certainly Morgana is its own "closed community," and hidden beneath the surface, its residents betray signs of uncertainty and self-blame—as we detect in Cassie's mother, for example. Although Mrs. Morrison is neither manless nor childless, she is not an image of the "good mother." Most of our glimpses of her occur as she walks out of the rooms where her children are: as the story opens, Mrs. Morrison leaves her son's room "and [goes] off to her nap" (20); shortly thereafter she leaves him again for a party (27); when Cassie tells her of the events at the MacLain house, she responds by "breaking from her" (92); and yet again she kisses Loch in his bed and "sway[s] out of the room" (94). Cassie "[bears] the dread that her mother might not come at all" (71), apparently expecting only leavetakings but not arrivals from her mother. In fact, Cassie's fears prove correct, as we learn in "The Wanderers": "After being so gay and flighty always, Cassie's mother went out of the room one morning and killed herself"

(261). Yet though Cassie's mother seems to resist, in her own small ways (until the final and most dramatic one), the ideal of Morgana womanhood, she nevertheless "could not help but despise Miss Eckhart. It was just for living so close to her, or maybe just for living, a poor unwanted teacher and unmarried. And Cassie's instinct told her her mother despised herself for despising" (64). Miss Eckhart is, in fact, *too close* to Mrs. Morrison, who deals with her own gender dis-ease by laying it on the head of the unmarried teacher. Miss Eckhart thus becomes the sign of deviance, the rejection of which grants the comforting illusion of stability in the system of beliefs underlying Morgana's social order.

Whenever the women of Morgana are faced with the threat of possibility, they attempt to recontain that threat through representations that eliminate its threatening nature, or else to expel it from the community, "closing ranks" in opposition to it. In "June Recital," Missie Spights reveals the tension between containment and expulsion, suggesting that Miss Eckhart "would have been like other ladies . . . if she had been married to anybody at all, just the awfullest man—like Miss Snowdie MacLain, that everybody could feel sorry for" (66). Snowdie MacLain is herself an example of the community's attempts at containment. Morgana's women must tell stories about Snowdie's separation from her husband in order to accept her aberrant position within the community. The first story in *The Golden Apples*, "Shower of Gold," consists precisely of Katie Rainey's storytelling efforts about Snowdie's marriage. Although she takes great pains to present Snowdie as the abandoned, silently grieving woman, there are nevertheless disturbing elements that cast doubt on her own version of events: "She must have had her thoughts and they must have been one of two things. One that he was dead—then why did her face have the glow? It had a glow—and the other that he left her and meant it. And like people said, if she smiled then, she was clear out of reach. I didn't know if I liked the glow. Why didn't she rage and storm a little—to me, anyway, just Mrs. Rainey? . . . I'll tell you what it was, what made her different. It was the not waiting any more. . . . We were mad at her and protecting her all at once" (8). Uncomfortable with Snowdie's potential difference (which, as we have seen, can also be taken as a mark of secret resemblance in *The Golden Apples*), the Morgana women construct the story of Snowdie's longing for her husband's return, thus recontaining her difference: the specter of threat to their own systems of belief.

It is apparent in "June Recital" that this strategy is also attempted on Miss Eckhart. Thus, the town tells the story of her love for Mr. Sissum and her grief at his death. The reliability of this version of events is undermined, however, by the constant emphasis on its construction *as a story*:

> *People said* she might have thrown herself upon the coffin if they'd let her; just as, later, Miss Katie Rainey did on Victor's when he was brought back from France. But Cassie had the impression that Miss Eckhart simply wanted to see—to see what was being done with Mr. Sissum. . . . It was strange that in Mr. Sissum's life Miss Eckhart, *as everybody said*, had never known what to do; and now she did this. . . . After the way she cried in the cemetery—*for they decided it must have been crying she did*—some ladies stopped their little girls from learning any more music. (54–55; emphasis added)

Despite the influence on her of Morgana's stories, Cassie can still see an alternative explanation for Miss Eckhart's behavior—one that suggests an emotional distance and detachment from Mr. Sissum.[8] The community, however, interprets her behavior—at least aloud— through the lens of a heterosexual desire that it can understand; simultaneously, and paradoxically, it acts on an increased sense of moral threat to its children. This scene makes no sense as a catalyst in the community's expulsion of Miss Eckhart if it is characterized merely by her crying at a funeral, a perfectly "normal" behavior. (Indeed, her "grief" is compared to that of Katie Rainey—one of their own—at the funeral of her son.) It is the way Miss Eckhart "cries" that gives the community pause, precisely because it is not crying at all. The people of Morgana seem to sense that their efforts to contain the threat of Miss Eckhart by rewriting her in the image of a "normal" woman have failed. The community cannot close around Miss Eckhart, as it does around Snowdie, so finally it must close against her.

It is given its excuse for doing so in the incident of the attack on Miss Eckhart (perhaps rape—Miss Eckhart is clearly meant to be ashamed of what has happened to her) by a "crazy nigger": "Miss Perdita Mayo . . . said Miss Eckhart's *differences* were why shame alone had not killed her and killed her mother too; that differences were reasons" (57). In point of fact the attack is another instance in *The Golden Apples* of violence done to women; but apparently such an act is not mythologized in the same way by the people of Morgana if it is committed by a black man against a white woman. In this case, rather than a magnificent rapist in the guise of a swan or a shower of gold, we get simply a "crazy nigger." The event is highly threatening to Morgana's inhabi-

---

[8] Critics, apparently not knowing what to make of Cassie's secret glimpse into Miss Eckhart, tend to ignore it and accept at face value the "romance" with Mr. Sissum. See, for example, Schmidt 89, McHaney 117, Skaggs 223.

tants, perhaps because it forces them to confront the underlying similarity between King MacLain and "crazy nigger," and the community's complicity (through myth-making) with both: "They wished [Miss Eckhart] had moved away . . . then they wouldn't always have to remember that a terrible thing once happened to her" (57). Cassie later thinks "that perhaps more than anything it was the nigger in the hedge . . . that people could not forgive Miss Eckhart" (58), possibly because the incident threatens to unravel the community's constructions of masculine and feminine, of whiteness and blackness. Indeed, there are also obvious parallels between Miss Eckhart and the black rapist: both are marked by their "differences" from that community (Miss Eckhart explicitly, the "crazy nigger" by implication), and "differences were reasons" for the exclusion of both. Like her attacker, Miss Eckhart is ultimately judged "crazy," a signifier that, as we shall see, marks her powerlessness within the white southern community as effectively as it does for the "nigger." The analogy suggests the role of stories in the production not only of an ideology of gender but of an ideology of race as well. It is not that myths are operative in interpretations of King MacLain but not in those of Miss Eckhart's attacker; rather, the community's stories construct the latter as "nigger" just as surely as they construct King as Zeus or Miss Eckhart as madwoman.

The mythologizing of Miss Eckhart, then, is the means by which the community contains her difference. But there is a ritual in her life which marks her own effort at containment, and that is the June recital: "For the recital was, after all, a ceremony. . . . Both dread and delight were to come down on little girls that special night, when only certain sashes and certain flowers could possibly belong. . . . A blushing sensitivity sprang up on [Miss Eckhart] every year at the proper time like a flower of the season. . . . Miss Eckhart stirred here and there utterly carried away by matters that at other times interested her least—dresses and sashes, prominence and precedence, smiles and bows" (70). Miss Eckhart, at this single time as at no other, is the picture of femininity, likened to blooming flowers as at other moments she is compared to witches and spiders. The "ceremony" of the recital is in fact a substitute for that ceremony which could ensure Miss Eckhart's position within the community. It takes place in June, the traditional month for weddings; Miss Lizzie Stark attends in "her most elaborate hat, one resembling a large wreath or a wedding cake" (75); most significantly, the dress that Miss Eckhart requires of each of the girls as uniform is "like a flower girl's dress in a wedding" (68). The purpose of uniforms is, naturally, to ensure uniformity; and Miss Eckhart seems at these times to be actively engaged with the rest of the community in the construction of gender. She herself draws the line of exclusion by which "only certain sashes and certain flowers could possibly belong," and she apparently ascribes that line to a sort of natural order: "Think of God's rainbow and its order" (67), she exhorts the young girls. At the June recital, Miss Eckhart symbolically takes up a position among "all female Morgana" (71) through a distorted image of the ritual that would in fact allow her to be accepted by them.

The recital, through which Miss Eckhart perhaps postpones her rejection by the community, also marks the incompatibility within that community of the roles of artist and woman. Miss Eckhart is portrayed as caring next to nothing about her art during the recital: "Except Virgie, all played their worst. They shocked themselves. . . . But Miss Eckhart never seemed to notice or to care. How forgetful she seemed at exactly the moments she should have been agonized!" (73). At the recital Miss Eckhart is completely distanced from her power and potential voice as an artist and is concerned only with the form of the pseudo-marriage ritual. A sharp distinction is made in Welty's story between the "art" of the recital, which substitutes clichéd images of femininity for music, and the single instance when Miss Eckhart truly performs on the piano: "Her skin flattened and drew across her cheeks, her lips changed. The face could have belonged to someone else—not even to a woman, necessarily. . . . And if the sonata had an origin in a place on earth, it was the place where Virgie, even, had never been and was not likely ever to go. . . . Coming from Miss Eckhart, the music made all the pupils uneasy, almost alarmed; something had burst out, unwanted, exciting, from the *wrong person's* life. This was some brilliant thing too splendid for Miss Eckhart" (56; emphasis added).

This is more than a modernist representation of artistic alienation; Miss Eckhart is the "wrong person" to be an artist. As an artist she disrupts the constructed category of woman, and the girls around her immediately react with the same sense of threat implicit in the rest of the community's response to her. But as Peter Schmidt has rightly noted, the "disturbing memory of Miss Eckhart is . . . buried within her female pupils and may surface even when they are acting most conventionally" (108). Reproduced in the young girls' tie-dyed scarves is "a design like a spiderweb" (Welty 36); the resurfacing of the spider imagery in Cassie's endeavor to make a pretty piece of feminine fashion parallels the resurfacing of memories of Miss Eckhart herself and suggests that these memories may ultimately disrupt Cassie's unproblematic positioning within a gender system.

Yet Miss Eckhart fundamentally misunderstands the radical possibilities of her own art. She either subordinates it to the reproduction of the dominant culture, as in the recital, or she conceives of it as offering potential escape, becoming Elizabeth Kerr's figure of the "creative artist who cultivates [her] powers to escape from and transcend conventions which bind men and women and waste lives" (148). Miss Eckhart hopes, further, for Virgie to make her own escape through art: "Virgie Rainey, she repeated over and over, had a gift, and she must go away from Morgana" (60). Several readers have taken up the proposition that the artist in Welty's fiction can serve a disruptive function simply by being on the outside of society.[9] This possibility is supported by the almost offhand mulling of Eugene MacLain in "Music from Spain" that "an artist, or a foreigner, or a wanderer, [are] all the same thing" (204). Yet serious doubt is cast on Miss Eckhart's faith in the "escape" provided by music: "Virgie would be heard from in the world, playing that, Miss Eckhart said[;] . . . 'the world'! Where did Miss Eckhart think she was now?" (60). Miss Eckhart fails to understand that she herself is in the world—that is, that there is no "outside of" or "away from" the conditions she suffers in Morgana: the various stories that "hold" and "place" subjects in particular ways. If Miss Eckhart is an artist figure, she nevertheless cannot simply *transcend* ideology through the sheer force of imagination. (We may speculate that, having failed to escape the world through art, Miss Eckhart finally escapes it through madness.)

Nor can she straightforwardly *destroy* ideological representation. The setting for Miss Eckhart's plunge into madness is an image of an image: the former piano teacher reconstructs the scene of the recital, "dressing up the parlor with ribbons of white stuff" (30) just as once she decorated it "like the inside of a candy box . . . with streamers of white ribbons . . . dividing and redividing the room" (72). Re-creating the representation of her own femininity in order to obliterate it by setting it on fire, Miss Eckhart seems to be undertaking an act of symbolic power which in fact has no power. Her fire is so pathetic that Old Man Moody and Mr. Fatty, the representatives of "law and order," evince more astonished surprise than fear, and are absurd in their leisurely efforts to put it out (80). Caught in a vicious double bind, Miss Eckhart—rejecting the memory of her complicity with the town's image of femininity—becomes the image of the unstable spinster that Morgana always harbored. How very little subversive force her madness has is indicated by Old Man Moody's exhortation to her to "come on lady-like[,] I'm sure you know how," and by Fatty Bowles's joking comment

---

[9] See, for example, Kerr 146–147, Demmin and Curley 244, 249. For a discussion of the "closed society," see Silver 154–55.

that perhaps Miss Eckhart aimed "mischief" because "she's a she, ain't she?" (87). Madness and constructions of the feminine, as depicted in Welty's story, are by no means mutually exclusive; they are finally, and paradoxically, two aspects of the same phenomenon.

When Miss Eckhart and Virgie encounter each other at the story's end, they are both portrayed as accomplished wanderers: "What [Cassie] was certain of was the distance those two had gone, as if all along they had been making a trip. . . . It had changed them. They were deliberately terrible. They looked at each other and neither wished to speak. . . . No one could touch them now, either. . . . Both Miss Eckhart and Virgie Rainey were human beings terribly at large, roaming on the face of the earth. And there were others of them—human beings, roaming, like lost beasts" (96). Wandering, in this representation, is hardly a manifestation of power; it is the complete *absence* of power. Far from being "heard from in the world," neither Virgie nor Miss Eckhart even wishes to speak. Thus, they have no way of countering the stories Morgana will tell about them in order to place and hold them, even as they wander—whether geographically or within their own minds. If no one can touch them now, they also can touch no one; they are outside the range of discourses. Virgie will get a second chance to confront the significance of storytelling and representation—in "The Wanderers"—but for Miss Eckhart, this silence is final. Miss Eckhart's fate strongly indicates that the wanderer, the foreigner, and the madwoman must finally be distinguished from the artist who works to transform ideological constructions by working within them. (This figure, I might add, is quite different from that of the alienated modernist artist who can shatter constructs and escape ideology through the sheer power of *his* imagination.) We can see in Welty's story the beginnings of a postmodern perspective characterized by Toril Moi's position that "we can only destroy the mythical and mystifying constructions of patriarchy by using its own weapons. We have no others" ("Representation" 198).

Cassie will never learn how to deconstruct Morgana's representations, for which she has so often been a mouthpiece; but her own position as a female subject has been jarred, and thus she does experience an initiation of sorts.[10] As she re-collects the fragments of her memories of Miss Eckhart, she begins to be dimly aware of her own share, as a receiver and transmitter of Morgana's stories, in Miss Eckhart's fate: "She thought that somewhere, even up to the last, there could have been for Miss Eckhart a little opening wedge—a crack in the door. . . . But if I had been the one to see it open, she thought slowly, I might

---

[10] See Kerr 135 for a description of feminine initiations in Welty's writing.

have slammed it tight for ever. I might" (67). By the end of her musings, she is able to name Morgana's collective responsibility for Miss
Eckhart's fate ("Then Morgana could hold them, and at last they were
this and they were that"). Although Cassie will always partake in
Morgana's representations to some degree—she never seems to be able
to see through the myth of the geographic wanderer, for example—she
will not become the paradigmatically "feminine" woman that she
promises to be in "June Recital," making tie-dyed scarves and going on
a romantic hay ride (perhaps, symbolically, her last) with boys. In "The
Wanderers," we learn that Cassie has in fact become another Miss Eckhart, an unmarried piano teacher, who spells out her mother's name in
flowers every spring on her grave (271) "as if subconsciously trying to
compensate for her mother's not being able to make her mark on the
world when she was alive" (Schmidt 176).

Virgie, in contrast, seems to be the recipient of a much more profound insight into the nature of representation in "The Wanderers."
The image of Perseus and Medusa which Virgie contemplates at the
end of this story, so strongly associated with Miss Eckhart, is one of the
most difficult to make sense of in all of *The Golden Apples*. As we have
seen, Miss Eckhart is represented as Circe, Sibyl, fairy-tale witch, and
sinister spider, suggesting her connection to Medusa, yet another monstrous woman. Although in Virgie's mind Miss Eckhart "had absorbed
the hero and the victim" (276), how Miss Eckhart constitutes a "hero"
seems to me a far more perplexing question than how she constitutes
the victim: she is the woman to whom violence has been done, both in
rendering horrible what was once beautiful, and then in slaying that
created horror as a menace to society. All the myths that surround Miss
Eckhart have an underside which the narrative of "June Recital" works
to reveal. Medusa, the Sibyl, Arachne: all are women whose hideous
appearance is, we might say, "constructed"; they have been made horrible as punishment from the gods, but need not have been so. Furthermore, it is worth noting that it is Medusa's *image* that is dangerous,
turning those who see it to stone; Medusa is the *constructed* spectacle
of threat. Perseus, capturing that image in the confines of his
mirror/shield, can control and contain the threat that she poses; in this
sense the Perseus-Medusa myth is emblematic of the desire to conquer
what appears threatening. Miss Eckhart is as much Perseus as Medusa
at this level of interpretation: she is her own Perseus, accepting her
constructed position as psychologically unfit spinster and thus de-
stroying herself in madness.

But at the same time the myth operates at another level in the story.
Perseus' flaunting of Medusa's head can be understood as a dramatic

revelation of the horrible workings of myth. Virgie's insight is that "cutting off the Medusa's head was the heroic act, perhaps, that *made visible* a horror in life, that was at once the horror in love" (275; emphasis added). The scene of Medusa's slaying is the spectacle that makes visible the potential horror of myths, including myths of "love"; for love, itself constructed through a multitude of myths, can mark exclusion as much as inclusion. Although the community can accept Miss Eckhart's supposed heterosexual love for Mr. Sissum, her love for Virgie Rainey is far more disturbing and threatening because it has no place in the town's myths of love, characterized largely by Zeus' rapes of various women: "Her love never did anybody any good" (65). In Virgie's final reworking of the Perseus myth her own community seems to hold so dear, Perseus is heroic not as a conqueror but as a figure for the artist who makes visible the potential violence of representation; the Persean act is in "identifying [Medusa] as an image, a cultural fiction" (Schmidt 250). Miss Eckhart, both defeated "victim" and, in Virgie's retrospective account, artistic "hero," has made visible to Virgie the horror implicit in the town's storytelling efforts. Furthermore, Virgie associates this making visible with Miss Eckhart's art, the Beethoven she played for her pupil. Art, Welty's story indicates, has the potential power to work against myth—that is, against repeated stories which have hardened into "barriers"—by offering an alternative understanding of reality, as the memory and image of Miss Eckhart do for Virgie, and as the narratives of *The Golden Apples* do for us.

Ironically, Welty's use of myth in her fiction has resulted in comparisons of her work to the writings of Joyce and Yeats. As a result, Welty received a fair degree of critical attention even before feminist critics began to recover women's writing from obscurity. In contrast, Jean Stafford and Hortense Calisher have received scant critical attention; indeed, their writing places them at odds with dominant strains of feminist criticism that might have "rescued" them. One of the few commentators on Jean Stafford's "Beatrice Trueblood's Story," Maureen Ryan, notes the appealing escape of madness in her fiction: "For Stafford, the withdrawal from the horrors of modern society—and for women, from the oppressions of a patriarchal culture—is a powerful temptation; her fiction demonstrates that the most dangerous and enticing of avoidance techniques is the retreat to one's own mind" (99). For Ryan, however, Stafford's ultimate rejection of madness is a sign of a chink in Stafford's feminist sensibility: "[Stafford's] contemporary, feminist attitudes," as suggested by her attraction to the liberatory potential of madness, "are undercut by her traditional, conservative impulses," which pull her back toward the "woman's life of compromise" (83). Thus Ryan reveals her alignment with feminist discourse that valorizes madness. But madness itself, as we have seen, is a "compromise"—or, to use another word, is complicitous—with the ideological systems that surround it.

Madness in "Beatrice Trueblood's Story" takes the form of the protagonist's temporary deafness, a classic manifestation of what Freud would no doubt have identified as a hysterical symptom. Stafford's use of hysteria must immediately invoke a whole set of fraught representations on psychological "illness" and femininity dating back to the nineteenth century, when hysteria was understood as an abdication (sometimes a willful one) of the woman's role within the family:

> The effect of hysteria upon the family and traditional sex-role differentiation was disruptive in the extreme. The hysterical woman virtually ceased to function within the family. No longer did she devote herself to the needs of others, acting as self-sacrificing wife, mother, or daughter: through her hysteria she could and in fact did force others to assume those functions. . . . As an impartial and professionally skilled observer, [the doctor] was empowered to judge whether or not a particular woman had the right to withdraw from her socially allotted duties. At the same time, such a physician accepted as correct—indeed, as biologically inevitable—the structure of the Victorian family and the division of sex roles within it. He excused the woman only in the belief that she was ill and that she would make every effort to get well and resume her accustomed role. (Smith-Rosenberg 208–9)

Paradoxically, although hysteria as described names a state of resistance to the feminine gender role, it has also traditionally been conceived as inextricably connected to femininity itself. Carroll Smith-Rosenberg suggests as much when she asks, "Why did large numbers of women 'choose' the character traits of hysteria as their particular mode of expressing malaise, discontent, anger, or pain?" The answer is, of course, that those "traits" were consistent with predominant notions of femininity; they were in fact "the embodiment of a perverse or hyper-femininity" (Smith-Rosenberg 198). S. Weir Mitchell, a prominent American neurologist during the Victorian period, "ended one of his treatises on hysteria with the comment that doctors, who knew and understood all women's petty weaknesses, who could govern and forgive them, made the best husbands" (Smith-Rosenberg 211–12). During a 1970–71 lecture series, a "nationally-known psychoanalyst" and clinical director at a psychiatric teaching hospital commented that "all good women are a little hysterical, that's why we marry them and pay for their therapy" (Pleck 17). Although a "good" woman (i.e., one who represents herself as appropriately feminine) was seen as "a little hysterical," she nevertheless needed to be cured of her hysteria, first, by acquiring a husband, and second, by seeing a therapist. (The two apparently served similar functions.)

Pauline Bart and Diana Scully further underscore the alliance of notions of hysteria with the stereotypical feminine image, not just in the Victorian period but into the late 1960s. They compared therapists' descriptions of psychologically "healthy" women in a 1970 study with the description of the hysterical personality in the *Diagnostic and Statistical Manual of Mental Disorders* and found the traits listed in each category to be fundamentally similar (369, 373). The supposed "threat" posed by hysteria, in the twentieth century as in the nineteenth, could be juxtaposed to descriptions, definitions, and symptomatology that positioned it firmly inside the feminine realm—indicating that hysteria is hardly an effective site for disruption of the sex/gender system.

Freud's patient Dora, the paradigmatic hysteric for the twentieth century, reinscribed the same basic formula: once again, the "cure" for hysteria as posited by Freud was a repositioning of the hysterical subject as feminine, though the feminine "role" was implicitly redefined as one of sexual satisfaction of male desires rather than as one of domestic duties. Although Freud recognized Dora's insight into her situation— her understanding that she was being exchanged between two men as currency in a "deal"—he nevertheless diagnosed her as "ill" for claiming not to want to be a participant in this exchange. Hysteria, Freud argued, resulted from repression of sexual desire; thus, he interpreted Dora's hysterical symptoms (pressure on upper body, cough) as manifestations not of disgust but of suppressed desire. Freud's fundamental goal in Dora's treatment, as many subsequent readers have pointed out, was to make her realize her hidden desire for Herr K.—that is, her secret wish to participate in the exchange.[11]

In an alternative interpretation of Dora's cough, derived from recent feminist reexaminations of hysteria, we might conjecture instead that it signaled her perception of her inability to speak. Dora's situation required of her a tacit acceptance, a pact of silence of sorts. Freud's narrative about Dora's symptoms conjures up an image of fellatio, which Dora denied desiring but which Freud insisted on, ignoring her

[11] See especially Moi, "Representation." Moi observes that, though Freud does mention the crucial factor of Dora's erotic attachment to Frau K., he concentrates not on this attachment but on her heterosexual desire for Herr K. and its connection to her oedipal feelings for her father.

words; the penis thus inserted forcibly into Dora's mouth literally stopped up her story. In a related context, Elaine Showalter observes that in nineteenth-century England, "psychiatrists believed that their therapeutic authority depended on domination over the patient's language. . . . The globus hystericus, which doctors had interpreted as the rising of the womb, may have been a physical manifestation of this choked-off speech" (154). Claire Kahane has noted the highly problematic nature of the "story" of hysteria:

> Since hysterics suffered from gaps in their memories, holes in their stories—the sign of repression—Freud's aim was to fill those gaps. Listening closely to the patient's communications—words, gestures, tone—Freud suggested meanings of which the patient was unaware, meanings which, extended to the symptoms, made of them signifiers—i.e., coded representations, that, when understood, formed part of a coherent narrative. When his patients came into possession of their own stories, Freud believed, they would not have to speak across the body. Yet Freud neglected to ask how a woman comes into possession of her own story. (21)

Hysteria is the site of a battle for representation which, for the woman, can be won only by being lost; she can, for Freud, come into possession of her own story only by ceasing to cling to her interpretation of events, with its denials, rejections, and repressions, and accepting that of the therapist. The underside of Freud's text is Dora as the figure of womanhood silenced—first by Herr K., Frau K., and her father, and then by Freud himself.

In light of this enforced silence, the feminist argument that Dora's hysteria was in fact a subversive speaking through her body has a certain persuasive power. Hélène Cixous, for example, wishes to reclaim the hysteric as a "force that works to dismantle structures. . . . Dora broke something" (Cixous and Clément 156–57). But Catherine Clément responds that "what she broke was strictly individual and limited" (Cixous and Clément 157), and Toril Moi agrees that this can hardly be seen as a successful revolt: "Hysteria is not, *pace* Hélène Cixous, the incarnation of the revolt of women forced to silence but rather a declaration of defeat, the realization that there is no other way out. Hysteria is, as Catherine Clément perceives, a cry for help when defeat becomes real, when the woman sees that she is efficiently gagged and chained to her feminine role" ("Representation" 192). Dora's symptom of coughing, then, can also be interpreted as a manifestation of her sense that she is gagged, that she will not be listened to. Her "cure," given that Freud "exhorts Dora to accept herself as an object for Herr K." ("Representation" 191), is to enter into a (hetero)sexual relationship that will gag her permanently.

The current debates over interpretations of hysterical symptoms can help us to understand why hysteria must have seemed particularly compelling to Stafford in the postwar period, as women were called on to leave the work force to make room for returning veterans—to beat a retreat to domesticity, taking up once again, without protest, the "traditional" feminine role. Remarkably anticipating subsequent feminist debates, Stafford represents hysteria in "Beatrice Trueblood's Story" as a battleground on which is waged the struggle between the construction and the deconstruction of gender. Beatrice, temporarily "manless" as she pauses between marriages, suddenly manifests a hysterical symptom—she literally can no longer hear her fiancé—in what clearly seems to "symbolize . . . female resistance to male oppression" (Goodman 214). Indeed, Beatrice's deafness can with good effect be read as a revolt against enforced feminine silence much like Dora's. Yet I would argue that the story ultimately works against any notion of the subversive possibilities of madness, whatever the "reason" the symptom might have for manifesting itself in the first place. Indeed, Stafford violently denounced retreats into hysteria and silence as a response to postwar conditions: "We are not entitled to be slovenly and *hysterical* because the world is a mess nor to be *incoherent* because governments do not make sense" (quoted in Hulbert 250; emphasis added). Instead, "Beatrice Trueblood's Story" focuses attention on the ways in which hysteria both contests and ultimately supports conservative notions of femininity.

The community that surrounds Beatrice, like that which surrounds Miss Eckhart, tells stories that define femininity and produce the feminine subject. (In de Lauretis's terminology, the stories are "technologies of gender" which point to other "technologies," such as the popular fiction they mimic and the medical and psychiatric establishments they call upon.) Romanticized representations of Beatrice Trueblood's engagement to Marten ten Brink, resembling fairy-tale plots or the domestic fiction of the eighteenth and nineteenth centuries, are repeatedly invoked; in them her marriage is the reward, described in Edenic, Elysian, and pastoral terms, for a heretofore troubled life bravely endured. These mini-plots, which seem to be produced by a communal chorus of voices and opinions, construct quite specific gendered positions: "[Observers might] have said that the man was animated and that his fiancée was becomingly engrossed in all he said, that ten Brink was in a state of euphoria as his wedding approached, while Beatrice moved in a *wordless* haze of happiness . . . [;] women thanked goodness that Mrs. Trueblood had come at last into a safe harbor, and men said that ten Brink was in luck" (391; emphasis added). As the community tells Beatrice Trueblood's story, it (re)produces gender as a position within which the woman's happiness is strongly linked to her "wordlessness." This representation further relies on notions of a feminine "norm" (Beatrice is said to be "becomingly engrossed"), from which the deviance, as we shall see, is the province of madness.

The community's high-flown, idealized stories about Beatrice are easily exposed as ideological—in contrast, for example, to the more ostensibly insightful musings of Jack Onslager, whose perspective the narrator most often presents, or even to the story told by Beatrice herself. Nevertheless, the more obviously "fictional" representations reveal behind them not a stable "truth," but only a series of more subtle fictions in which faith is more easily invested, with the result that they have far more profound effects. The extravagant parties which Onslager attends aid him in the construction of elaborate stories about the guests:

> He always felt on these occasions that he was static, looking at a colossal *tableau vivant* that would vanish at the wave of a magic golden wand. He was bewitched by the women[;] . . . he heard and saw among these incredible women moving in the aura of their heady perfume their majestic passions—tragic heartbreak, sublime fulfillment, dangerous jealousy, the desire to murder. When, on the next day, he had come back to earth, he would reason that his senses had devised a fiction to amuse his mind, and that in fact he had witnessed nothing grander than flirtations and impromptu pangs as ephemeral as the flowers in the supper room. (390)

The melodramatic scenes Onslager constructs from the "text" of these evenings, described in terms of magic and witchcraft, is dismissed as obvious imaginative creation (a "tableau vivant" with the status of "fiction"); but behind them is assumed to be a more stable truth which Onslager had in fact "witnessed." Nevertheless, romantic clichés appear here as well, in the depiction of women's passions and emotional entanglements as "ephemeral as flowers." Similarly, the "romantic mist" with which the community surrounds Beatrice is apparently dispelled by Onslager's ostensibly more accurate and reliable perception; but the narrative as a whole, I shall show, undermines our grounds for investing greater faith in Onslager's "truth." "Figures of speech" (397), by their very nature, represent something as something else. The ubiquitousness of such language in "Beatrice Trueblood's Story" suggests not that the characters are all misguidedly misrepresenting reality, but that re-presentation is inescapable, and always ideologically laden. Hysteria, then, in this story as in Dora's, becomes the focal point in a conflict over who tells the stories and what effects they may have.

Even in the single instance when Beatrice tells her own story, she nevertheless acts according to a fundamental principle of "wordlessness": her narrative is governed by the construct that, as "a reticent woman [she] . . . had too much taste to bare all these grubby secret details" (403). At the moment of self-representation, then, Beatrice reveals her own "interpellation" as a gendered subject: on the face of it, she uncritically accepts her feminine position and represents herself to her community as a woman, with all the social expectations that accompany that word. Nevertheless, the movement of the narrative as a whole centers on a slippage which Beatrice encounters in her subjectivity when her representations of herself suddenly cannot be made to fit with those of her community. Within "Beatrice Trueblood's Story" there is a veritable fugue of voices that invoke Beatrice's femininity, including the community's often collective voice, an ironic narrator who mimics that voice (for example, in the first paragraph of the story), a subtly different narrative voice identifying with Jack Onslager, who considers himself the only one with a "true" understanding of Beatrice's situation, and a narrator who appears to present Beatrice's thoughts. The ambiguity of the story's title, "Beatrice Trueblood's Story," suggesting simultaneously "the story about Beatrice Trueblood" and "the story that Beatrice Trueblood tells," indicates that the crux of the narrative is the juxtaposition of these various representations and the measure of correspondence between Beatrice's story about herself and the story told about her by others, including the story of her femininity.

Beatrice's hysteria is perceived by the community around her as being an obstacle to her desire for a happy marriage, in the same way that Dora's hysteria, perceived as suppressed desire, keeps her from permitting herself to serve as the object of Herr K.'s desire. The narrator, opening the story, takes on—clearly ironically—the perspective of the community: "When Beatrice Trueblood was in her middle thirties and on the very eve of her second marriage, to a rich and reliable man—when, that is, she was in the prime of life and on the threshold of a rosier phase of it than she had ever known before—she overnight was stricken with total deafness" (385). The narrator's opening then blends seamlessly in tone with the voice of one of the members of the chorus that constitutes Beatrice's community: " 'The vile unkindness of fate!' cried Mrs. Onslager" (385). For the community, Beatrice's inability to marry Marten ten Brink is nothing less than a tragedy.

The censure that is focused on Marten suggests that this tragedy is directly related to a violation of gender position on his part as well as on Beatrice's: " 'If he was in love with her,' preached Mrs. Fowler rabidly, 'he would have stuck by her. He would have refused to let her break the engagement. He would have been the one to insist on the specialists, he would have moved heaven and *earth*, instead of which he fled like a scared rabbit at the first sign of bad luck.' " And when another neighbor interjects, "Remember it was *she* who dismissed *him*," Mrs. Fowler retorts, " 'Yes, but if he'd had an ounce of manliness in him, he would have put up a fight. No decent man, no manly man, would abandon ship at a time like that.' Mrs. Fowler hated men so passionately that no one could dream why she married so many of them" (387–88). The narrator's ironic comment on Mrs. Fowler's hatred of men underscores the fundamental importance that the category of "man" has to this member of the chorus. "Manliness" apparently consists of vigorous activity which quite specifically opposes itself to Beatrice Trueblood's own expressed will, in order to position her correctly, with the help of the "specialists" of the medical and psychiatric institutions. Marten should have "put up a fight" and "moved heaven and earth," stereotypical enough expressions of the image of the chivalrous man coming to the rescue of the maiden in distress, with the addendum that what Marten is fighting against is the distressed maiden herself. A "manly man" would have *"refused to let her* break the engagement" (emphasis added), would have prevented her from having a "say" in the matter, as it were, for the sake of inserting her into her appropriate subject position. Crucial to Mrs. Fowler's construction of gender is a complete eliding of Beatrice's will and her own active involvement in her situation: she will not acknowledge that "it was *she* who dismissed *him*."

Mrs. Fowler supervises the neighborhood's plot—which verges on satire—to reclaim Beatrice as a social subject who will get over her hysterical deafness and "patch up things with Marten ten Brink." As Mrs. Fowler emphatically states, "I think she ought to have a husband"—this in spite of her low opinion of Marten. When the narrator tells us that "the whole gathering . . . agreed that this proposal made sense" (397), we begin to see the role of this tight community as more than merely a chorus; for they have a collective, vested interest in ensuring that their members do not rupture the system by which they understand the world. The potential disruption posed by Beatrice Trueblood, and even Marten ten Brink, to the constructed categories of gender are immediately countered by moves to reproduce those categories via the mediation of the psychiatric institution: someone must "get [Beatrice] to a good man" (397), meaning here not a husband but a psychiatrist. (As I have noted, the two roles were elided into each other in the medical discourse of the time.) Just as Freud ultimately allied himself with Dora's immediate community in its efforts to reinsert her into an appropriate feminine position (the object of Herr K.'s desire), so the psychiatric community is seen to work jointly with the expectations of Beatrice's community, for cure will lie only in the elimination of deafness. It must follow that Beatrice will then be gotten—since she is denied the power to get herself anywhere—to a "good man" who will be her husband.

Given that psychiatric intervention seems so important to the community, it is certainly notable that, at the onset of Beatrice's symptoms, Priscilla Onslager, Jack's wife, vigorously rejects the possibility of mental disorder, insisting that Beatrice's deafness is not "psychosomatic" or "hysterical" (386) but simply a "thunderbolt [which] comes out of nowhere" (386), an instance of "fate" (385). Mrs. Onslager's denial seems a bit extreme. Why this convulsive withdrawal from the possibility of hysteria? We might begin to answer this question by noting that hysteria had long been linked with some sort of willed stubbornness: "Even doctors sometimes interpreted [it] as a power grab rather than a genuine illness. . . . The hysterical 'type' began to be characterized as a 'petty tyrant' with a 'taste for power' over her husband . . . and, if possible, her doctor" (Ehrenreich and English 39–40). The treatment prescribed for hysteria accordingly involved the suppression of the hysteric's will: "Much of the medical literature on hysteria is devoted to providing doctors with the means of winning this war of wills. Physicians felt that they must dominate the hysteric's will; only in this way, they wrote, could they bring about her permanent cure. . . . 'Assume a tone of authority which will of itself almost compel submission,' Robert Carter directed. 'If a patient . . . interrupts the speaker, she must be told to *keep silent and to listen*' " (Smith Rosenberg 210; emphasis added).[12] It is of course extremely significant that this "war of wills" took place on a battlefield of *speech*, that is, of symbolic exchange. To secure submissiveness of will, the doctor need only ensure that the patient "keep silent" and "listen"—that is, accept the doctor's production of meaning, and implicitly its construction of reality, without engaging in her own.

Marten ten Brink espouses the view that the hysteric is being willful, as Beatrice reports to her kindly advocate, Jack Onslager: "He doesn't

---

12 Quoting from Robert B. Carter, *On the Pathology and Treatment of Hysteria* (London: John Churchill, 1853), 119.

believe that I am deaf but thinks it's an act. He says I am indulging myself, but he is willing to forgive me if I will only come to my senses"
(403). In a way, of course, Marten is right: Beatrice is not deaf, if deafness is defined as the condition in which hearing is physically im-
paired. There is nothing in Marten's own perception of Beatrice that
would negate a psychological explanation; he is asking her to "come to
her senses"—that is, to cease being mad—by coming to her sense of
hearing. (He is implicitly telling her "to keep silent and to listen.") Similarly, Priscilla Onslager resists calling Beatrice hysterical precisely because, according to the popular conception, hysteria would be a form
of "indulging" herself—Marten's accusation. Although Mrs. Onslager
rejects psychological explanations outright, while Marten alludes to
them, both depict madness as something that is in some sense willed,
and that can be left behind through an act of character.

Significantly, the community's construction of Beatrice as quintessentially feminine and romantic seems to be the factor that propels her
again and again into relationships in which the man dominates, replac-
ing her will with his own. The story concludes with Beatrice's "happy"
union with a man who quite clearly makes his own will the absolute
priority: "I have told you a thousand times that my life has to be exactly as I want it" (405). And though Mrs. Fowler disparages Beatrice's
earlier choice, Marten, because if he were a manly man, he would have
overridden her desire to end the engagement, Marten matches Mrs.
Fowler's expectations of manliness well enough at other times, such as
when he declares to his fiancée: "You mustn't think you can shut your
mind to these things. . . . [Y]ou can't shut your ears to them" (392).
Beatrice's hysteria is finally a desperate response to this forcible control
of her faculties (according to Marten's command, she cannot shut her
mind or ears). Beatrice takes control of her own senses, making her will
supreme:

> Her wish to be deaf had been granted. This was exactly how she put it,
> and Onslager received her secret uneasily. . . .
> "You are being fanciful," Onslager wrote, although he did not think she
> was at all fanciful. "You can't wish yourself deaf."
> But Beatrice insisted that she *had* done just that.
> She emphasized that she had *elected* to hear no more, would not permit
> of accident, and ridiculed the doting Priscilla's sentimental fate. (400)

It is, notably, the idea that Beatrice has enacted her own will that makes
her sympathizer Jack Onslager so nervous. Furthermore, to this extent
he acts with his community in trying to construct Beatrice differently—
by serving as a mirror through which Beatrice will see herself as with-

out control in this situation, even though he uncomfortably senses the challenge she poses to his own conception of her ("he did not think she was at all fanciful"). In other words, it would seem that Beatrice's hysteria, if viewed as an exercise of will, is construed by the community as a threat to its constructions of gender.

Nevertheless, the potentially disruptive power of hysteria, which Cixous would like to claim as a positive subversive move, finally disrupts nothing in this story. In the words of Catherine Clément, "[Hysteria] mimics, it metaphorizes destruction, but the family reconstitutes itself around it. . . . [Hysteria] introduces dissension, but it doesn't explode anything at all; it doesn't disperse the bourgeois family, which also exists only through its dissension, which holds together only in the possibility or the reality of its own disturbance, always reclosable, always reclosed. It is when there is a crossing over to the symbolic act that it doesn't shut up again" (Cixous and Clément 155–56). Although Beatrice's hysterical deafness "introduces dissension" to the extent that it resists the position in which her community's idealizing remarks have attempted to place her, such dissension is present only as a metaphor, while its real effects are to leave her more powerless than before. For Beatrice can have power, or the semblance of power, only in isolation.

Beatrice Trueblood comes to realize the dangers of withdrawal: "She had not bargained for banishment she said; she had only wanted a holiday. . . . 'And now I'm sorry because I'm so lonely here, inside my skull. Not hearing makes one helplessly egocentric'" (400–401). Her attempt at control—the will to deafness—has become helplessness. The "holiday" from hearing immediately transforms itself into the "banishment" of the transgressor from the systems of discourse through which any real power must be exerted. Even Douglas Clyde, the "cynical expastor" who, along with Onslager, is the only member of the community to admit the possibility of will in Beatrice's "fate," points out that Beatrice has gained no true agency through it: "[Though] the will is free and very strong. . . . I believe further that it can cease to be an agent and become a despot. I suspect hers *has*" (397). The model of hysteria we are presented with in Stafford's story is one of a willed strike, aimed at the praxis of an ideological system, which—because it is in fact firmly embedded in that system—strikes the self. Furthermore, the entire community and the mechanisms of madness upon which it calls immediately consolidate, circle, and close in on Beatrice in an attempt to reconstruct her in appropriately gendered terms. Even Clyde goes along with the rest of the community in agreeing with Mrs. Fowler's plan to "get [Beatrice] to a good man and then patch up things with

Marten ten Brink [because] . . . I think she ought to have a husband" (397). Neither Clyde nor Onslager ultimately escapes the ideology of gender. Beatrice's only options, apparently, are a good man or helpless banishment to a world of silence.

The story's presentation of these alternatives and their double bind is of course an indictment of the construction of femininity—and of the complicity of psychiatry, diffused into public concepts and practices, in that construction—as fundamentally similar to the construction of madness. The paradox posed by the narrative is that it is already a condition of the feminine gender to be silenced by the male will. Problematically, Beatrice's loss of hearing—which would appear subversive in its silencing of the voices that have collectively constructed her—renders her own voice tentative; she speaks "only approximately" and in a "far, soft, modest voice" (396). The deaf Beatrice is thus viewed as quintessentially feminine, even as her hysterical symptom manifests her single attempt to transgress gender. It is surely not a coincidence that Beatrice receives Jack Onslager's most ardent thoughts of praise after she has acquired her hysterical symptom. For in her first encounter with deafness, on the morning when she first fails to engage in conversation with her neighbors because she cannot hear their words, Onslager idealizes this silence as a demonstration that Beatrice "has risen above their fatuous questions and compliments. That woman was as peaceful as a pool in the heart of a forest. He turned to her, . . . looking directly into her eyes (blue and green, like an elegant tropic sea), and he said, 'I have never seen you looking prettier' " (395).

How we ought to regard Onslager's sense of superiority to his neighbors' "fatuous compliments" may be surmised from the juxtaposition between his voice and theirs. Those who encircle Beatrice repeatedly use idealizing representations in their readings of her experience. Beatrice and Marten, for example, are generally described as "dancing on air," and their tactful withdrawal from other party guests to have an argument is perceived as the understandable desire of lovers for privacy, represented in terms of an idyllic paradise: the neighbors "fondly sped them on their pastoral way, [and] the two walked down across the lawn and presently were gone from sight in the romantic mist. Their friends watched them and sighed, charmed, and went inside to drink a substitute for nectar" (391). The overblown images of Arcadia, jarring so demonstrably with Beatrice's own subsequent story, provide us with a clue for reading not only the community's constructions of reality but also those of Jack Onslager. The narrator intrudes on such a series of pseudo-poetic passages in order to call attention to their specific function in the narrative:

"I wish this day would never end," said Lucy Allingham. "This is the kind of day when you want to kiss the earth. You want to have an affair with the sky." . . .

Onslager's own wife, just as foolishly given to such figures of speech but with a good deal more style, simply through being older, said, "Look, here comes Beatrice. She looks as if her eyes were fixed on the Garden of Eden before the Fall and as if she were being serenaded by angels." . . .

. . . [E]veryone was watching Beatrice as she came slowly, smiling, down the stone steps from the terrace and across the lawn, dulcifying the very ground she walked upon. . . .

"You look as fresh as dew, dear," said Priscilla. (393)

The "figures of speech" which the narrator's commentary under-scores become a marker for representations of Beatrice's experience which do not account for her own understanding of that experience. The first figures of speech we encounter are those that repeatedly sketch Beatrice and Marten as a deliriously happy couple. When such figures appear again here, on the first morning of Beatrice's deafness, we may deduce that the community's rendering of what turns out to be Beatrice's confinement to a world of silence as paradisal is similarly in conflict with "Beatrice Trueblood's [own] Story."

There is of course no substantial difference between Onslager's con-struction of a (nonspeaking) Beatrice as "peaceful as a pool" and "like an elegant tropic sea" and his wife's version, in which she looks "as fresh as dew" and "as if she were being serenaded by angels." Sharing fundamental assumptions about femininity with his community, de-spite his various mental attempts to differentiate himself from them, Jack Onslager conceives of Beatrice as "the embodiment of everything most pricelessly feminine" at exactly the moment when "he remem-bered that she would not hear" (399)—a circumstance that has the paradoxical effect of rendering her speech increasingly tentative. In-deed, as Beatrice finally tells her own story, Onslager's image of her is momentarily disrupted; no longer "as peaceful as a pool," she "was frankly wringing her hands, and the terror in her face was sheer" (403). It is at this juncture that the ever-admiring Jack Onslager feels "un-manned" (perhaps because Beatrice has temporarily been "unwom-aned") and takes his confused leave.

Hysteria, then, appears to be a closed circle, an inescapable paradox: it is a rebellious move that leaves one powerless, an attempt to escape positioning as feminine even as it is a caricature of femininity. Beatrice wills not to hear, with the result that she is to some degree excluded from symbolic exchange; she deploys a hysterical symptom to escape her feminine role, with the result that she appears to others as more feminine; she refuses to have her will controlled or effaced by that of others, with the result that her own will becomes a "despot." To escape such a vicious circle, the story hints, more than madness is needed. In the struggle for control over storytelling, some distinction is made between the possible subversion offered by hysteria, as a muted form of communication—as "body language, or the vocabulary of the powerless" (Bart and Scully 373),[13] always therefore easily subject to appropriation by others—and the use of language itself, spoken or written, which wages the battle on the grounds of representation and the spaces it constructs. While Beatrice's hysterical symptom, and the demureness that seems to follow naturally from it, only make Onslager the more enamored of her, her self-representation, her "story," is nevertheless the single point at which Onslager—the "good man" sent to bring her back into the fold of the community by inducing her to see a psychiatrist—is "unmanned." That is, it is Beatrice's single attempt to represent her own life story, rather than her hysterical symptom (which, as a subversive move, seems finally only to reinscribe her in feminine silence), that holds the potential to disrupt gender positions.

Nevertheless, even if Beatrice's own story demonstrates some subversive potential, it never fulfills that potential; it is subsumed by the larger story in which it is embedded. (In contrast to Clément's hopeful assertion, Stafford depicts a brief "crossing over to the symbolic act" that is in fact "shut up again.") The community's general responsibility for Beatrice's fate is clear enough from the passage leading up to the conclusion:

> Everything was all right for Beatrice[;] . . . when she began treatment with a celebrated man, her friends began to worry less, and to marvel more at . . . the diligence with which she and the remarkable doctor hunted down her troublesome quarry. During this time, she went about socially, lent herself to conversation by reading lips, grew even prettier. Her analysis was a dramatic success. . . . Some months later, she married a man, Arthur Talbot, who was far gayer than Marten ten Brink and far less rich; indeed, a research chemist, he was poor. Priscilla deplored this aspect of him, but she was carried away by the romance (he looked like a poet, he adored Beatrice) and at last found it in her heart to forgive him for being penniless. . . . [W]hen his wife, who had now become a fervent supporter of psychiatry, exclaimed after the second evening that she had never seen Beatrice so radiant, Onslager agreed with her. (404)

---

[13] Bart and Scully draw on the arguments of Thomas Szasz in *The Myth of Mental Illness*.

Beatrice's treatment by a "good man" shows signs of immediate success—she is reintegrated into society, becomes "even prettier," and engages in conversation by reading lips (but does she say
anything?)—and demonstrates its ultimate accomplishment in the evidence that she is finally happily married (to a "good man"). Her circle
of friends have continued to tell Beatrice's story in such a way that for
Beatrice to take up a subject position within the community is necessarily to find herself again in the same sort of unhappily dominating
relationship. And we have seen that, though Beatrice's hysterical
symptom marks a crisis in her subject positioning, she nevertheless is
to some degree consistent in understanding and representing herself as
a feminine woman; she thus has some stake in taking up that position
which is created by the community's repeated versions of her story.
From the community's standpoint, the end to Beatrice Trueblood's
story is a happy one: she has been successfully reinterpellated into an
ideology of gender.

Onslager's version of the end of Beatrice Trueblood's story, as it is
presented by the narrator, is in its own way just as dangerous as the
community's, and perhaps more insidious: "Beatrice . . . and Onslager
travailed in the brief look they exchanged. It was again an enrapturing
day. The weather overhead was fair and bland, but the water was a
mass of little wrathful whitecaps" (405). Onslager's belief that he understands Beatrice's true situation and that he has secretly communi-
cated with her in the exchange of glances is enough to paint the day as
"enrapturing" in his memory and to assure him that he and Beatrice,
like bittersweet lovers or soul mates, have "travailed." For Onslager,
Beatrice is the romantic heroine of a tragic tale, a fiction as powerful as
those of his wife, whose happy ending would still find Beatrice
wrapped in the arms of a good man. Thus, Stafford's story marks a
shift in tone from Welty's "June Recital," published six years earlier.
Although Miss Eckhart may not survive, her story and its legacy do.
Beatrice's story, however, is lost just as surely in Jack Onslager's tragic-
romantic narrative as in Priscilla Onslager's fairy-tale ending; she is silenced equally by femininity and by hysteria, with no third alternative
presenting itself.

The early 1960s marked the upsurge of the antipsychiatry movement,
spearheaded by R. D. Laing. Setting himself up as a challenge to traditional psychiatry, Laing insisted on seeing madness within a social
context; he searched for causes of mental illness within the troubled
person's immediate environment (the family unit) as an alternative to
emphasizing a functional "failure" of the individual (*Divided Self* 27).

In his early work he paid close attention to how discourses, representations, and other modes of social interaction might position the individual. Laing's investigation of the production of madness within and by the family no doubt dealt a serious challenge to the operation of postwar psychological discourses and practices in support of the bourgeois family structure. In this sense, Laing's "revolt against the claustrophobic family" (Mitchell, *Psychoanalysis* 230) was radical indeed. But he inadvertently supported the prevailing ideological system by laying the blame for the child's madness at the feet of the bad mother: "There may be some ways of being a mother that impede rather than facilitate or 'reinforce' any genetically determined inborn tendency there may be in the child towards achieving the primary developmental stages of ontological security" (*Divided Self* 189). Laing's colleague David Cooper agreed: "If the mother fails to generate the field of reciprocal action so that the infant learns how to affect her as another, the child will lack the precondition for the realization of his personal autonomy. He will forever be a thing, an appendage, something not quite human" (*Psychiatry* 138–39). Although Laing's increasingly popular model of madness emphasized social construction, he remained oblivious to the role of technologies of gender in that construction.

Hortense Calisher's short story "The Scream on Fifty-Seventh Street," appearing in 1962 just as the antipsychiatry movement was getting under way, shares many of that movement's basic premises regarding the social construction of madness, while filling in what the antipsychiatry model left out: the interrelation of gender and madness as social productions.[14] Constituting madness in order to exclude it, Calisher's fictional community thus reaffirms the order and stability of what is included: the nuclear family, the wife and mother. The notion that the older woman left without a husband and family is likely to become slightly "funny in the head," and will then of necessity no longer be a functioning part of society, is the starting point for Calisher. The story suggests that what gives that stereotypical image a degree of "truth" is the threat that manlessness poses to the nuclear family. The community acts to expunge the threat. Thus the manless woman, receiving no confirmation from others about her own constructions of meaning, finally loses the ability to produce meaning within society altogether: that is, she becomes mad.[15]

[14] I am arguing here not for a direct influence by the antipsychiatry movement on Calisher, but more generally for a set of shared assumptions and a similar perspective on madness, produced out of a common historical experience.

[15] My reading of this story thus differs substantially from that of Kathleen Snodgrass. In her full-length published study of Hortense Calisher, Snodgrass invokes as her guid-

Mrs. Hazlitt, the widowed protagonist of "The Scream on Fifty-Seventh Street," certainly does not wish to play a subversive or threatening role; she wants only to represent herself as part of the (admittedly ill-defined) community of New Yorkers among whom she lives. It is ironically her desire to maintain some kind of social identification that leads Mrs. Hazlitt to recognize her new position—her widowhood, described explicitly in terms of her manlessness—as problematic with relation to the "community" of the city. Insisting on her status as a New Yorker "born . . . and raised" (108), when she hears a scream in the night, she considers her knowledge of city ways "all the more reason why what she had heard, or thought she had heard, must have been hallucinatory. A harsh word, but she must be stern with herself at the very beginnings of any such, of what could presage the sort of disintegrating widowhood, full of the mouse-fears and softening self-indulgences of the manless, that she could not, would not abide. . . . No, the fault, the disturbance, must be hers" (108–9). At some level, then, Mrs. Hazlitt already identifies a potential difference between the average New Yorker, with a "hive-sense of never being utterly alone" (108), and the "manless" woman who might "disintegrate." Her own construction of the manless widow as potentially disintegrating leads her to monitor herself sharply; her recognition of her driftings toward "madness" will presumably enable her to distinguish herself sharply from the truly mad. Thus she attributes "the fault, the disturbance," to herself in order to represent herself to herself as still capable of making important distinctions between, for example, the real and the hallucinatory—as still, that is, being a rational person. Later, when Mrs. Hazlitt clearly hears the scream once again, she still implicitly clings to belief in her difference from the screamer, whose cry in the night is "a madness expanded almost with calm" (110): she is "brought . . . to her senses" by the "vision of herself in her blue robe creeping down the front of a building on Fifty-Seventh Street" (111).

We can read Mrs. Hazlitt's efforts to distance herself from the "clearly" mad as a form of self-monitoring. Foucault identified the origins of a shift toward the social encouragement of *self*-regulation in

---

ing theme the image of "an open-ended journey," echoing Laing's later writing, in which he conceived madness as a liberating journey (although Snodgrass never mentions Laing or antipsychiatry). For Snodgrass, Calisher's fiction is about "rites of passage" and the "movement from stasis to mobility"; any movement is apparently "forward movement" (12, 61, 54). But if madness in "The Scream" can be construed as an open-ended journey, it certainly is not a journey forward or a voyage of insight. Considerations of the position of the "crazy old woman" in society seem to have rendered such idealizations less appealing to Calisher than to the antipsychiatrists.

Pinel's nineteenth-century asylum: "The madman recognizes himself as in a mirror in this madness [that is, of his fellow madmen in the asylum] whose absurd pretensions he has denounced. . . . He is now pitilessly observed by himself. And in the silence of those who represent reason, and who have done nothing but hold up the perilous mirror, he recognizes himself as objectively mad" (Focault 264). Although Mrs. Hazlitt "denounces" madness, her words imply that she is beginning, like Pinel's madman, to see her own madness reflected in the screamer's. For in attributing to herself "the fault, the disturbance," and suggesting that these are the products of "disintegrating widowhood" and "the self-indulgences of the manless," Mrs. Hazlitt suggests a connection between manlessness and a disruption of the social ("disturbance") and attributes to that disruption a certain moral judgment ("fault"). She begins to suspect herself of a violation, in Foucault's words, of "moral and social uniformity" (268).

Figurative mirrors in the story are the regulators of such uniformity, and thus hold immense power. Mrs. Hazlitt worries obsessively about how she appears to others: "One had to tidy one's hair, spruce a bit for the possible regard of someone in the hall, and when she did see someone, although of course they never spoke, she always returned feeling refreshed, reaffirmed . . . her day had begun in the eyes of others, as a day should. . . . Curious how, when one lived alone, one began to feel that only one's own consciousness held up the world, and at the very same time that only an incursion into the world, or a recognition from it, made one continue to exist at all" (115). The paradox is that only by being confirmed in the eyes of others can Mrs. Hazlitt rely on the truth of her own perceptions about the world, for if "only one's own consciousness held up the world," then one's perceptions have no external reality. Mrs. Hazlitt's search for someone else who has heard the scream is, similarly, a search for confirmation of her own construction of reality. R. D. Laing and A. Esterson detailed their model of mental illness in precisely these terms: a lack of confirmation of one's experience could result in the inability to distinguish "illusion" from "reality"—a primary "symptom" of madness (96, 73–74). In much the same way that the original mirror stage of our childhood, according to Lacan, gives us a sense of our bodies as an integrated whole and thus starts us on the road to subjectivity, "confirmation" for Laing and Esterson—the reflection of our interpretation of reality by others—serves as a subsequent metaphorical mirror stage, which continually secures our subjectivity.

Since the regard of others is crucial to Mrs. Hazlitt, her encounter with her neighbor Reginald Warwick is potentially shattering, not be-

cause Warwick fails to confirm the scream (concealing his own deafness, he suggests that he actually did hear a scream), but because, at
the end of their exchange, he refuses to look at her again: "Coco [the
dog] looked back at her; but his master, back turned, disentangling the
leash from the doorknob, did not, and went out without answering"
(116). The negation of acknowledgment implied by the turned back is
overwhelming to Mrs. Hazlitt, who cannot know herself except
through the gaze of others. Thus she immediately puts herself in
Warwick's place, regarding herself with the harsh critical eye of Pinel's
madman/judge: "So I've done it after all, she thought. Too friendly. Especially too friendly since I'm a woman. Her face grew hot at this probable estimate of her—gushy woman chattering over-brightly, lingering
in the hall. Bore of a woman who heard things at night, no doubt
looked under the bed before she got into it" (116–17). The descriptive
images she draws of herself, as she becomes the object of her own spec-
ulations, depend absolutely for their power and possibility on the fact
that she is a woman without a husband—lonely for male company,
afraid, needing protection. As she measures every instance of seemingly aberrant behavior against the image of "disintegrating widowhood," that image cannot fail to become the mirror by which she sees
herself. That is to say, her self-judgments cannot be separated from
the popular conceptions which she knows are attached to her new position as a widow.

The little boy whom Mrs. Hazlitt hires to help her carry her groceries
provides another mirror. When she offers him an éclair, the boy, "after
an astonished glance, . . . wolfed it with a practical air, peering at her
furtively between bites, and darted off at once, looking askance over
his shoulder at her. . . . Obviously he had been brought up to believe
that only witches dispensed free gingerbread" (119). The emphasis on
the boy's seeing Mrs. Hazlitt—he glances, peers, and looks askance at
her—suggests that the "witch" image is somehow reflected to Mrs. Hazlitt in his gaze. Mrs. Hazlitt once again internalizes the judging glance
of the other by becoming her own observer: "In front of the bathroom
mirror . . . [she] regarded her image, not yet a witch's but certainly a
fool's, a country-cookie-jar fool's" (119). Despite her ostensible rejection of the boy's perception of her, this moment marks a stage in the
process of becoming—of seeing herself as—what others see in her.
She is "not yet a witch"—or, more to the point, a crazy old woman—
but she might well become one.

Furthermore, the story's construction of Mrs. Hazlitt as a fairy-tale
witch suggests, once again, a social function similar to that of historical "witches": defense against "unknown or feared phenomena." We

might productively ask such questions as: What are those feared phenomena that beset the community around Mrs. Hazlitt? What specific
function can her construction as a madwoman or witch serve? Indeed,
how can she pose as a threat to a community that is barely a community at all? For the sense of responsibility to its members is virtually
absent, as Mrs. Hazlitt notes: "Here, in the city, the sense of responsibility has to weaken. Who could maintain it, through a door, an eleva-
tor, a door and a door, toward everyone, anyone, who screamed?"
(112). Nevertheless, there is, if not a principle of active inclusion, then
one of exclusion still operative even in the city, as Mrs. Hazlitt discovers. Indeed, in the face of social disintegration and isolation, the gesture of exclusion draws a circle around, and thus defines, the existing
community. Just as the "disordered" society of the witch-hunts needed
a scapegoat, not simply to blame but also to create the illusion of its
own order, a city notable for its absence of community relies on outcasts to define an illusory community, and to define it negatively:
those who are defined by the community's collective gaze as being
"no longer in the fold" (130) provide the only marker that there is a
fold.

Significantly, although Mrs. Hazlitt is aware that "in the city, the
sense of responsibility has to weaken" (112), she is comforted by
thoughts of organizations such as the hospital board to which she
gives her time. The faith in the servants of medicine as "an antidote to
that dark, anarchic version of the city" (118) underscores even further
the relation of medical discourses and practices, including those surrounding madness, to the maintenance of community through the
image of chaos controlled. Hospitals emblematize a model of service; it
is presumably their responsibility to attend to cries in the night. The
negative, coercive aspects of this form of responsibility are hinted at in
Mrs. Hazlitt's meditation that "everywhere, on flight after flight of the
city's high, brilliant floors, similar groups of the responsible were con-
vening, could always be applied to, were in command" (118). But
though Mrs. Hazlitt still accepts at face value the ideology by which
the perception of contained threat justifies a certain power, she no
longer has a secure position within that ideology: the "high, brilliant
floor" is figuratively swept out from under her when she learns that
her presence at the afternoon board meeting is not required. Mrs. Hazlitt has herself become the specter of anarchy against which the community defines itself.

Even in the country, Mrs. Hazlitt has observed a similar phenomenon, though on a more subtle level. She recalls the " 'people next door'
with their ready 'casserole' pity, at worst with the harbored glow of

their own family life peering from their averted eyelids like the lamp-light from under their eaves" (112). Although gestures of ostensible inclusion are present here, they are bracketed off by quotation marks ("people next door," "casserole" pity), suggesting an act of exclusion inherent within those gestures. This exclusion is based precisely on Mrs. Hazlitt's superfluousness to the family structure. She cannot see herself in the "averted eyes" of her country neighbors, which, reflecting only "the harbored glow of their own family life," offer her no recognition.

The idealized family structure is equally vital to the city's constitution of itself as a community. The multitude of "middle-aged and elderly, seemingly either single or the remnants of families," who occupy Mrs. Hazlitt's building, are clearly oddities "clinging to ceiling rents in what had become a fancier district" (113). And Mrs. Berry, the widowed owner of Mrs. Hazlitt's New York apartment, has, like Mrs. Hazlitt, been sent wandering "in search of recommended change" (109). Mrs. Hazlitt conjures an image of a long chain of nomadic, manless women like herself and Mrs. Berry, cut loose from their anchors in the heterosexual couple and family structure—an "imagined procession of women inhabiting each other's rooms, fallen one against the other like a pack of playing cards" (109). The evocation of the "fallen" woman cliché cannot fail to hint at a vague, lingering sense of moral trespass. Although the women are "fallen" for no other reason than that they no longer support, or are supported by, the structure of the bourgeois family, this is regarded with the same taint as a trespass of a more active sort.

Even as Mrs. Hazlitt straggles not to be defined as the disintegrating widow, the glances of others, inextricable from the way in which she "sees" herself, refuse to recognize her as anything but an Other—that which is unrecognized in the dominant ideology except by its difference. Mrs. Hazlitt's attempts to overcome this lack of recognition eventually take a desperate form, as she substitutes herself for the absent other: "Across from her, in another mirror, the full-length one, herself regarded her" (125). The shifting of pronouns, by which the direct object has become a separate subject, suggests that the self-monitoring gaze by which Mrs. Hazlitt regards herself has become reified into an imagined other who observes Mrs. Hazlitt, with the ostensible function of confirming her position within a community. Or perhaps we might say that Mrs. Hazlitt's regard of her image marks a stage in the process of her un-becoming. Whereas, earlier in the story, her glances in the mirror have been preparations for her entry into a social world (reminding us of each person's initial progression from Imaginary to

Symbolic, as described by Lacan), the process is now slowly reversed, as Mrs. Hazlitt retreats from social interaction to an imagined interaction with her mirror image: " 'Oh well, you're company,' she said" (119). Recall that the mirror stage for Lacan is still located in the Imaginary (736); in Terry Eagleton's gloss, "No clear distinction between subject and object, itself and the external world, is yet possible" (164). The necessary end of the mirror stage, in both temporal and teleological terms, is a sense of the difference and distance between self and others. It is, further, through this process that we acquire language, entering into the realm of symbolic representation which is founded on the exigencies of difference and absence. Not to enter this realm—to remain trapped in an imaginary bond with one's image—is, literally, madness.

In *The Divided Self*, published two years before Calisher's short story, Laing explained, in terms that can be seen as complementing Lacan's, how we develop a sense of ourselves as separate individuals (or what Lacan would call subjects). Laing returned to Freud's description of the young boy's game of "fort-da," in which the boy learns to overcome his anxiety at separation from his mother, in order to hypothesize the importance of being seen: "It seems that loss of the mother, at a certain stage, threatens the individual with loss of his self. The mother, however, is not simply a thing which the child can see, but a person who sees the child. Therefore, we suggest that a necessary component in the development of the self is the experience of oneself as a person under the loving eye of the mother" (116). In a footnote to the description of the "fort-da" game, Laing noted, Freud had mentioned that the boy learned to play the game with his own image in the mirror. Laing suggested that the importance of the mirror is not only that the boy sees his reflection, thus precipitating the process by which he will come to understand the image to be both him and not him, but also that the reflection "sees" him as well: "In overcoming or attempting to overcome the loss or absence of the real other in whose eyes he lived and moved and had his being, he becomes another person to himself who could look at him from the mirror. . . . [W]hen he could no longer see that other reflected image of his own person in the mirror he himself disappeared, possibly in the way he felt that he disappeared when he could no longer feel that he was under scrutiny or in the presence of his mother" (117). That is to say, for the very young child, the image of himself in the mirror might substitute for the gaze of others in giving him a sense of himself as a subject—the implication being, of course, that subjectivity depends on a social context. Furthermore, this is a continuing dependence for Laing, not one foreclosed by the successful passage through a particular "stage." He writes: "The sense of identity requires the existence of another by whom one is known . . . [it is not] finally possible to be human without a dialectical relationship to others" (139). In the schizoid personality, Laing observed, the child's willingness to allow the mirror image to substitute for the absent or nonrecognizing other is reproduced and magnified: "The schizoid person seeks in the boy's way of being a mirror to himself, to turn his self, a quasi-duality with an overall unity, into two selves, i.e. into an actual duality" (117). The more carefully Mrs. Hazlitt watches herself in the mirror, the more she will become what she fears, by substituting imaginary relations for symbolic ones.

We can read Mrs. Hazlitt's imaginary conversation with her double, Mrs. Berry, as a version of Laing's "schizoid" experience:

> She told her everything. At first she stumbled, went back, as if she were rehearsing in front of a mirror. Several times she froze, unsure whether a sentence had been spoken aloud entirely, or had begun, or terminated, unspoken, in the mind. But as she went on, this wavering borderline seemed only to resemble the clued conversation, meshed with silences, between two people who knew each other well. By the time she had finished her account she was almost at ease . . . so nearly could she imagine the face, not unlike her own, in the chair opposite, smiling ruefully at her over the boy and his gingerbread fears. (127)

What is internal to Mrs. Hazlitt's mind becomes externalized as a "conversation . . . between two people." Mrs. Berry is slowly transformed from a reflection in the "mirror"—an image of Mrs. Hazlitt herself, into which is projected Mrs. Hazlitt's own characteristics—to an externalized and observing other who, through her very similarity to Mrs. Hazlitt (a "face . . . not unlike her own"), can provide the recognition Mrs. Hazlitt seeks. Ironically, it is this act of inventing an other, for the purposes of confirming her sanity, which marks the boundary into madness that will ensure her exclusion from "the fold," just as her brief return to "sanity" once again deprives her of the comforting gaze of others: "There is nobody in the chair. Never was, never had been. It was sad to be up at this hour and sane" (129).

Here lies a contradiction: madness begins to provide a sense of community, while sanity for the manless woman denies it. When Mrs. Hazlitt finally acknowledges that she is "alone"—that is, unseen by others—the verbal acknowledgment of her separation from "the fold" propels her directly into the perception of a new and differently constituted community, consisting of all the Others unrecognized, except in their otherness, by society: "She had recognized it. She had identified the accent of the scream. . . . What had summoned her last night would have been . . . audible only to those tuned in by necessity—the thin, soaring decibel of those who were no longer in the fold. . . . There must be legions of them, of us, she thought" (129–30). "Them," the figures of disintegration from whom she has been trying throughout the story to distinguish herself, finally becomes "us," a separate group whose cries will be heard, recognized, and responded to only by one another. The self-regulating mechanisms that have finally succeeded in constituting her, in her own eyes, as an outcast from "the fold" simultaneously position her within a new "community," and the resolution of conflict that comes to her with this new position explains her earlier characterization of the screamer's tone as "a madness expanded almost with calm" (110).

But just what is the status of this community? Are we to view the calm that comes with madness as a triumph? Is the community of lonely madpeople somehow a viable alternative to the ill-defined community of city dwellers in New York? Mrs. Hazlitt's own reaction would seem to indicate an affirmative response to these questions, and thus to support those who argue for the subversive force of madness: "She brought her fist to her mouth, in savage pride at having heard it, at belonging to a race some of whom could never adapt to any range less than that. *Some of us*, she thought, are still *responsible*" (131). At some point Mrs. Hazlitt's vision of "those high convocations of the responsible" (118), such as the hospital board, clearly fails her—perhaps because such convocations are unable (in a larger sense than simply the canceled meeting) to provide her with the opportunity not only of "seeing people" but also of being seen by them. At any rate, by the story's conclusion, it is only the "race" of night criers who are "still responsible," because they can recognize and attend to one another's screams.

Yet if a myth of subversive madness constitutes a solution here, that solution is Mrs. Hazlitt's rather than one posed by the narrative as a whole. The importance of speech as a social act in the story suggests a pattern to Mrs. Hazlitt's disintegration marked by her increasing willingness to substitute imaginary communication for symbolic exchange. At first she mimics social interaction in a way that still posits the potential presence of another, whose absence is only temporary: "She shook herself with a reminiscent tremble. . . . It was a gesture made more often to a companion, an auditor" (112). In her comments to herself she still recognizes the outlines of "addressing a vis-à-vis, so deeply was the habit ingrained" (124). Although she speaks to herself, she takes on the "accent" of others—her husband, her neighbor Mrs.

Finan—so as to insist on the fundamental importance of the other, for which the self is but a poor substitute in the exchange of meaning (118, 124). It is for this reason that she is so frightened by the development of her habit of talking to herself: " 'Come on, Millie,' she said, using the nickname her husband always had. 'Get on with it.' She started to leave the room, then remained in its center, hand at her mouth, wondering. Talking aloud to oneself was more common than admitted; almost everyone did. It was merely that she could not decide whether or not she had" (118). It is not so much the talking aloud which disturbs Mrs. Hazlitt as it is her confusion between speech— essentially still social in nature, particularly as she plays the role of other people—and private thought.

Although her imagined conversation with Mrs. Berry seems to be yet another manifestation of this habit, it bears a marked difference: Mrs. Hazlitt has never met Mrs. Berry. Mrs. Berry is not a representation of an other so much as she is a "mirror" of Mrs. Hazlitt herself. Whereas earlier Mrs. Hazlitt had attempted to imitate the accents of others, Mrs. Berry is made in Mrs. Hazlitt's image, and is thus suggestive, in Lacanian terms, of a retreat from the realm of the "Symbolic" to "imaginary" reflection. The semblance of meaningful exchange with another now masks an increasingly internalized "conversation," beginning and ending in Mrs. Hazlitt's mind. We must judge Mrs. Hazlitt's final interpretation of the scream in the context of this detachment from the social production of meaning. It is notably in her own accent—her spoken word "alone"—that she "identified the accent of the scream" (129), suggesting that the process of substituting the self for all other possible auditors is complete. Furthermore, as Mrs. Hazlitt waits for the repetition of the scream at the story's end, she stands with her "hand clapped to her mouth" (131)—a gesture used twice earlier to mark her uncertainty about whether or not she has spoken and powerfully indicative of the stoppage, not the production, of speech. Locked once and for all in a replaying of the Lacanian mirror stage, Mrs. Hazlitt is also trapped outside of language. Whether or not the original scream was in fact Mrs. Hazlitt's own, the story's structure cannot fail to indicate that any "community" of the mad is a community of one. Precisely when Mrs. Hazlitt most strongly feels that she has found a new mode of meaningful exchange, the story hints that her speech has been stopped up in her own throat. This is the marker of her final "madness."

Once again, we may look to Laing's model of madness as closely congruent with Calisher's, this time in his early views on the relation of madness to "effective" action: "When the 'self' becomes more and more a participant in phantasy relationships, in doing so it loses its own reality. It becomes, like the objects to which it is related, a magical phantom. . . . The self can be 'real' only in relation to real people and things[;] . . . losing reality, it loses its possibility of exercising effective freedom of choice in the world" (*Divided Self* 141). Laing, arguing in existential terms, saw in madness the loss of "freedom of choice," through which the individual becomes unable to act effectively in the world. Calisher's picture of madness also, finally, suggests the loss of one's ability to act effectively. But for Calisher this aspect of madness hinges on the estrangement from production of socially intelligible meaning. Although power is not overtly dealt with in either formulation, we might translate Laing's arguments into a vocabulary of resistance by positing that one can wield power only in relation to others—that is, in a field of discourses and practices. We might also "translate" Calisher's representation, as I have argued, by suggesting that the mad can have no real power, though their illusory power may ensure their continued subordination to others. There is no space for subversion offered by a community of night screamers in blue bathrobes whose cries are intelligible only to themselves.

As we have seen, madness in these postwar stories is the final threat for protagonists who, whether deliberately or not, find that they have strayed outside the prescribed notions of womanhood. Whatever resistance is enacted in that straying is effectively contained by the community's production of madness, which reduces the women to absolute silence and deposits them far outside any arena for communal transformation. In this sense, the stories are entirely consistent with the testimony of the women discussed in Chapter 1, who actually experienced the incapacitating effects of madness. Any feminist criticism or theory that does not ground itself in these experiences risks losing sight of its subjects and the real, sharply felt constraints on their empowerment.

Yet it is one thing to say that the stories discussed in this chapter reject disempowering solutions and another to say that they offer empowering ones. In 1949, when the memory of women's active participation in the work force during World War II and corresponding changes in popular attitudes about women were fairly fresh, Eudora Welty could reject the non-solution of madness and still suggest in her writing a more potent symbolic solution, a means of transforming gender ideology: the making visible of the effects of past representations. Not only is Welty's "June Recital" itself a making visible, but also in "The Wanderers" Virgie Rainey comes to recognize the imperative to make visible and begins the process of reconceiving representation. Coming as it does at the end of *The Golden Apples*, this insight is a wholly hopeful one through which we as readers can envision an alternative solution to that of madness. That is, ideology can be transformed through an active engagement in the act of representation—through any discourse that challenges previous representations by exposing their ideological function.

By the mid-1950s, women had been safely relocated in the "private" sphere of domesticity and in many ways excluded from the social production of meaning. (We might even conjecture that this set of circumstances goes some way toward explaining Stafford's and Calisher's consignment to critical oblivion.) The changing climate takes its toll on the heroines of Stafford's and Calisher's narratives. Beatrice Trueblood's power to engage in representation—that is, to tell her own story—is highly circumscribed by the stories of others, which ultimately engulf her. And for Mrs. Hazlitt, whose construction as a (non)subject takes place primarily at the specular level—for whom glances implying particular discourses take the place of the discourses themselves—there simply seems to be no way out; she is trapped, as it were, in a mirror. It is perhaps because, by 1962, an active engagement in alternative representations with a transformative potential was so hard to envision that Mrs. Hazlitt's illusion of power in madness seems so much more compelling than those of Miss Eckhart or of Beatrice, who both give indications of recognizing the severe limitations on their power. Poised at the threshold of what would become an invigorated women's rights movement, "The Scream on Fifty-Seventh Street" presents by far the darkest view of the three stories—one in which, though madness is clearly depicted as the last gasp of the powerless, the narrative offers no more positive alternative. Ideological transformation cannot take place purely through critique, however. Thus it becomes crucial to ask, and examine, how subsequent women's texts felt their way out of the dead end of madness.

3
Multiple Personality and
the Postmodern Subject
Theorizing Agency

In the midst of the 1950s recasting of femininity, the image of the madwoman took a startling new form in American popular culture: the female multiple personality. Between 1954 and 1957 this disorder was the subject of fiction, film, and a nonfiction case study; in all of them the "patient" was a woman.[1] The sudden interest in the topic was all the more remarkable because professional diagnoses of multiple personality had gone markedly out of fashion at some time in the early twentieth century (Wilkes 331). How, then, are we to understand the resurgence of this particular form of madness and its hold on the popular imagination?

Decidedly, attention to all forms of mental illness was a hallmark of postwar American culture; never before had the disordered mind been to such a degree a topic for popular consumption. As I observed in Chapter 2, the country seemed to turn to a science of individual psychology at just the point when the international situation had become particularly bewildering and frightening; furthermore, psychological explanations for tragedies such as the Holocaust often gave those tragedies a manageable aspect. We have seen how the explosion of

---

[1] Despite the fact that popular representations of the disorder in the 1950s, as well as the most prominent of those that would follow (the famous "Sybil" case), invariably depicted the divided self as a woman, and that the diagnosis has consistently been handed out to women far more frequently than to men, the landmark feminist works reviewing the intersections of madness and gender (see works by Chesler, Showalter, and Ussher) have failed so much as to mention multiple personality. They have thus unintentionally demonstrated a persistent reliance on categories of discussion defined by men. Arguably the two most prominent male figures in the historical development of discourse on madness—Freud and R. D. Laing—focused on hysteria and schizophrenia, respectively; these are, in turn, the forms of "madness" that are most often attended to in revisionist feminist analyses.

popular interest in matters psychological was used to particular effect in the social rearrangement of gender roles after the war. As veterans rushed to seek stability in an idealized image of domesticity, women's wartime occupation of traditionally male jobs needed to be suppressed in the service of male employment and a stable, secure, already nostalgic vision of family life.

Postwar representations of female multiple personality seem to have participated at some level in the reconfiguration of women's roles through the depiction of contradictory selves which could not coexist in a healthy, "normal" woman. For example, Glenna Matthews describes a feature in the April 1945 issue of the Ladies Home Journal that told the story of a woman who "had had a promising career on the concert stage, but the tension of trying to fill multiple roles had induced a nervous breakdown" (Matthews 208). The image of divided or multiple woman, who could be several things at once, was used to suggest a potential threat to the precarious sense of social order, and to the traditional gender relations which provided a domestic haven from the atrocities of the war. Thus, a reviewer of Lizzie, the 1957 MGM movie based on The Bird's Nest, Shirley Jackson's novel of multiple personality, quipped, "Lizzie will probably be pretty confusing to the old-fashioned kind of moviegoer who thinks that when a girl isn't single, it's because she's married" (Lizzie 109). Another reviewer disparaged the film version of The Three Faces of Eve by objecting: "We never know from one moment to the next just what sort of girl [Eve] is going to be. . . . It develops that when she isn't a drab housewife, she is a low-life girl who . . . sneers at her husband, neglects her child, and takes up with any male who will give her a big hello. Her husband, an innocent in psychiatric matters, can't figure out why she is mousy one minute and wanton the next, and presently he says the hell with her and gets a divorce" ("Kiss" 134). A third review was accompanied by a cartoon depicting a naked man being torn in three different directions by women tugging at his arms and legs; the caption reads "I Never Knew a Woman Like You"(Fig. 2). The focus in all cases was on the complications that multiplicity in woman presented for normative gender relations; the figure of multiple personality, in the hands of the media, intimated a vague threat to the sexual contract which was the cornerstone of 1950s domestic life.

If such representations betokened a lingering anxiety that women might not ultimately be satisfied with the reduction in their "roles," that anxiety was easily calmed by the suggestion that woman in her traditional role was already many things at once. In September 1957, when the multiple personality fad was in full swing, Bell Telephone

© Abner Dean

"I NEVER KNEW A WOMAN LIKE YOU."

used it as a trope in an advertisement. A picture of the same woman, duplicated five times and dressed differently in each, appears over the caption "This Is Your Wife." The copy reads: "This is the pretty girl you married. She's the family chef. And the nurse. And the chauffeur and maid. And when she's all dressed up for an evening out—doesn't she look just wonderful!" (Fig. 3).The multiple roles so feared in popular representation for their potential threat to domesticity had been, literally, domesticated. Even when personalities like the startling Eve Black (in *The Three Faces of Eve*) could not be made to fit the "good wife" image, they were nevertheless described and judged in terms of feminine stereotypes ("mousy," "wanton," and so on). A male gaze simply assigned a cliché of femininity to each manifestation, establishing a comforting range of labels by which this strange phenomenon of the psyche could be understood.

In this respect, multiple personality as experienced by women is not significantly different from other forms of female "madness," such as hysteria a century ago or anorexia nervosa today, which enact a protest against the socially constructed category of femininity even while they reside fully within that category. James Glass, a political theorist who has interviewed women clinically diagnosed with multiple personality disorder, observes that "in none of the accounts offered [in his study] . . . did I see that the phenomenon of [multiple personality] was a creative or playful or regenerative experience. . . . Multiplicity of identity becomes for these women an ongoing torment, a horror that . . . totally incapacitates them" (xvi). Multiple personality, in other words, reduces women to even greater powerlessness. Whatever the threat to dominant gender ideology posed by a figure of multiple feminine selves, that figure is easily reappropriated in the service of the production of gender, as I will show.

Yet there is still another issue complicating any discussion of multiple personality *as representation*, and that is its close affinity with conceptions of the postmodern subject. Certainly it is difficult to view the phenomenon of multiple personality from a postmodern perspective *without* considering its relation to the postmodern subject. At least one discussion of the latter has used the figure of multiple personality as a metaphor (Dunning 137), and many of the adjectives used to describe current conceptions of subjectivity make equal sense in a discussion of multiple personality: "fragmented," "multiple," "shifting," "decentered." Glass finds the parallels so disturbing that he uses the clinical category of multiple personality disorder to debunk conceptions of a liberatory "multiplicity." He suggests that "the most powerful evidence against the postmodernist concept of self comes not from theory

This Is Your Wife

How the telephone helps her to be five busy people

This is the pretty girl you married.

She's the family chef. And the nurse. And the chauffeur and maid.

And when she's all dressed up for an evening out—doesn't she look just wonderful!

How does she do it?

Of course she's smart and it keeps her busy, but she never could manage it without the telephone.

When the "chef" needs groceries, she telephones. Supplies from the drugstore? The "nurse" phones her order.

A train to be met? The telephone tells the "chauffeur" which one. A beauty shop appointment? A call from the "glamour girl" makes it easily and quickly.

Handy telephones—in living room, bedroom, kitchen and hobby room—mean more convenience and security for everybody.

Working together to bring people together... **BELL TELEPHONE SYSTEM**

but from the words and lives of individuals actually experiencing the terrible psychological dislocation of "multiplicity," women with the psychiatric diagnosis of multiple personality disorder. . . . Postmodern philosophers such as Baudrillard and Lyotard . . . create an aesthetic that celebrates a certain limitlessness. . . . But for a real person the psychological reality of being multiple, of actually living it out, is an entirely different issue" (xii, xviii–xix). Glass's account suggests that the only way multiplicity can be experienced in "real people" is through multiple personality, implying a fundamental lack of distinction between the postmodern subject and the victim of multiple personality disorder (a point I will return to). Some feminist critics, sharing Glass's unease with current theories of subjectivity and their implications for the concept of subject-as-agent, have also felt it necessary to jettison the notion of the postmodern subject. Nancy Hartsock writes, "Somehow it seems highly suspicious that it is at the precise moment when so many groups have been engaged in . . . redefinitions of the marginalized Others that suspicions emerge about the nature of the 'subject'. . . . Why is it that just at the moment when so many of us who have been silenced begin to demand the right . . . to act as subjects rather than objects of history, that just then the concept of subjecthood becomes problematic?" (163). On the other side of the debate, critics such as Ruth Leys and Jacqueline Rose seek an alternative "to the argument that feminism needs access to an integrated subjectivity more than its demise" (Rose 15, quoted in Leys 167); the unified subject is a fiction, and a nostalgic wish that things were different will not make them so.

Given the figural similarity I have noted between multiple personality and the postmodern subject, it should not be surprising that Leys, who wishes to rescue that subject for feminism, should focus on representations of multiple personality. She sets up her own thesis by looking to Rose for a way to conceptualize the nonintegrated, postmodern (female) subject as potentially subversive *because* she is not integrated:

> For Rose, the psychic as an "area of difficulty" is important for feminism because it involves a concept of the subject as structured by unconscious fantasies that always exceed the rigid gender positions that are defined as the norm for women and men. . . . "What distinguishes psychoanalysis from sociological accounts of gender . . . ," Rose writes, "is that whereas for the latter, the internalization of norms is assumed roughly to work, the basic premise and indeed starting-point of psychoanalysis is that it does not." . . . For Rose, the necessary "failure" of identity—the inability of the patriarchal "law" fully to determine human actions and beliefs—is also virtually a condition of possibility for a feminist politics as she understands it. (Leys 167–68, quoting Rose 90)

Multiple personality constitutes an even more vigorous and visible "failure" of identity, and thus (according to Rose's logic) would presumably even further elude "patriarchal 'law.' " As we shall see, Leys's argument is that multiple personality can resist or challenge gender ideology by undermining any notion of an "original" self.

Leys turns to a landmark text in multiple personality, Morton Prince's *The Dissociation of a Personality* (1905), in an attempt to move beyond a "theory of the trauma, understood as an external historical event that befalls the already-constituted female subject" (168). Such a theory, she claims, is part of "a discourse which in effect denies the female subject all possibility of agency" (204 n.3). Leys is taking issue with prominent factual representations of multiple personality such as Prince's—and, fifty years later, that of Drs. Corbett Thigpen and Hervey Cleckley, authors of *The Three Faces of Eve*—which relied on an assumption that some originary trauma inflicted on the subject caused the initial fragmentation of personalities. Both of these accounts assume an original integrated subject who had existed before the trauma; interestingly, in both accounts the doctors proceed by trying to identify which personality comes closest to the original self and then by enabling that personality to have dominance over the others. Leys argues that the theory of trauma is problematic because it posits the female as a passive non-agent, to whom things happen from outside; she challenges Morton Prince's (humanist) notion of an original, integrated self by suggesting that the "personalities" manifested by his patient Miss Beauchamp were actually products of a particular mimetic identification produced by hypnosis: "The hypnotized person is . . . given over body and soul to the hypnotist's suggestions such that she is the other" (174). That is, the hypnotized subject identifies with the doctor and, particularly under strong suggestion from him, can view herself as a "she" rather than an "I"; hence the effects of multiple personality. This model, serving as a paradigm for how all subjectivity is formed (i.e., by identification and imitation), is potentially subversive according to Leys because "the mimetic paradigm expressly holds that no 'real' self exists prior to mimesis, [whereas] the concept of the self as a multiple of component traits or dispositions lends itself to the common-sense, essentialist idea that there exists a 'real' or 'normal' self that can be identified and recuperated" (191). Leys's argument emphasizes the ideologically loaded nature of any concept of a "normal" self, which can lend itself to notions of "natural" gender traits that must be recovered. (For example, the normal self who is to be rescued by the male doctors is inevitably the appropriately feminine one, as we shall see.) The mimetic model, in contrast, is potentially able to disrupt gender, since it suggests that gender is always a social construct assumed by imitation. By identifying with a male doctor, a female personality is traversing gender boundaries in a manner that cannot be viewed as trespass, since there is no "natural" female self to begin with.

Nevertheless, I would argue that there is a fundamental problem for feminism with Leys's formulation. Certainly her mimesis argument moves beyond concepts of a natural feminine self and allows multiple personality to intimate gender disruption; but in the model Leys holds up as paradigmatic, that disruption comes about through a female patient's imitation of her male doctor and extreme acquiescence to his suggestions. Consequently, although Leys argues against a theory of trauma partly on the basis of its construction of the feminine as without agency, it is hard to see how her model of mimesis-suggestion restores agency, for the female "subject" is reduced to a product of a (male) doctor's suggestions. Furthermore, how is any agency possible without a sense of subjectivity—without, that is, being able to identify oneself as an "I" rather than a "she"? How can a woman's view of herself as absolutely "other," and her identification with a male doctor as the only legitimate subject, be viewed as a figure for transgression, much less transformation of the gender system? Does it not rather duplicate—or imitate—the doctor's view of the woman as an object for study rather than a subject? As Teresa de Lauretis notes: "The discourse of the sciences of man constructs the object as female and the female as object. That . . . is its rhetoric of violence" (45). It is not my purpose here to reject Leys's hypothesis that hypnosis may actually bring about, or at least exacerbate, the phenomenon of multiple personality. I am, rather, taking issue with her postulation of the mimesis-suggestion model of multiple personality as a means to theorize *more* agency for women. Her countermodel holds far more serious problems for me than a trauma model because it claims subversive potential while continuing to imply a lack of agency.

In response to such a model, we might offer de Lauretis's formulation of the possibilities for agency in the postmodern (female) subject. If gendered subjects are constructed by discourse and representation, they can nevertheless participate in the (de)construction of gender through the "ongoing effort to create new spaces of discourse, to rewrite cultural narratives." These counternarratives constitute "a view from 'elsewhere,' " de Lauretis observes, although such a view is "not [by way of] . . . a movement from one space to another beyond it, or outside: say, from the space of a representation . . . to the space outside the representation, the space outside discourse." For if we are constructed within and by discourse and representation, we cannot simply move outside them and somehow start anew. The "elsewhere," the space for our transformative representative practices, is to be found within hegemonic discourses themselves. In other words, any counternarrative must strategically begin with the space opened by existing discourse and must work to reveal the fundamental assumptions and "givens" which are simultaneously revealed and obscured by such discourse. As I discussed in the Introduction, de Lauretis calls this the "space not represented yet implied (unseen)" in dominant discourse (25–26).

The novel that marks a starting point for the post–World War II fascination with multiple personality, *The Bird's Nest* by Shirley Jackson, can be seen as just this kind of counternarrative. Jackson had thoroughly researched her subject, and had made herself particularly familiar with Morton Prince's once famous study, *The Dissociation of a Personality*, from which her novel drew much of its material (Oppenheimer 161–62). Through her reimagining of Prince's account, Jackson makes central to her text the "elsewhere" of his narrative: the violence his rhetoric inflicts on his subject, Christine Beauchamp, in the service of the (re)production of gender. For as Leys has pointed out, "Prince's writings . . . join[ed] the increasingly abrasive turn-of-the-century debate over the 'crisis' of masculinity associated with the New Woman's appropriation of male roles and the breakdown of the traditional separation between male and female spheres" (188), in part by presenting the various personalities of Miss Beauchamp as "a virtual typology of early twentieth-century concepts of the feminine" (182). But Jackson's model of multiple personality also persuasively suggests the lack of real agency in such a phenomenon, as I will show later in this chapter, for though multiple personality can be understood as a demand for the recognition of subjectivity, it ultimately demonstrates the absolute powerlessness of one who cannot completely claim the "I" for herself.

If Prince's text was reacting to "the breakdown of traditional separation between male and female spheres" associated with the emergence of the New Woman in the early twentieth century, Jackson's novel was in many ways responding to the postwar reinscription of those spheres. Multiple personality—a figure of femininity out of control—had the potential to disrupt this rigid ideal. We have seen the anxiety it seems to have caused the reviewers of books and movies on the phenomenon. Certainly it disrupts the complacency of Jackson's Dr. Wright, who, in a parody of Morton Prince, scrambles to defend his precarious worldview by shoring up each portion of the disintegrated personality into a distinct, and wholly separate, image of woman—an activity, as we shall see, that dramatizes what de Lauretis calls the violence of rhetoric. Wright declares of the patient who first walks into his office that "I wasn't much inclined to her at first. . . . 'Colorless' was a word [that] came to my mind when I looked at her" (176). This is the "first" Elizabeth Richmond, who has been—as the doctor also admiringly notes—"well brought up and taught that a lady seats herself quietly" (178). She is, in other words, a Victorian woman—a "lady," but without sexuality by virtue of that construction, and therefore wholly without interest for the doctor. Notably, Wright (who seems to fancy himself a Victorian gentleman) remains blind to the fundamental 170 conflict suggested by his own, actually quite contemporary representations of gender. Postwar representations that positioned woman in a "private" domestic sphere—on which both male veterans' fantasies of a safe domestic haven and male participation in the "public" economic sphere depended—were characterized by a lack of sexuality, paradoxically rendering this ideal potentially uninteresting to the very men who envisioned themselves running home to it.[2]

But if Elizabeth (or R_1) bores the doctor sexually, Beth (R_2) brings out his manliness by being the figure of the maiden in distress; it is Beth, Dr. Wright tells his imagined audience, "who, although weak and almost helpless, was at least possessed of a kind of winsomeness, and engaging in her very helplessness" (275). It is in the cause of saving Beth that the doctor imagines himself a Prince Charming in a fairy tale: "I saw myself . . . as setting free a captive princess" (195). Into this chivalric fantasy intrudes Betsy (R_3); the doctor now notes: "I found myself . . . much in the manner of a knight . . . who, in the course of bringing his true princess home, has no longer any fear, but only a great weariness, when confronted in sight of the castle towers by a fresh dragon to slay" (198). The appearance of a new personality is presented not as a medical complication but as an unwelcome interruption in the resolution of a romance. Furthermore, Wright's chivalric discourse distracts from, but never completely occludes, a discourse of aggressive male sexuality which everywhere colors his representations of psychiatric treatment: "I may liken [Elizabeth Richmond's] state and its cure to . . . a stoppage in a water main. . . . [T]he only way in which I might accomplish [its] removal was by going myself . . . down the pipe. . . . [The metaphor] does, I fear, portray most vividly my own diagnosis of Miss R.'s difficulty and my own problem in relieving it. Let us assume, then, that the good Doctor Wright is steeling himself to

---

[2] See Friedan 174 for a discussion of how the predominant feminine image for returning veterans was the (asexual) mother, Halberstam 280 for a discussion of the infuriated public reaction to Kinsey's *Sexual Behavior in the Human Female*.

creep manfully down a sewer pipe" (186). Miss Richmond's problem, then, must be "relieved" through a manful creeping down her pipe; all she really needs is a good screw, and the doctor is presumably just the one to provide it.

In Wright's catalogue of feminine types, Betsy is the dragon to Beth's princess; more often Betsy is described by the doctor as demonic, the feminine Hyde to Beth's Jekyll: "She was not, I saw, at all handsome, and as I watched her in horror, the smile upon her soft lips coarsened, and became sensual and gross, . . . and she laughed, evilly and roughly, throwing her head back and shouting, . . . a devil's mask. . . . What I saw that afternoon was the dreadful grinning face of a fiend, and heaven help me, I have seen it a thousand times since" (192). Wright's image of Betsy as a she-demon possessed of a horrible, evil sensuality is difficult to sustain, however, when held up against the narrative of her escape to New York, in which she appears to be little more than a lost child searching for a mother who has been dead for years.

But to stamp Betsy as a creature of no sexuality is as gross a simplification as to accuse her of wantonness. The hints Jackson provides regarding Betsy's sexuality suggest instead that it is highly contradictory. For example, her memories of her mother's lover, Robin, are tormented; identifying closely with her mother, she courts Robin's sexual attentions at the same time that she fears him in a manner which suggests a previous rape. In one flashback during which she mistakes a stranger for Robin, something she does repeatedly during her runaway trip to New York, she manifests both attitudes at once in a dizzying manner suggestive of a personality split within Betsy herself: " 'I won't let you, not ever any more,' Betsy said to Robin, 'and neither will my mother.' . . . And she could hear him after her, down the hall and down the stairs, praying not to stumble, not Robin again, it wasn't fair . . . no one could do that again, praying to move quickly enough, to be safely out of it and away before he could touch her, to be safely out of it; 'Robin,' she said, 'Robin darling, call me Lisbeth, Lisbeth' " (259). Yet "Lisbeth," Betsy's mother's nickname, is not another personality; it is an aspect of Betsy herself, that part of her which wishes to be her mother. This counternarrative, exposing the contradictions, the fragmentation, within a single "self," suggests a subjectivity which indeed escapes Dr. Wright's efforts to fix and hold it.

In contrast, Elizabeth Richmond's multiple personalities seem to play into the doctor's hands. Presented with the opportunity to label each separate personality, he can suppress disturbing contradictions in the service of a categorical worldview: Betsy becomes "the hateful, the enemy" (198) and "our villain" (204). Elizabeth's Aunt Morgen, Dr. Wright's competitor for control over his patient, also uses such rhetoric in an attempt to gain authority over the phenomenon of multiple personality, comparing her niece's ailment to her own "Jekyll-and-brandy personality" (327), and then immediately distancing herself from Elizabeth through a rhetoric of morality: "[The] cruel and vicious manner [of her niece] . . . would automatically set a distinction between the reasonable, regular alterings of a sensible person—Morgen—and the unreasonable, erratic alterings of a non-sensible person—Elizabeth" (328). Unreason is thus linked to evil—a remnant of the concept of moral insanity—and, by implication, reason to moral rectitude.

Although notions of moral madness presumably had been succeeded by more scientific explanations in the late nineteenth and early twentieth centuries (witness Freud's vehement claims to the "science" of psychoanalysis), the rhetoric of morality lingered on, even in discourses that, claiming objectivity, seemed to distance themselves from moral judgments. A wartime study of multiple personality provided a list of characteristics in which the various personalities of a case might differ from one another, including "propriety or good behavior," which was the distinguishing factor (the study reminded readers) in "Jekyll-Hyde differences between the personalities" (Taylor and Martin 289). The rhetoric of moral dichotomy could be used to particular effect in the postwar construction of femininity; for if the Russians were our enemy abroad, our enemy at home was the woman who was not a willing participant in a chivalric fairy tale (soldier returns home, rescues princess, marries her, and sets up house). In *The Three Faces of Eve*, a "true" story of a multiple personality case published three years after Jackson's novel, moral rhetoric, used as a strategy for managing undesirable aspects of woman, seems to govern the entire narrative. The pseudonyms by which the first two personalities are designated in the account, Eve White and Eve Black, are blatantly suggestive of a Jekyll-and-Hyde division of "Eve," the first and paradigmatic woman. Indeed, the authors go on at some length about Stevenson's novel, explicitly feminizing his construction, and in the process betraying their own anxieties about the potential disruption of the domestic haven suggested by multiple personality: "The two famous names [Jekyll and Hyde] in conjunction serve as a rough equivalent for such popular expressions as 'she's a street angel but a home devil' " (Thigpen and Cleckley 42).

In the writers' brush strokes, Eve White, a housewife, is the "figure of propriety" and (therefore?) a "colorless" woman with a "monotonous voice" (9). Eve Black, in contrast, is a trampy seductress, a "creature of ... passion and erotic potentiality and inclination"; the "average man," we are told, "might have found it difficult to avoid the fundamental reactions conveyed in the vernacular by such phrases as *this girl is really stacked, there's something about her that let's* [sic] *you feel she could be a mighty hot dish"*(167). Certainly the authors attempt to mask the effect of their own sexual impulses on their presumably objective account: an "average" man might think such things about Eve Black, but the good doctors stay at least one step removed by reporting on *his* reaction to her. Nevertheless, their hypothetical reconstructions of a scene between Eve Black and Ralph White, the husband of Eve White, leave little room for doubt about their own implicatedness in 1950s gender ideology: "As they sat talking, Eve Black crossed her legs. It is very reasonable to believe that Ralph found what had seemed wantonly flirtatious when directed toward another could be delectable and rich with thrilling promise when directed toward himself.... Some men, after being bitterly disillusioned or icily rejected by what they regard as the sacredly good manifestation of femininity, have been known to fling themselves wildly into the arms of despised harlots" (166–67). The male dilemma could not be made more explicit; the "sacredly good" woman is in fact *too* good; lacking any sexuality, she is boring. (Remarkably, Eve White is the only one of the three personalities who does *not* consider herself a virgin, acknowledging her marriage to Ralph; her representation by the doctors as without sexuality thus suggests yet again the conflict inherent in the 1950s construction of the feminine position.) Her counterpart, the wanton Eve, may provide "thrilling promise" in the short term, but her very wantonness makes her ultimately a threat to domesticity—for she does not direct her sexual charms solely to their proper recipient, her husband, but freely disperses them. It is for this reason that she must be "despised," whatever momentary relief she may offer.

Into the stalemate between two equally unsatisfactory Eves steps "Jane," an answer to the male fantasy produced as though on demand. She is, on the one hand, "far more mature, more vivid, more boldly capable, and *more interesting* than Eve White .... Beside this genuinely impressive newcomer, Eve White appeared colorless and limited" (119; emphasis added)—as if she had not before! Unlike Eve White, Jane is perceived as a sexual being; yet, she *contains* her sexuality in appropriate ways rather than distributing it "wantonly" like Eve Black: "Everything about Eve Black seemed designed specifically to attract ... attention. Though many polite eyes were likely to note with appreciation Jane's progress along any sidewalk, even a fool would automatically restrain his impulse to whistle. There was about her no flaunting whatsoever of erotic charm, but dull indeed would be the man who would not on second glance surmise that here was an authentic potentiality for what is naturally sensuous" (126). The doctors, disingenuously tentative in their claim that "there was some choice open to the psychiatrist as to which personality he should try to reinforce" (123), predictably "choose" Jane; their motivation for doing so is made apparent in their observations that "her mind . . . suggested the *tabula rasa* of John Locke, the empty sheet upon which experience is to write but which now is blank and without content" (125). As the real "Eve," Chris Costner Sizemore, would observe later in her own account, "Jane" stood for "Jane Doe," meaning "brand new, blank"; and though this suggested a "pallid and colorless anonymous" to Sizemore (274), in search of her *own* identity, it certainly did not to her doctors. To them Jane was, for all practical purposes, waiting to be written on, and Thigpen and Cleckley wrote upon her the text of their own male fantasies, thus revealing the degree to which their scientific "choice" was conditioned by sexual considerations.

In Jackson's novel, the rhetoric of moral dichotomy which embues Dr. Wright's psychiatric choices is undermined precisely as the product of his own gendered position. Her somewhat caricatured portrayal of the doctor can be understood, in this context, as an attempt to write from "the space not represented yet implied" in psychiatric discourse. Jackson provides strong cues for reading the moral rhetoric that continually creeps into Wright's account. Such rhetoric betrays not simply Wright's acceptance of particular "norms" of gender but also his personal investedness in those norms. His moral condemnation of some of Elizabeth Richmond's selves is, for example, clearly as much a direct response to challenges to his own (masculine) authority as it is an ideologically loaded ideal of proper feminine submissiveness. Since even Wright acknowledges the difficulty he experiences as a "man of science" in being "impartial, and sensible, and invulnerable" (273), it is difficult to accept at face value his characterization of Betsy as a manifestation of evil, wanton femininity without taking into account his anger at her lack of submission to his will. He recounts with indignation the fact that Betsy demonstrates "an air of mockery" (196) toward him, "felt and showed [him] no respect" (200), and, most grievously, "called [him] a damned old fool!" (200). Wright's backhanded admissions serve as a warning that we should not accept his reductive and clichéd characterizations of his patient(s) as "objective." Jackson, however, does not allow us to regard Wright's "morality play" classifications merely as a benign reflection of the ideological contexts in which he finds himself. As we shall see, his emphasis on his own creative powers betrays psychiatry's complicity in reproducing that ideology, and in producing subjects who would be appropriately interpellated by it.

Psychiatric discourse typically obscured (and still obscures) its own position within ideology, including gender ideology—and therefore its own interest in the reproduction of particular forms of subjectivity— with a rhetoric of scientific neutrality. De Lauretis (citing the work of Wini Breines and Linda Gordon) notes the operation of such rhetoric in "gender-neutral methodological perspectives on incest." She explains:

> In spite of the agreement among statistical studies that, in cases of incest as well as child sexual abuse, 92% of the victims are females and 97% of the assailants are males, "predictably enough, until very recently the clinical literature ignored this feature of incest, implying that, for example, mother-son incest was as prevalent as father-daughter incest." . . . Such studies . . . obscure the actual history of violence against women. . . . Put another way, even as those studies purport to remain innocent of the ideology or of the rhetoric of violence, they cannot avoid and indeed purposefully engage in the violence of rhetoric. (de Lauretis 34, quoting Breines and Gordon 523)

We can use de Lauretis's pertinent discussion as a means to understand how the figure of multiple personality constructed by psychiatric discourse deflects attention from the gendered content of particular forms of violence.

For example, the language in which Drs. Thigpen and Cleckley construct their narrative in *The Three Faces of Eve* suggests unimpeachable neutrality while repeatedly obscuring the violence Ralph White inflicts on his wife, "Eve." They write: "Though ordinarily a kind and agreeable man, [Ralph] eventually became impatient and at last angry with [Eve]. . . . As Ralph remembered the scene, Eve had seized him by the arm in an effort to make him stay home with her. In freeing himself, he had inadvertently pushed her in such a way that she interpreted his action as a slap or a blow. He did not realize this at the time" (29). Eve's subsequent miscarriage on that same night is presented as a coincidence, only tangentially related to Ralph's misinterpreted struggle for freedom. The doctors' empathy with Ralph is palpable: "The husband's role in this situation was undeniably difficult. . . . It is doubtful if any ordinary man could have successfully solved the problems that confronted him. . . . He regretted having struck her lightly in the ensuing quarrel. But who could be sure of controlling himself under such circumstances?" (84–86). Although they take great pains to assure their readers that their view is balanced ("It is difficult to reconstruct the incident in detail through two differing accounts" [29]), their own representation of Eve's malady as one that would place a husband in an "undeniably" bad situation subtly locates the fault in the bewilderingly multiplied woman, not her beleaguered husband. Ralph is, after all, only doing what the authors themselves are doing: attempting to control an excessive profusion of femininity. The doctors' narrative thus testifies to the violence of postwar psychiatric rhetoric which, in masking gender violence through the guise of scientific neutrality, also served to legitimate its perpetuation.

The violence "implied (but unseen)" in these psychiatric discourses is the space in which Jackson builds her characterization of Dr. Wright, who takes a blatantly obvious, and specifically gendered, pleasure in his power over his female patient, whom he describes as "a vessel emptied." He asserts, "*Our* responsibility [i.e., his and Aunt Morgen's] is, clearly, to people this vacant landscape—fill this empty vessel, I think I said before—and, with our own deep emotional reserves, enable the child to rebuild. . . . She will owe to us her opinions, her discriminations, her reflections; we are able, as few others have ever been, to recreate, entire, a human being, in the most proper and reasonable mold" (374). Although Wright is here conspiring with Aunt Morgen over the "rebuilding" of Elizabeth, the vocabulary he uses is his alone, and is clearly conditioned by his masculine position; he views Elizabeth as the biological "empty vessel" of womanhood, waiting to be filled by life-giving male seed and then "peopled" with babies. Psychiatric authority becomes, in Wright's hands, a quite literal authorship: he longs to *write*, to *create* his feminine heroine from the materials of his own desire.

Wright's self-conscious insistence on the creation of his narrative is almost inevitably connected to his position as a sexual pursuer. His extended metaphor likening his treatment of Elizabeth to a manful creeping down her pipe, for example, is interjected with parenthetical statements such as "if my reader will forgive such an ignoble comparison" and "gracious heaven, how I have caught myself in my own analogy!" which repeatedly call attention to the status of his narrative as a particularly literary writing (186); and his fantasy about rescuing the distressed and helpless Beth is, as we have seen, delivered in the language of chivalric romance and fairly tale. He is quite explicit about the connections between psychiatry and authorship, observing that "a good writer is much the same as a good doctor," and admitting his propensity for "fancying myself Author" (176). The capitalized "Author" suggests, of course, that Wright is God as well as Adam: he is a

God who wishes to create the essential Eve for *himself*. His authorship, in other words, is driven by a particularly masculine desire. Authority, Jackson will not let us forget, is inevitably conditioned by gender relations.

At the same time, since Wright wishes to create his feminine ideal, he must deny his patient the powers of authorship he allows himself. In this way his rhetoric "constructs the object as female and the female as object" (de Lauretis 45); hence its violence. When Betsy rejects the numerical designation with which the doctor has fixed her, declaring, "I certainly don't choose to be called R₃[;] . . . [y]ou can call me Rosalita, or Charmian, or Lilith, if you like," Wright inwardly mocks "the thought of this grotesque creature naming herself like a princess in a fairy romance" (202–3). In general, the doctor does not respond well to challenges to his narrative, attempting to compensate through compulsive assertions regarding his position as an author. His report to Aunt Morgen on the condition of her niece is marked by a defensive reaction to his uncomfortable sense of loss of control:

> As I spoke—and I spoke well, having so thoroughly rehearsed myself, and having my notes besides—Miss Jones listened attentively, with every appearance of great fascination; she interrupted me once. . . . [D]uring her interruption I was strongly afraid of losing the thread of my own narrative, and its perfect balance, and had at last to cut her off in order that I might continue. Again, she asked and insisted on a more detailed and simpler description of the dissociated personality, as described by Doctor Prince, and again I must break off and give it to her. We were wasting time, I thought, since I knew the subject perfectly and she need not know any more than she did (305–6).

Wright's anxiety over the loss of narrative control, as well as his focus on narrative *form*, suggests his precarious hold on the *content* of his narrative; Elizabeth's various selves present the specter of that which might not be containable by the doctor's efforts. Periodically the specter is loosed. When Wright discovers that the personality he believed to be the sweet and malleable Beth is actually Betsy *imitating* Beth—that is, representing her, and thus exerting control over her own narrative—he beats a retreat: "I was badly frightened and unwilling to jeopardize my own health" (218). And once again his loss of control over his subject matter is immediately suppressed through a renewed attention to narrative form, as his focus shifts to his explanatory letter to Morgen, a piece of prose in which he takes great pride: "I wrote . . . very well (indeed, I have saved the letter, and it is before me now)" (218).

But the doctor's attention to form in the face of unmanageable content is only a stopgap measure; ultimately he must regain control over his material through an authorship characterized by violence. Wright's desire to inflict such violence on his patient when she does not conform to his narrative is barely disguised. The language he uses to refer to his professional care of Elizabeth—"her treatment at my hands" (265)—suggests not therapy but brutality; a few pages later he confesses his "sympathy for whoever had gotten a hand around [Bess's] throat" (267). Indeed, the very form of his treatment is brutality, figured in quite graphic physical images. Engaged with Morgen in a literal tug-of-war over Elizabeth's body, he expresses his desire to "rip her in half" (356); and he describes his own psychiatric goals through yet another self-consciously literary metaphor: "I saw myself, if the analogy be not too extreme, much like a Frankenstein with all the materials for a monster ready at hand, and when I slept, it was with dreams of myself patching and tacking together, trying most hideously to chip away the evil from Betsy and leave what little was good, while the other three stood by mockingly, waiting their turns" (276). Once again Wright's emphasis on authority (here through literary allusion) occurs amidst—and as a reaction to—extreme anxiety regarding his ability to manage his subject matter; he fears that his patient is a monster who will escape his control. Notably, even in this image of the creation of a monster, Wright is more a Pygmalion than a Frankenstein, fantasizing an object of desire sculpted from his own hands. His efforts to regain control over his unwieldy creation thus take the additional form of an image of chiseling and chipping which cannot fail to suggest violence when applied to what is after all not stone but flesh and blood.

If the doctor can contemplate selectively preserving some aspects of each personality while doing away with others, then it should be no surprise that he also contemplates the extermination of entire personalities, as he warns Bess in a moment of anger: "Consider that it is only through my misguided sufferance that you continue to exist at all. . . . [D]o you think that you may with impunity bring your pert words to bear against a power like [mine]? . . . [Y]ou are at best, young lady, only a slight, only a poor and partial creature, and for all your fine words, you will not stay long; . . . I promise you, here and now, that you as a person will, with the knowledge of you I have, cease, absolutely and finally and without possibility of petition, cease I tell you, unalterably cease to exist!" (316). The Godlike power of creation which Dr. Wright assumes is also a power of destruction, justified by his psychiatric determination that, since each personality is (to quote Prince along with Wright) "a part only of a normal whole self" (quoted in Jackson 199), that self is not a real person with the right to exist but "only a poor and partial creature" which Wright is within his moral bounds to extinguish at will. The psychological "ripping" Wright wishes to inflict on his patient is meant to preserve his preferred personality, the charming and dependent Beth, at the expense of the other three. "My present hope," he tells us, "was to strengthen Beth, by whatever means, and bring her slowly to a complete open realization of the whole personality" (281). (Wright, of course, does not acknowledge the contradiction in his desire to make Beth, who by his own determination is only a part of the whole, dominant over the entire person.) In response to the dangerous specter of feminine multiplicity, in other words, Wright ultimately wishes, whatever his theoretical claims to the contrary, not to reintegrate the personalities into a single (but necessarily shifting and contradictory) self, but to sever them more violently, salvaging one and doing away with the others. Wright's strategy thus indicates how the figure of multiple personality can be easily reappropriated by, and made to function in the service of, the ideology of gender—whatever its initial challenges to that ideology. Under the guise of psychiatric therapy, Wright takes an active hand in the re-creation of a model of femininity that will stand for the natural, normative state (Beth, he tries to convince us, is "Miss R. . . . as she was meant to be" [186]); what his own metaphors reveal is that the hand of ideological production is also a hand of violence, wielded against women.

On one level, of course, Wright is merely continuing a tradition of the denial of full "personhood" to women based on certain (male) criteria of normalcy; the general outlines of his ideological assumptions and legitimating rhetoric were already at hand in Prince's text. Although Prince (as well as Thigpen and Cleckley half a century later) had a certain stake, for reasons of maintaining his medical reputation, in proving the existence of separate personalities in his patient and therefore the authenticity of his case, he was also ultimately committed to denying the subjectivity of some of those personalities for reasons both professional (he needed to assert that he had "cured" his patient) and—as we shall see—ideological. Prince's oft-quoted explanation of multiple personality—"each secondary personality is a part only of a normal whole self" (3)—suggests that he believed any one personality was as "real" (or unreal) as another. But his practice throughout much of his 570-page record corresponds to a quite different, and overtly stated, assumption: that *one* of the personalities was the "real, original or normal self, the self that was born and which [the patient] was intended by nature to be" (1), and that it was Prince's job to discover which personality this was and to extinguish all the others. Arguments based on what "nature intended" thus justified what Prince boldly admitted amounted to murder of those personalities that were not the "real" self (conflated uncritically with a "normal" self): "Plainly, if B IV were the real self, she must be kept and the others annihilated. Poor Miss Beauchamp . . . must no longer be allowed to live. . . . In my thoughts the annihilation of Miss Beauchamp seemed in no way different from saying that she must be satisfied with death. . . . [I]t seemed like a crime we were committing. It was a psychical murder" (245, 248). Prince's self-described task was "to determine which personality was comportable with abnormality and which with normality, and so find the real self" (241). What was not "normal" presumably could not be "real."

Predictably enough, the criteria on which Prince based determinations of normalcy were shaped largely by gender ideology. For example, during the course of Prince's narrative, B IV temporarily becomes a candidate for the "real self" because she dispenses with a traditionally "feminine" emotionality in favor of cool-headed rationality: she "explained her point of view so logically, that the hypothesis that she was the real and original self gained greatly in favor" (245). Unlike B I, B IV "had no shattered ideals, no intensity of sentiment, no discouragement from overwhelming obstacles, but [was] content with the conditions as she found them" (249). Emotion and sentiment thus mark B I as sick and therefore unreal, in comparison to the cool logic of B IV. (No consideration is ever given to whether the obstacles in Miss Beauchamp's life do indeed call for discouragement as an appropriate or understandable response.) Buried behind this evaluation is a larger indictment of the status of women in general; if, as the wisdom of the day had it, women were indeed emotional and men rational, then by Prince's criteria women must be seen as less deserving of a claim to "real" personhood than men.

But Prince's evaluations also reveal the double bind of madness as a technology of gender which labels women mad simultaneously for their difference from a male model and for their deviations from their feminine position. For B IV is also potentially "real" because she is "so natural and simple" (245). Sally, "mistress of herself" from the moment she is "truly born into this world" (95–96), is "rebellious" and "[fights] to counteract [Prince's] influence" (138); Prince arguably retaliates by judging her from the very first as not a real person. Increasingly, Prince notices that B IV, too, "yielded to no one, [and] demanded to be mistress of herself" (412), as she fiercely pits her own will against Prince's (493). Not surprisingly, then, B IV turns out not to be the "Real Miss Beauchamp" in Prince's estimation after all. The Real Miss Beauchamp is a modified version of B II, who is absolutely malleable in Prince's hands and lets his will reign supreme even over her own: "B II begged pathetically . . . that I would help her, protect her from herself, from every one" (434). Thus those personalities who attempt to assert their own wills and control their own lives are, seemingly for that very reason, declared not "real" people and therefore without the right to self-determination.

Prince arguably was responding to the threat of the New Woman with a humanist discourse of a real, natural, and original self that would serve rigidly to recontain gender by excluding certain types of womanhood from his construction of a "real" and "natural" self. (Leys makes essentially this argument.) Jackson's reimagining of Prince's narrative foregrounds its violence. When placed in the mouth of Dr. Wright, appeals to the assumption of an integrated, original, noncontradictory subject (through, for example, assertions about what Elizabeth Richmond was "meant to be") ring remarkably false, juxtaposed as they are with his blatant Pygmalion fantasies. In Jackson's hands, psychiatry's appeals to a humanist subject are a discourse violently wielded—a hammer and chisel hacking away at troubling contradiction—against the threat of a potentially uncontrollable feminine self.

It is possible to read the symptoms of multiple personality as a signpost for this sort of rhetorical violence.[3] For those symptoms offer a compelling (one might even say an exaggerated) demand for recognition of subjectivity, precisely when the denial of subjectivity by another has constituted a violent act of silencing. The rebellious personality Sally in Prince's account provides one such counternarrative by composing an "autobiography" about her existence from childhood as a separate personality. The text of her autobiography is preceded on the page by this odd bracketed introduction:

SALLY'S STORY

[The autobiography begins in a somewhat flowery, childish style with a few brief memories of infancy, while she was in her cradle. When I refused to accept the accuracy of her memory she went on as follows:] (371)

---

[3] It is also, of course, quite possibly a sign of literal violence. As Kathleen Wilkes points out, "a repressed, puritanical childhood, often including neglect and physical abuse, seems a pattern common to many cases of multiple personality" (332 n.2). It seems to me, however, that the "neglect" to which Wilkes points as a cause might be as crucial as physical abuse to an understanding of the counternarrative offered by the symptoms of multiple personality.

Sally's memories blatantly contradict Prince's theory that the fragmentation of self was effected by an incident of much more recent occurrence. Her narrative, that is to say, challenges the accuracy of his. In consequence, Prince must struggle to neutralize the potentially damaging effects of Sally's counternarrative with a counter-counternarrative; he frames her text with this discrediting introduction, concludes it with hypotheses about why Sally "thinks" she remembers events from childhood (396–7), and interjects a footnote pointing out an "error" (390) in her account at just the point when she is explicitly challenging his narrative of personality disintegration. Remarkably, Prince later writes of Sally's "unaccountable anxiety to recover possession of the manuscript of her autobiography" (468), but seems oblivious to her desire to regain possession of her *story*, though that desire is surely what is intimated by her urgency about recovering her manuscript from Prince's hands. Prince is, in fact, betraying a Wright-like anxiety over narrative form at the very moment when his story is beginning to escape his control. He wishes to posit an exact beginning, middle, and end to Christine Beauchamp's personality disintegration, and can do so only through a violent suppression of her own experience. In the end, that suppression includes the "murder" of Sally, who is allowed by Prince to play no part in the final, ostensibly integrated personality. Prince, that is to say, refuses to recognize Sally's claim to subjectivity, even while, contradictorily, he insists upon it: Sally exists as a separate person, though not a "real" one.

Thigpen and Cleckley enact a similar violent silencing of "Eve." Like Prince, these doctors contain the ways in which she contests their authoritative account of her disorder by imposing rigid narrative form on her story, this time in the shape of a happy ending. In her subsequently published autobiography, Chris Costner Sizemore (the real "Eve") details a long history of attempts, in her co-author's words, to "tell *her* story, the way *she* lived it and felt it, not the way someone else saw her live it and assumed she felt it" (342–43). Sizemore reveals that this story had for years been forcibly silenced (through both legal means and psychological coercion) by Drs. Thigpen and Cleckley, who had wished to give "the world . . . the impression that I had recovered from my dissociative problem, multiple personality" (Author's Note x). The doctors were aware that Sizemore had experienced subsequent personalities; but, despite her wishes, they had not "included the material, because a book cannot be written with a 'lady or the tiger' conclusion, it had to have a resolved ending" (371).

In Shirley Jackson's account the figure of multiple personality suggests a potential defense against just the sort of discourse that would deny subjectivity—although, as we shall see, that potential proves to be a false one. The Elizabeth we meet at the beginning of Jackson's novel is an "anonymous" person. If her subjectivity is not actively denied by others, it is also not recognized: "The letters signed 'per er' and the endless listings of exhibits vouched for by E. Richmond were the outstanding traces of her presence.... She was not even interesting enough to distinguish with a nickname; where the living ... kept a precarious hold on individuality and identity, Elizabeth remained nameless" (151–52). Elizabeth is not confirmed as a subject by another, and we may usefully recall here R. D. Laing's contention in *The Divided Self* that "the sense of identity requires the existence of another by whom one is known" (139).

But there is one other who recognizes Elizabeth, writing her letters: "watch out for me lizzie watch out for me and dont do anything bad ... dont think i wont know lizzie because i do—dirty thoughts lizzie dirty lizzie" (151). This other is Betsy, one of the personalities of Elizabeth Richmond and therefore a part of Elizabeth's self; and despite the nasty tone of her letter, it is a confirmation of subjectivity, for it both acknowledges that Elizabeth's thoughts are "known" by another and demands a reciprocal recognition of an alternative subjectivity—Betsy's—from Elizabeth ("watch out for me").

Elizabeth's obvious fondness for Betsy's letters, regardless of their abusive tone, is clearly motivated by her sense that someone is confirming her existence as a subject: "Someone had written her lots of letters, she thought fondly, lots of letters; here were five. She kept them all in the red valentine box and every afternoon now, when she came home from work, she put the new one in and counted them over. The very feel of them was important, as though at last someone had found her out, someone close and dear, someone who wanted to watch her all the time; someone who writes letters to me, Elizabeth thought, touching the papers gently" (164–65). Elizabeth treats Betsy's epistles as love letters; indeed, in spite of their contempt, they are love letters of a sort, expressing the primary importance of Elizabeth's existence for some other person. Nevertheless, the substitution of the self for an absent confirming other is ultimately not a viable solution; if multiple personality is a protest against subjectivity denied, it also, to use Susan Bordo's terms, works "as if in collusion with the cultural conditions that produced" it ("Anorexia Nervosa" 105) For the multiple personality completely misrecognizes the self as an other—a distinction crucial to subjectivity—and thus negates the essential precondition of effective agency.

In Prince's classic text, the personalities of Miss Beauchamp manifest an inability to speak (that is, an inability to engage in the symbolic order) at just the moment when Prince is most insistent on the existence of separate persons in his patient. In a discussion devoted to proving the coexisting consciousness of Sally Beauchamp, Prince describes "contests of wills" between two personalities, which "Sally usually won," with the result that "Miss Beauchamp's will would be paralyzed. . . . [O]ften, after vain effort to speak, [Miss Beauchamp] has given it up, remarking, 'Well, it doesn't matter.' . . . This was nothing more nor less than *aboulia*. Arising in the manner described, it was of importance in that it showed the existence of a secondary consciousness, concomitant or coexisting with the habitual consciousness. For two wills to contend against each other they must exist" (122–23). The intent of Prince's discussion, ironic though it may seem, is to *assert* Sally's existence as a separate will—to use Leys's words, to "guarantee the status of the subject as a subject" (195)—although what Leys never recognizes is that this is the vital precedent to then *denying* her subjectivity on the grounds that she is not "real." Yet Prince's narrative actually gets ahead of him, offering the disturbing suggestion that, in spite of his insistence here to the contrary, the phenomenon of multiple personality does not magnify the potential for agency (through the coexistence of several "wills") but actually undermines agency—perhaps most drastically the agency of speech. Prince does not define "aboulia" for his lay readers, merely pointing out its "importance" in proving Sally's existence. Jackson, by contrast, makes a point of highlighting the negative, rather than the positive, nature of aboulia. She places its definition, provided by Dr. Wright, in a footnote that calls attention to itself through its separation from the rest of the text: "*aboulia*; a state which I can describe for the layman who reads and runs as an inhibition of will, preventing a desired action; Miss R. showed this largely in speech, almost as though she were *prevented* from uttering a syllable" (176). Far from being a magnification of will, as Prince seems to suggest through his depiction of a "contest of wills," aboulia—a commonly reported effect of multiple personality—is an *inhibition* of will, depriving the subject of any agency while (in such manifestations) presenting the illusion of a contest.

In *The Bird's Nest*, multiple personality may provide Elizabeth with a comforting sense of recognition by "others," but ultimately her inability to recognize *herself* as such threatens to destroy Elizabeth Richmond's subjectivity—a threat played out in terms of her ability to use language. Betsy, who has been carrying a dictionary with her during her New York escapade "in case she needed help in talking or writing or spelling" (220), suddenly discovers that "the big dictionary she had brought with her . . . was lying just inside the suitcase, its binding torn off, its pages pulled out and crumpled, its millions of good, practical, helpful words hopelessly destroyed" (249). Already, Betsy's extreme tentativeness with regard to her use of words (she carries a dictionary with her) indicates that her place as a separate subject in the symbolic order is highly problematic. Yet another personality within the self provides no better access to language but rather symbolically destroys what access there is. (Bess has torn apart the dictionary.) Finally, in a scene that cannot fail to remind postmodern readers of the Lacanian "mirror stage," Betsy participates in what may be regarded as an exit from language, which is also an exit from subjectivity: "Suddenly, madly, she took up the book, and rising and turning, threw it as hard as she could at the mirror. 'There,' she said out loud, through the crash, 'that'll show you I'm still worse than you are, whoever you are!' " (249). The Lacanian mirror stage is marked by *"an identification"* (Lacan 735) which prefigures "the alienating function of the *I*, the aggressivity it releases in any relation to the other" (737). In other words, seeing her image in the mirror begins the process by which the subject will understand herself as separate (alienated) from all others. But Betsy's aggressivity toward an other is directed toward *her own* image in the mirror—an image with which she utterly fails to identify.

Once again, this scene has its corollary in Prince's narrative, which receives an astute commentary from Leys: "The person with whom I identify is immediately converted into my rival who is seen to occupy my place. . . . [T]he specular as such is linked to the assertion of difference, of essential otherness, indeed of *violent rivalry* with that other who is, as the scene makes clear, a version of the same" (180). But while the image in the mirror is certainly "a version of the same," what is crucial in both Prince's account and Jackson's re-vision is that the personality who looks in the mirror acts as though this identity did not exist. When Betsy is engaged in "violent rivalry" with an other who occupies her place in the mirror, she in no way understands the rival as an aspect of herself. We need no more vivid example of the fundamental *lack* of identification among Elizabeth Richmond's separate personalities than Bess's attempt to choke Betsy (262), an indication that the disorder has begun to function in collusion with psychiatric violence. Furthermore, in the process of so totally misrecognizing herself in the mirror scene, Betsy retaliates with renewed destruction of the dictionary (249), even though it provides her key to the use of language. Betsy might block Elizabeth from speech, but Bess blocks Betsy from speech, and Bess herself finds that a note written by Beth "turned into meaningless markings when she brought it close enough to read" (261). Multiple personality, Jackson's story suggests, signals the disintegration of the *speaking subject*.

The problematic nature of multiple personality in terms of agency is also suggested by the trope of naming in *The Bird's Nest*. As we have seen, the failure of others to recognize Elizabeth's subjectivity at the opening of the novel is indicated by her namelessness. Presumably the determined claiming of distinct names by the various personalities might then indicate a renewed "hold on individuality and identity" (152). But naming is as much an attempt to control another as it is a recognition of that other. Dr. Wright suppresses the radical instability suggested by Elizabeth Richmond's multiple personalities by shoring up each personality into a separate feminine type with her own name. His original attempt to categorize the personalities through a numerical system is resisted, as I have noted, by Betsy, who offers her own system of categorization, based on a nursery rhyme: "Elizabeth, Lizzy, Betsy and Bess / All went together to see a bird's nest; / They found a nest with five eggs in it; / They each took one and left four in it" (Friedman 95).[4] The rhyme, however, suggests not how names keep things separate, but how names provide the linguistic illusion of discrete, clearly defined categories which always threaten to break down. For not only do all the names refer to the same person, but also all the names are really the *same* name.

Betsy, seeming to sense the power of naming, attempts to turn the tables on the doctor in her typically resisting manner. Just as he manifests his author-ity by naming the personalities in order to exert control over them, so Betsy struggles against his names (resisting his numerical system by suggesting, as alternatives, what Wright derisively refers to as the names of "a princess in a fairy romance") and attempts to reclaim authorship through naming. Thus she tags labels on the doctor— "question-asker" (207), "well-wisher" (208), "eye-closer" (209)—which, strung together, construct their own mini-narrative about him. Her most prominent exercise in naming as narrative control, however, is her dubbing of Dr. Wright as "Doctor Wrong." The name becomes part of an ongoing battle of wills with the doctor. In a highly comical scene, Betsy insists that he call himself by the name she has given him:

> "Then tell me who you are," said Betsy.
> "I am Doctor Wright."
> "Indeed you are not," said Betsy, laughing.
> I took a deep breath . . . "I am Doctor Wrong," I said. . . .
> "Who?"
> "Doctor Wrong," I said.
> "Who?" I could hear her laughing.
> "*Doctor Wrong*." (213)

4 In Jackson's version of the rhyme, the second name, Lizzy, becomes Beth.

By forcing the doctor to claim as his own the name that *she* has given *him*, Betsy effectively reverses their positions (if only momentarily), "authorizing" herself, as it were, in a counternarrative to his own Jekyll-and-Hyde constructions of her as a fiend, and forcing him to acknowledge his moral culpability (he is "wrong") in his efforts to control her. (As usual, this point is entirely missed by Wright.)

But Betsy's own exercises in naming are not a straightforward self-authorizing; they also can be viewed as a too easy adoption of Wright's strategy of naming in an effort to control the named. Assuming the power of naming, Betsy both echoes Wright's vision of a dichotomous moral universe (Wright/Wrong) and, more generally, uses naming as an attempt to fix and stabilize her own world—an attempt that can hardly be seen as different in kind from Wright's efforts to label each personality with a feminine cliché. Thus, at just the moment when Betsy's narrative seems to be challenging Wright's, it is also an *imitation* of his authorizing strategies. (Leys's discussion points toward just such a vexed relation between imitation and autonomy for Betsy's prototype, the "Sally" of Prince's case.)

Notably, Wright's strategies of naming are not effective means of agency for his patient. Betsy chants her name repeatedly during her escape to New York, as though the name will secure her identity: " 'I am Betsy Richmond,' she said over and over quietly to herself. 'I was even born in New York. And my mother's name is Elizabeth Richmond, Elizabeth Jones before she was married. . . . My name is Betsy Richmond, and I was born in New York. My mother loves me more than anything. My mother's name is Elizabeth Richmond, and my name is Betsy and my mother always called me Betsy and I was named after my mother. Betsy Richmond,' she whispered softly into the unhearing movement of the bus, 'Betsy Richmond' " (226). Betsy's chant of names, like Sally's "autobiography," is a claim to subjectivity; her name grants her the illusion of a stable sense of self, and this is essential during her first "solo" journey. But she is, simultaneously, suppressing what apparently are some very troubling aspects of her narrative; like Wright-as-author, Betsy imposes a rigid narrative form (the formulaic chant) on her materials in an effort to control them. Betsy's surprise that "two people who . . . had the same name liked two different things" (228), or her bewilderment at the multitude of listings for "RICHMOND, ELIZABETH" in the phone book (254), betrays a fragile sense of self preserved only by a naive faith in a one-to-one correspondence between signifier and signified (all "Elizabeth"s will refer to the same person) which is immediately confused by the customary uses of some names as forms of others: are Elizabeth and Betsy the same name, or different ones? Although she disclaims the name Elizabeth Richmond when it refers to the first of the four personalities—"I *hate* her name" (202)—she notes with pleasure elsewhere the similarity of the two names: "My mother's name is Elizabeth Richmond, and my name is Betsy and my mother always called me Betsy and I was named after my mother" (226).

Betsy discovers that names will not do what she wants them to; they continually slide from her control and suggest not the stability but the fluidity of her own identity: "If I had a husband then my mother could marry him and we could all hide together and be happy. My name is Betsy Richmond. My mother's name is Elizabeth Richmond, Elizabeth Jones before I was married. Call me Lisbeth like you do my mother, because Betsy is my darling Robin" (236). The tentative difference provided by the names Betsy and Elizabeth breaks down, and along with it Betsy's sense of her existence as a separate subject; the personal pronouns "I" and "my" now become loosed from exclusive reference to Betsy, the speaker, and float variously between herself and her mother. With her precarious identity thus destabilized, Betsy now views the whole world, or at least everyone she meets in New York, as extensions of herself, and the dramatic triangle involving Robin, her mother, and Betsy is replayed again and again in her mind as she interacts with people on the street.

To be a speaking subject requires a linguistic acceptance of one's own difference from others: "When the child learns to say 'I am' and to distinguish this from 'you are' or 'he is', this is equivalent to admitting that it has taken up its allotted place in the Symbolic Order and given up the claim to imaginary identity with all other possible positions. The speaking subject that says 'I am' is in fact saying 'I am he (she) who has lost something'—and the loss suffered is the loss of the imaginary identity with the mother and with the world" (Moi, *Sexual/Textual Politics* 99). Having lost her mother, Betsy seems to enact something like a regression to the presymbolic (i.e., imaginary) period in which she identified with her mother and with the world. And lest we suppose that this particular conception of fluid and shifting identity is in fact a means of resisting rigid gender boundaries and thus subversive, we might turn again to Moi. Using Lacan to argue against theories that posit a presymbolic realm of merged identities as a subversive site, Moi forcefully suggests that no truly subversive position can be reached "through a straightforward *rejection* of the symbolic order, since such a total failure to enter into human relations would, in Lacanian terms, make us psychotic. . . . There is no *other space* from which we can speak: if we are able to speak at all it will have to be within the framework of symbolic language" (*Sexual/Textual Politics* 170). In losing her sense of separate subjectivity, Betsy loses her linguistic ability, as suggested by her pronoun confusions. Without the power to speak, she can have no true agency; Betsy's New York escapade is portrayed not as a subversive act but as a ludicrous comedy of misidentifications. Multiple personality is simply the same problem in a somewhat different form: what should be an "I" is instead rendered as "she," or occasionally as "we." Betsy's inability to identify herself results in an impasse of agency: there are a multitude of actions which she cannot claim as her own (and which thus paralyze her with fear).

In contrast, the reintegrated Elizabeth Richmond at the novel's conclusion relishes her awareness of agency: "She looked down at her clothes, and remembered with an odd kind of tenderness that her own hands had torn this blouse when she was angry in New York, and ironed this skirt in a deep rush of love toward herself; she had scratched her own face" (364). No longer relying on an illusory other to grant recognition of her subjectivity, Elizabeth now takes joy in recollecting the simplest acts, not because the acts in themselves are pleasant—some, indeed, have been willful strikes at the self—but because they are evidences of agency, of her own ability to act in anger or love or violence. Her claim to agency is accompanied by a firm occupation of the "I." When Aunt Morgen asks, "Who put the mud in the refrigerator?" she can respond, "I did" (360). When she cuts her hair without "permission" (362), a symbolic act of independence from the doctor and the aunt who have attempted to mold her in their image (an act that is therefore a marker of a break from mimesis), she quite deliberately rejects the stylist's choice of pronouns—"Well, how do we like ourselves *now?*"—for the first-person singular: "So, that's what I'm going to look like" (362). The moment of reintegration is a moment full of potential: "She came out of the doctor's office laughing, feeling her head cool and aware for the first time of this day as separate from all other days; she walked lingeringly toward the corner where she would catch her bus, thinking, I am all alone and I have no name; I have cut my hair, I'm the gingerbread man, and wanting to prolong this time of perfect freedom" (365).[5] Elizabeth, once again, has "no name"; but in the light of the doctor's constraining moral labels, and even of Betsy's attempts to fix identity through names, this condition can be seen as

---

[5] Judy Oppenheimer argues, in contrast, that "the reintegration into 'sanity' . . . somehow feels like a loss—of potential, of possibility, of self," whereas "the madness itself is a far from miserable state; . . . [Elizabeth experiences] a heady rush of delight, exultation, a pure sense of power in its sway" (164). Thus, Oppenheimer shares in the valorization of madness-as-resistance so common to contemporary feminist criticism.

freeing. We must remember that Dr. Wright's compulsion to fasten a name on each personality has gone hand in hand with his desire to tag each one with a simple descriptive phrase in an attempt to control the threatening multiplicity that was Elizabeth Richmond.

Yet Elizabeth Richmond's reintegration need not stand for a valorizing of the integrated humanist subject, any more than her self-division need be read as a valorizing of madness. The text offers the possibility of a postmodern subject that can be *distinguished* from the mad subject. It is impossible to look at the Elizabeth Richmond of the novel's conclusion without remembering the cleavages in the self which once yawned into chasms. Furthermore, Jackson has provided enough other examples of the divided self (the doctor's frequent and unexplained mysterious illnesses; the contradictions and confusion within a single personality, Betsy) to warn readers against simply viewing the "final product" as a comforting model of wholeness in which all contradiction has been reconciled. Even the doctor's and Aunt Morgen's sinister attempts to rename the now nameless Elizabeth "Morgen Victoria" or "Victoria Morgen" after themselves (380)—thus suggesting their continued, authorizing efforts to mold her in their own images—are unintentionally ironic. Morgen and Wright have absolutely opposed tastes, as Wright's vigorous criticism of Morgen's house and her unfeminine person indicates, and the yoking of their names together thus constitutes a sort of oxymoron, implying contradiction and potential cleavage within itself.

But named Elizabeth must be. Naming is, after all, a linguistic act, an engagement within the symbolic order; it also suggests the ultimately limited nature of our subjectivity. While theories of the subversive potential of madness subscribe to what Susan Bordo calls "a postmodern ideal of narrative 'heteroglossia' [which] . . . celebrate[s] a 'feminine' ability to identify with and enter into the perspectives of others, . . . [that ideal] obscures the located, limited, inescapably partial, and *always* personally invested nature of human 'story making.' " Against what she calls the "dream of being *everywhere*," Bordo offers "the body [as] a metaphor for our locatedness in space and time" (Bordo, "Feminism" 143–45). But the *name* may serve just as well as such a metaphor. Jackson's early vision of a postmodern subject, in contrast to the ideal of everywhere-ness, fully recognizes partiality and limitation. Elizabeth's moment of complete freedom in namelessness must ultimately be replaced with the moment at which, personally invested (as Bordo would say) in her own story-making, she must name herself (308). Only by being a subject within the symbolic order can Elizabeth wield any agency whatsoever; Jackson's vision suggests that if we wish to locate subversive potential in the postmodern subject, we must separate that subject from figurings of it as "mad."

Furthermore, we will not find the subversive potential of the post-modern subject simply in its multiplicity. Terry Eagleton flatly rejects the notion that "the dismantling of the unified subject [is] a revolution-ary gesture in itself[;] . . . bourgeois individualism thrives on such a fetish" (191). If adjectives such as "multiple" and "shifting" character-ize certain practices having to do with the continual making and re-making of the self, then they are perfectly in keeping with a consumer society that relies on such self-redefinition (through cars, clothes, cos-metics, and so on). There is nothing subversive in the multiplicity of feminine roles (cook, chauffeur, maid) suggested in the Bell Telephone advertisement (Fig. 3) at the beginning of this chapter. It is the capacity of multiple "positions" to coexist simultaneously in a way precluded (and therefore repeatedly elided or obscured) by dominant ideology which offers a theoretical site for the disruption of dominant dis-courses. The postmodern subject challenges such discourses by having (to use Jackson's words) "too much detail" (372) for any one discourse adequately to fix and contain; or, to recall Ruth Leys's discussion of Jacqueline Rose, the subject "always exceed[s] the rigid . . . positions" (even if these are also *multiple* or *changing* positions) into which a given discourse would insert it (Leys 167). And the potentially transforma-tive power of the postmodern subject lies in the resulting possibility of creating counternarratives that will contest the dominant discourse in which she finds herself. Sally's autobiography, the force of which is never quite suppressed by Prince's efforts to reappropriate it; Elizabeth's naming of herself, which can never equal her doctor's and aunt's attempts to name her; Chris Costner Sizemore's desire to correct the record of her story: all are examples of counternarratives which re-sist at the micropolitical level the dominant discourses of gender and the violence en-gendered by them.[6]

[6] I paraphrase de Lauretis (see 9, 33).

4

Out-Hurting the Hurter
Morrison, Madness, and the Moynihan Report

A principal target of feminist thinking since the 1970s has been the traditional nuclear family; it is only quite recently that feminist scholarship has begun to revisit earlier analyses of the family. In a revised edition of *Rethinking the Family: Some Feminist Questions*, Barrie Thorne suggests that "during the 1970s feminists were so intent on criticizing the prevalent ideology of The Family that they paid insufficient attention to other meanings and experiences of 'family' " (8). In the same volume Linda Gordon points out the problematic connections between wholesale condemnation of family structures and an "uncritical individualism" within feminism (151–52). Feminists have not been the only ones to cast judgment on the family, however, nor have they been alone in construing the family as a structure pitted against the individual. The feminist critique in the 1970s constituted one aspect of a "radical" discourse calling, in different ways, for the "death of the family." Feminism shared the stage with antipsychiatry, a movement which, as I have discussed elsewhere in this book, made little of the relevance for gender issues of its own claims. In 1970 David Cooper protested that the family unit—supposedly so suffocating and oppressive "that one can separate from [it] over thousands of miles and yet still remain in its clutches and be strangled by those clutches"—was exclusively an instrument of social control which stifled "the free assumption of identity" (*Death* 18, 9, 23).

I certainly do not wish to take issue with the general premises of the critique of the traditional nuclear family as an institution instrumental in women's oppression; this critique was and is vital to any feminist perspective. Nor am I discounting the importance of individual self-fulfillment. Some articulations of the critique of family and of the valorization of "self-realization" are clearly problematic, however. For instance, to see the family, with Juliet Mitchell, as a "constant unit in relation to the entire course of social history" (*Woman's Estate* 159) is to be operating precisely within the ideology of the family, since one function of ideology is to make a particular historical condition seem universally true. Thus Mitchell (and others) assumed that what was to some degree true of white, middle-class women in the 1960s and 1970s had always been true of all women, of all classes and races, and in all places. Furthermore, to claim that the family—even the "traditional" nuclear family consisting of mother, father, and children—operates only hegemonically is to ignore the importance of context in evaluating any practice. As articulated by white, middle-class women, second-wave feminism often envisioned a utopian future in which the individual (woman) was liberated from family and community structures seen only as oppressive—a view largely conditioned by race and class. Such a perspective allowed no space for alternative historical understandings of family that might see it as anything other than one side of a family/individual dichotomy.

Let us consider as a challenge to that perspective the functions and conditions of the African American family under slavery. The commonplace that the African American family was fragmented by the institution of slavery has become a highly contested claim; but it is certainly true that the legal denial of slave families gave ideological sanction to the breakup of those families when owners deemed it economically necessary or beneficial to sell one member of the family. To preserve family structures in the face of such institutional pressures would thus have been a resistant or even subversive effort. Herbert Gutman argues, along these lines, that if slave owners were motivated by economic considerations to ignore slave family ties, slaves also manipulated owners' economic motivations in order to constitute themselves as families, despite white society's refusal to regard them as such (75–76). Furthermore, Gutman proposes, those families played a crucial role in the creation of larger communities that made "it possible to pass on slave conceptions of marital, familial, and kin obligation from generation to generation"—that is, to pass on a history and culture which differed from that of the white slaveowners. He writes: "Obligations rooted in kin ties also affected relations between slaves unconnected to one another by either blood or marital ties. . . . [O]n slave ships, according to Orlando Patterson, 'it was customary for children to call their parents' shipmates "uncle" and "aunt" ' and even for adults to 'look upon each other's children mutually as their own.' . . . [P]arents and other adult blacks also taught slave children to use such titles when addressing *older slaves unrelated to them by either blood or marriage"* (216–17).[1] By investing "non-kin slave relationships with symbolic kin meanings and functions," Gutman suggests, slaves built a community on the model of kinship: "Enlarged social obligation emerged out of kin obligation" (217, 229). Recognition and maintenance of family ties, in other words, were the bedrock of a slave community that resisted the imposition upon it of white culture and history.

Gutman's analysis highlights the problems with any ahistorical, uncontextualized critique of the ideological function of "family." And although Thorne optimistically suggests that (white) feminism has moved away from its single-minded focus on critiques of the family, thanks in large part to alternative perspectives that have been "especially insightful in revealing the white, middle-class assumptions embedded both in familial ideology and in much of the feminist critique" (8), I believe that a certain strand of feminist literary criticism continues in practice, if not in theory, to persist in a depiction of family structures—at least those involving men—as inevitably conservative, locked in a relation of direct opposition to the individual woman, whose emancipation lies in rejecting them outright. In ignoring issues such as race which may impact differently on the family, certain feminist critics remain trapped in positions staked out by the earlier radical critiques of the family.

Simultaneously, the same critics continue to be influenced by antipsychiatry's celebration of madness as perhaps the ultimate escape of the individual from constraining and ideologically conservative family structures. But the celebration of madness was (and is) as firmly embedded within a white, middle-class framework as was the wholesale rejection of family. Both aspects of the "radical" agenda—that is, the critique of family and the idealization of madness—are problematized, for example, by discourses of the 1960s and 1970s that represented the African American family as "pathological" and located the source of that pathology in African American women. White revolutionaries of all stripes might have had the privilege of metaphorically killing off their families for greater self-realization; but this privilege was not extended in public discourse to African Americans, for whom the purported absence of family resulted, if the researchers were to be believed, in a "tangle of pathology."

This phrase was coined in the 1965 report by Daniel Moynihan, *The*

---

[1] Quoted passages are from Orlando Patterson, *Sociology of Slavery: An Analysis of the Origins, Development, and Structure of Negro Slave Society in Jamaica* (London: MacGibbon & Kee, 1967), 150, 169–70.

Negro Family: The Case for National Action. The Moynihan report, as it came to be known, presented itself as a liberal perspective highly sympathetic to the condition of African Americans, whose difficulties were the pernicious result of the institution of slavery. As the title of the report indicates, it urged government action to improve that condition. And yet the report can be understood as quite simply a new incarnation of the sleight of hand whereby that which is seen as "Other" is labeled mental illness; for the black family's "pathology"—a word investing social problems with the connotations of disease—consisted simply of difference from the "normative" white family. Furthermore, this difference was identified as the organization of gender roles, thus marking the intersection of racial and gendered "norms" in judgments of social disorder: "In essence, the Negro community has been forced into a matriarchal structure which, because it is so out of line with the rest of the American society, seriously retards the progress of the group as a whole. There is, presumably, no special reason why a society in which males are dominant in family relationships is to be preferred to a matriarchal arrangement. However, it is clearly a disadvantage for a minority group to be operating on one principle, while the great majority of the population . . . is operating on another" (75). The term "pathology" apparently referred not simply to the ill effects, such as crime, poverty, and so on, for which Moynihan had arrived at the causal explanation of matriarchal families; the term also encompassed the deviant family structure itself (deviant, that is, from normative white standards). "Pathology" was unabashedly defined as difference from a white male norm, even though the inherent superiority or healthiness of that norm was explicitly rejected. Conversely, to "break out of the tangle of pathology" was equated with "living according to patterns of American society in general" (75). Moynihan's proposed solution was to teach African American males to be dominant once again—through military service: "Military service for negro men . . . is an utterly masculine world. Given the strains of the disorganized and matrifocal family life in which so many Negro youth come of age, the Armed Forces are a dramatic and desperately needed change: a world away from women, a world run by strong men of unquestioned authority" (88).[2]

Certainly, as bell hooks has observed, Moynihan's misogyny was part of the larger postwar backlash against the "career woman" (180), which I have discussed in previous chapters; but in the context of public discourse on African Americans, such arguments constituted a po-

---

[2] For a very different reading of the Moynihan report's implications and of its relevance for a reading of *Beloved*, see Berger.

litically loaded attack not only on women's rights but also on civil rights. Robert Staples and Leanor Boulin Johnson have noted that the construct of "the Black family as a pathological form of social organization [emerged] at precisely the time when Blacks were beginning to indict institutional racism as the cause of their lower status. The civil rights movement was entering a militant phase when the government-subsidized Moynihan study made public the assertion that weaknesses in the Black family . . . were responsible for poverty, educational failures, and lack of employment in the Black population. His efforts put Blacks on the defensive and diverted their energy into responding to his charges" (35). Andrew Billingsley draws out the implications of this timing, suggesting that "Moynihan's thesis seemed to reinforce the policy perspective that there was less need for changing the structure of society, less need for civil rights legislation and affirmative action, and more need for changing the internal structure of African-American families by putting a man in charge of every house" (78).

Such discourses were not limited to the 1970s. In an extended survey of the legacy of Moynihan's "deficit model" of black families, Robert B. Hill reports:

> In late 1983 the *New York Times* presented a series of articles on "The Black Family," which focused almost solely on poor, one-parent families on welfare—a group that comprises only about 15% of all black families. . . . In 1983 *The Baltimore Evening Sun* also ran a series of articles on "The Black Family" that was so full of stereotypes that the black community launched a boycott of that newspaper. . . . And in January 1986, Bill Moyers produced a documentary entitled *A CBS Report: The Vanishing Family—Crisis in Black America*. This documentary on black families characterized single-parent families as "vanishing" non-families. (5)

Nor has the notion of the African American woman as the source of "pathology" been limited to discussions by whites. Deborah McDowell has argued vigorously that some male African American writers, invested in maintaining the male position of dominance within a traditional family, have themselves espoused arguments regarding the black "matriarch" ("Reading" 85). The image of the African American as the victim of some vague form of mental dysfunction persists, as does the perception of the inappropriately powerful black woman as the source of the problem.

Granted, Moynihan's report traced black "pathology" to slavery itself, thus presumably suggesting the role of social conditions (76); nevertheless, to identify the source of white America's culpability solely, or even primarily, as slavery was to put that culpability at a safely distant remove, while firmly locating the continuing problems of African Americans in a context of their own shortcomings. As George Rawick has noted, the argument implied "that blacks in America are psychological victims, incapable of helping themselves and requiring virtual clinical help from those more fortunate to . . . become fully functioning adult human beings" (54). Assumed in this perspective was the notion that, while slavery was a past sin, white America in the present exemplified "the healing powers of the democratic ideal" (Moynihan 76) which had enabled blacks to come as far as they had—and which was presumably evident in the concerns of Moynihan's own report. Not surprisingly, some responded with vehement denials that slavery had any impact whatsoever on present circumstances. Laura Carper wrote: "My Negro landlady encountered a helpful woman who tried to tell her that Negro culture was rooted in the life style of slavery and fixed by history. In telling me about the conversation my landlady said, 'That woman thinks that if she handed me a bail [sic] of cotton, I'd know how to make a dress out of it!' The Negro is not grappling with the social system under which he lived over a hundred years ago, or even with the social system under which he lived ten years ago. He is grappling with the social system under which he lives today" (474). It would take two decades of distance from the Moynihan report for slavery to become the subject of novels by Toni Morrison, Sherley Anne Williams, and Charles Johnson.[3]

Morrison's return to the subject of slavery in *Beloved* reclaims the ground that had become so treacherous in the wake of the Moynihan report. Morrison insists on telling an alternative story of the inheritance of slavery from Moynihan's version, in which slavery reached out a transhistorical arm to render the African American family "pathological" generations later. Rather, for Morrison, that inheritance has to do with a continuing tradition of *representation* by dominant discourses which had legitimized slavery and which persisted into the late twentieth century in studies such as Moynihan's which continued to depict African Americans as "pathological" in comparison to whites. As we shall see, to read forward in Morrison's oeuvre from *The Bluest Eye* to *Beloved* is to trace backward—and thus to uncover—this legacy of slavery.

Part of the tradition of representation against which Morrison writes

[3] Gayl Jones's *Corregidora* (1975) preceded and anticipated these later returns to the slave narrative; the novel's explicit theme was the effects of past generations of slavery on one woman's present.

has to do with the silencing of alternative voices. Morrison has been quite explicit about her view of the purpose of legal prohibitions against teaching slaves to read or write: "One could write about [slaves], but there was never any danger of their 'writing back' " ("Unspeakable" 13). Harryette Mullen concurs, suggesting that the "institutionalized illiteracy" of slavery can be understood as "a mode of 'silencing' populations rendered 'voiceless' so long as their words are not written, published, or disseminated within a master discourse" (245, 249). For Mullen, as for Morrison, contesting this process of silencing, in the past as in the present, becomes critical.[4]

It is crucial to note, however, that Morrison's challenge to Moynihan and others does not lie in a recuperation of "pathology" as some sort of subversive strategy. Pecola Breedlove in *The Bluest Eye* is the most obviously "mad" character in all of Morrison's fiction; but it is impossible to rally around Pecola as a figure of subversion, for her madness consists of a denigration of her "blackness" and a desire so overwhelming for the blue eyes of little white girls and baby dolls that she believes her own eyes have actually been transformed. For Morrison, I will argue, madness consists not of subversion but rather of surrender to the representations of others; madness constitutes the inability to construct a counternarrative of any sort. To read *The Bluest Eye* is to be confronted with nothing less than a statement that the subversive powers of madness—particularly for a group of people already silenced within dominant discourse—can only be theoretical.

Remarkably, however, even readers of Morrison crucially concerned with how dominant discourses have "read black women" (Henderson, "Speaking" 158) or have attempted a "silencing" of them (Mullen 249) continue to claim a subversive quality for black women in madness, irrationality, and exits from language, revealing the continuing legacy of the "radical" discourses of the 1960s and 1970s which celebrated madness. Despite Mullen's investment in "resistant" representation that can counter a process of "silencing," for example, she participates in the prioritizing of a feminine "language" that is in fact non- or prelinguistic, and therefore subversive. Mullen writes of *Beloved* that "Morrison chooses to explore . . . women's power over life by constructing a supernatural character that has access to language, yet mimics the child whose 'relation to the pre-oedipal, phallic mother is prelinguistic, unspoken, and unrepresentable'. . . . The exorcism of the malicious ghost set loose by writing is performed by a chorus of black women producing a sound before or beyond words . . . perhaps moan-

---

[4] Mullen argues for a "resistant orality" in the texts of slave women (245).

ing, keening, ululating, or panting as in childbirth" (261, 263).[5] Following Kristeva, Mullen designates a prelinguistic realm associated with
motherhood as a site for feminist subversion, rendering her argument
immediately problematic in the context of historically grounded imperatives to *resist* a process of silencing by others. As Rebecca Ferguson
has observed, "While the language of the dominant culture and the
written word itself have all too often been potent instruments in . . .
oppression, not to have mastery of them is to be rendered impotent in
ways that matter greatly" (109).

Mae Gwendolyn Henderson, like Harryette Mullen, is deeply concerned with African American women's challenge to "silencing." Henderson has posited an illuminating and valuable model for reading
African American women's writings, based on an understanding of
the heteroglossia, or "creative dialogue," which characterizes their
texts. Black women's "social positionality . . . enables them to speak in
dialogically racial and gendered voices to the other(s)" of their own
multiple position ("Speaking" 146–47). Yet, in an attempt to develop
fully the trope of "speaking in tongues," Henderson too turns to ideas
of a prelinguistic (and thus noncommunicative) feminine realm: "Inac-
cessible to the general congregation, [glossolalia] . . . is outside the
realm of public discourse and foreign to the known tongues of hu-
mankind. . . . [S]peaking in tongues connotes both the semiotic,
presymbolic babble (baby talk), as between mother and child—which
Julia Kristeva postulates as the 'mother tongue'—as well as the diver-
sity of voices, discourses, and languages described by Mikhail
Bakhtin" ("Speaking" 149–50). Henderson then reads the character of
Sula in Morrison's writing as subverting the discourses that attempt to
construct/represent her—by howling: "Howling, a unitary movement
of nondifferentiated sound, contrasts with the phonic differentiation
on which the closed system of language is based. . . . [T]he howl, signi-
fying a prediscursive mode, thus becomes an act of self-reconstitution
as well as an act of subversion or resistance to the 'network of signification' represented by the symbolic order. . . . Sula's silences and howls
serve to disrupt or subvert the 'symbolic function of the language' "
("Speaking" 158).[6] This privileging of "silences and howls" is precisely
the sort of critical move that reinscribes women's inability to be intelligible, to make (linguistic) sense. There is no subversiveness in such an

---

[5] Quoted passage is from Elizabeth Grosz, *Sexual Subversions* (London: Allen and
Unwin, 1989), 87.

[6] Quoted passages are from Nelly Furman, "The Politics of Language: Beyond the
Gender Principle?" in *Making a Difference; Feminist Literary Criticism*, ed. Gayle Greene
and Coppelia Kahn (New York: Methuen, 1985), 72–73.

abdication of the field of representation. When Pecola in *The Bluest Eye* substitutes "conversation" with a hallucinated self for conversation with others, her withdrawal from language ("How come you don't talk to anybody?" [153]) can hardly be read as an "act of subversion or resistance to the 'network of signification' represented by the symbolic order." Rather, what Pecola "says," but does not really say, in the recesses of her mind participates most fully in the network of signification which has constructed her: "Suppose my eyes aren't blue enough?" (157). Pecola's "silence" thus becomes a blank in which others may write their own inscriptions of her.[7]

In contrast to Pecola, her counterpart Claudia tries to construct a story with the potential to challenge dominant representations—representations that might, for example, portray Pecola's madness as a "typical" product of the pathology of the African American family. Claudia, who narrates portions of *The Bluest Eye*, tells us that as a child she was given a white, blue-eyed baby doll every Christmas, which she was obviously expected to love although she could not understand its charm: "I had only one desire: to dismember it. To see of what it was made, to discover the dearness, to find the beauty, the desirability that had escaped me, but apparently only me" (20). Dismembering the white doll, which Claudia believes will tell her the story of its power, simultaneously offers a gruesome figure for the dismantling of such power. But by the end of the narrative, Claudia's attention has turned away from the white doll. The story she really wants to understand is the story of Pecola and her baby, and she can do this only through an act of remembering: "Little by little we began to piece a story together.... Properly placed, the fragments of talk ran like this" (147); then readers are given a reconstituted conversation, apparently seamless and uninterrupted but in fact pieced together out of many parts. The suggestion that Claudia is literally re-membering is emphasized by the juxtaposition of her sentiments about Pecola's baby with her memories of the white baby doll: "I felt a need for someone to want the black baby to live—just to counteract the universal love of white baby dolls" (148). While she wanted to dismember the doll, her desire to remember Pecola's story is given, as it were, a bodily form. The image of reattaching fragments to form a physical body, then, comes to suggest the remembering of a story. (Implicitly, dismembering is the opposite, which is why Claudia's plan to dismember the white baby doll in order to understand the story of its appeal presumably would not have worked.)

Claudia's act of remembering seems, at least at the fictional level, to be a failure ("it's much much much too late" [160]), because her per-

---

[7] See Morrison, "Unspeakable Things" 22–23, for a discussion of Pecola's madness.

spective is limited. She does not know the full story behind Pecola's eventual madness—that is, the individual story of each person who, touching Pecola's life, contributes to that madness. Thus Claudia's recollections must be supplemented with the help of an omniscient narrator who provides what one reader has called "cameos" of the various characters (Turner 362). "Cameos" is a good description for the individual, isolated portraits with definitive boundaries that constitute much of *The Bluest Eye*. This form strongly indicates that the members of Claudia's community cannot see how their stories interconnect with and depend on one another; the community remains willfully blind to its complicity in Pecola's fate. As Claudia observes, everyone in that community wants Pecola's baby—the potential embodiment of a communal story—dead. Beloved, as the literal embodiment of a memory that has been "disremembered [read: dismembered] and unaccounted for" (Morrison, *Beloved* 274), will suggest at least the possibility of a more hopeful remembering (and, thus, representation).

Like Claudia, who wishes to challenge the white baby doll's story with that of Pecola's black baby, Morrison constructs her novels as challenges to dominant representations such as the discourse of African American pathology highlighted by the Moynihan report. And, as I have argued of other women writers, Morrison must first strategically inhabit such representations in order to reveal the spaces "not represented yet implied (unseen) in them" (de Lauretis 26). Significantly, Morrison's early novels, *The Bluest Eye* (1970) and *Sula* (1973), both contain striking representations of pathology, in the form of madness. Michele Wallace wrote of the former work: "When I first read this book, I was deeply troubled by Pecola's characterization as a victim of incest and by her subsequent loss of the ability to communicate rationally. It seemed to me such a story was hopelessly negative" (63). Like Wallace, we are understandably reluctant to read madness in Morrison's writing as confirmation of African American "pathology"; perhaps it is just such a critical problem that motivates Cedric Gael Bryant's argument that "in Morrison's novels madness itself is a survival strategy that empowers individuals with the means to order chaos in unusual ways. Madness, then, is power to the black community" (Bryant, "Orderliness" 733). But to turn to a specific portrayal of madness in Morrison's writing—Pecola's, or Shadrack's in *Sula*—is immediately to undermine any theory about the empowering nature of madness in her fiction. One of the most vivid images of Shadrack's madness involves his efforts to complete the simplest of tasks—untying his shoes:

Uncoordinated, his fingernails tore away at the knots. He fought a rising hysteria that was not merely anxiety to free his aching feet; his very life

depended on the release of the knots. Suddenly without raising his eyelids, he began to cry. Twenty-two years old, weak, hot, frightened, not dar-
ing to acknowledge the fact that he didn't even know who or what he was
. . . he was sure of one thing only: the unchecked monstrosity of his hands.
. . . Through his tears he saw the fingers joining the laces, tentatively at
first, then rapidly. The four fingers of each hand fused into the fabric,
knotted themselves and zig-zagged in and out of the tiny eyeholes. (11)

Hands, a paradigmatic image of instrumentality (we must rely on
them for any sort of "ordering" at the literal level), are hopelessly em-
broiled in knots from which they cannot extricate themselves.
Shadrack may wish to "order chaos," but he cannot. National Suicide
Day is his way of attempting to order the chaos he perceives in death:
"If one day a year were devoted to it, everybody could get it out of the
way and the rest of the year would be safe and free" (12). But this effort
to control chaos backfires horribly when, one National Suicide Day,
scores of people playfully following Shadrack parade to their deaths
inside a collapsed tunnel which had once embodied their hopes for
employment.

Bryant has (accurately, I think) equated madness in Morrison's texts
with the impulse to order; but the obsession for ordering in *The Bluest
Eye* is a coded signal for the acceptance of dominant representations
that esteem whiteness over blackness. Ordering is for Pauline
Breedlove an act of classification and segregation: "Jars on shelves at
canning, peach pits on the step, sticks, stones, leaves. . . . Whatever
portable plurality she found, she organized into neat lines, according
to their size, shape, or gradations of color. Just as she would never
align a pine needle with the leaf of a cottonwood tree, she would never
put the jars of tomatoes next to the jars of green beans" (88–89). This hierarchical ordering extends to people, with negative effects for herself:
"She was never able, after her education in the movies, to look at a face
and not assign it some category in the scale of absolute beauty, and the
scale was one she absorbed in full from the silver screen" (97); that is, it
was one in which blackness is low on the scale, if it even appears there
at all. It is when Pauline goes to work for a more well-to-do white family that she finds "beauty, order, cleanliness, and praise" (97), with the
result that she nurtures the family's little girl like a daughter while despising—at least outwardly—her own daughter Pecola. Finally, we are
told, Pauline Breedlove "assigned herself a role in the scheme of
things" (100); her impulse to order has resulted not in subversion but
in a complete acceptance of the dominant white values of her society.

Soaphead Church, who believes with Shadrack that "to name an evil was to neutralize if not annihilate it" (*Bluest Eye* 130), also longs for "a triumph of cosmic neatness . . . the orderly sectioning and segregating of all levels of evil and decay" (136). But this orderly segregating has racial implications. Soaphead is one of a long line of West Indians with a "white strain" running through their family, who have made their "life's goal the hoarding of this white strain" (132). When Pecola comes to Soaphead asking for blue eyes, he is immediately sympathic to her wish—"Here was an ugly little girl asking for beauty. . . . A little black girl who wanted to rise up out of the pit of her blackness and see the world with blue eyes" (137)—with the result that he exacerbates her own self-hatred and ultimate destruction. For Soaphead, as for Pauline Breedlove, the compulsion to orderliness is intimately connected to a contempt for his own blackness, with destructive results. If madness, as Bryant proposes, is a "means to order chaos," then surely it is highly suspect as a strategy of empowerment. Self-directed scorn can be seen in Morrison's writing as a thwarted (not a successful) attempt to manage the "chaos" created by the cultural products of racism. As Claudia explains of her confusion over the appeal of blond hair and blue eyes, she eventually "learned . . . to worship [Shirley Temple], just as I learned to delight in cleanliness, knowing, even as I learned, that the change was adjustment without improvement" (22). Morrison suggests that the pain of racist representations requires some strategy other than superficial "ordering."

Indeed, madness in all of Morrison's fiction is consistently linked with destructive impulses directed inward, which thus become another aspect of the already oppressive situation of racism. Teresa de Lauretis has shown (drawing on the writings of Althusser) that subjectivity involves the "process whereby a social representation is accepted and absorbed by an individual as her (or his) own representation, and becomes, for that individual, real, even though it is in fact imaginary" (12). Although de Lauretis is referring to the formation of gender, her succinct explication can be applied just as well to the formation of race, that is, of one's understanding of race. If to become a racial subject means taking on representation as self-representation, then one devastating product of a society saturated with racist practices and representations is the self-hatred that becomes, in *The Bluest Eye*, a virtual given of black subjectivity.

One such representation—indicting Moynihan's brand of sociology almost directly—is of the "normative" white family. The narrative of *The Bluest Eye* is preceded by a sequence drawn from what was at one time a standard children's reader, the "Dick and Jane" text. This "quotation" presents an image of the idealized nuclear family: "Here is the house. It is green and white. It has a red door. It is very pretty. Here is the family. Mother, Father, Dick, and Jane live in the green-and-white house. They are very happy" (7). The passage is set on the page a second time without capitalization or punctuation, and then a third without spaces between the words—"undercutting," as Michele Wallace observes, "the very basis of the alphabet's power to signify" (64). The suggestion here, of course, is of Pecola's descent into madness, where madness means not power but what it has meant in so many other texts: the inability to produce meaning for others. Obviously, then, Morrison means to suggest that the Dick and Jane text is implicated in the process of Pecola's madness; it functions ideologically to construct an ideal as the natural and universal shape of things. Morrison drives this point home by using every detail of the Dick and Jane story (mother, father, dog, cat) to reel out another strand in the narrative of collective self-hatred which, taken together, brings about Pecola's madness. The technique of juxtaposition, by which each mini-narrative is introduced by and set against its counterpart in the "representative" family, reduplicates the strategy of dominant discourses such as Moynihan's, even while it suggests that it is precisely this mode of representation that is at fault. The dysfunctional family at the center of the story is a sort of ruse by which Morrison mirrors back to us the discourse of pathology that has constructed and represented "the black family" in particular ways, in order to explode the confines of that space. Moynihan's use of the white family as a yardstick by which to measure black pathology is thus turned on its head: it is the existence of the ideal, and its ideological function as representation, that brings about whatever "pathology" we may find.

Herein, perhaps, lies the "secret" that is both gestured toward and displaced by the first narrative sentences of *The Bluest Eye*: "Quiet as it's kept, there were no marigolds in the fall of 1941. We thought, at the time, that it was because Pecola was having her father's baby that the marigolds did not grow" (9). Morrison has commented of these opening lines that "the words are conspiratorial. 'Shh, don't tell anyone else,' and 'No one is allowed to know this.' It is a secret between us and a secret that is being kept from us" ("Unspeakable Things" 20–21). On one level, of course, the "secret, terrible, awful story" (*The Bluest Eye* 147), which Claudia has learned and is passing on to readers, is that of Pecola's pregnancy and madness, and behind these the immediate source of both: the rape by her father. And yet this secret is really a non-secret; it is common knowledge in the neighborhood. It is also not a secret to readers. Morrison points out that "the book can be seen to open with its close," so that there are no surprises in the novel's structure. Indeed, the "secret" of Pecola's rape by her father is given away on the book's jacket ("Unspeakable Things" 22, 20). Finally, that rape seems to be a confirmation of theories about the "pathological" nature of the black family. A "nasty bit of scandalmongering" turned into "golden confidence," it is an example of what Marianna Torgovnick has called the "secret of the primitive" which is always "whatever Euro-Americans want it to be. It tells us what we want it to tell us" (9). This secret that is no secret points behind itself, to yet another (non)secret: "that the earth itself might have been unyielding" to the prosperity of African Americans (9). Although the existence of racism in the present is no secret, saturating popular representations from movies to children's books, it is denied—or secreted—by discourses such as Moynihan's. Morrison herself has indicated the role of institutionalized discourses of madness in obscuring racism's significance: "The trauma of racism . . . has always seemed to me a cause (not a symptom) of psychosis"; but this causal relation is "strangely of no interest to psychiatry" ("Unspeakable Things" 16).

The representation of the African American *woman* as a source of pathology also seems to be accepted and internalized by Morrison's characters. Ascriptions of "craziness" are common to the talk of the women overheard by Claudia and her sister Frieda in *The Bluest Eye*. Such conversation is worth quoting at length for what it reveals about the women's collective constructions of madness:

> "You know him," [Claudia's mother] said to her friends. "Henry Washington. He's been living over there with Miss Della Jones on Thirteenth Street. But she's too addled now to keep up. So he's looking for another place."
>
> "Oh, yes." Her friends do not hide their curiosity. "I been wondering how long he was going to stay up there with her. They say she's real bad off. Don't know who he is half the time, and nobody else."
>
> "Well, that old crazy nigger she married up with didn't help her head none."
>
> "Did you hear what he told folks when he left her?"
>
> "Uh-uh. What?" . . .
>
> " . . . Well, somebody asked him why he left a nice good church woman like Della. . . . Said he wanted a woman to smell like a woman. Said Della was just too clean for him."
>
> "Old dog. Ain't that nasty!"
>
> "You telling me. What kind of reasoning is that?" . . .
>
> " . . . But you know, none of them girls wasn't too bright. Remember that grinning Hattie? She wasn't never right. And their Auntie Julia is still trotting up and down Sixteenth Street talking to herself."

"Didn't she get put away?"

"Naw. County wouldn't take her. Said she wasn't harming anybody."

"Well, she's harming me. You want something to scare the living shit out of you, you get up at five-thirty in the morning like I do and see that old hag floating by in that bonnet. Have mercy! . . ."

"Well, I hope don't nobody let me roam around like that when I get senile. It's a shame."

"What they going to do about Della? Don't she have no people?" (15)

Virtually everyone the women mention is labeled "crazy," "addled," "not right," or "senile"; yet there are marked differences in the weight given to these words, depending on the context of the conversation. Della Jones's husband is an "old crazy nigger" with questionable "reasoning," but these words seem to be meant as a sort of lighthearted critique of his scoundrel-like acts and words rather than a serious imputation of madness. In contrast, every woman to whom craziness is ascribed is represented as truly troubled. And while Della's husband has simply taken up with a new woman (and therefore is still rooted in a relationship of some kind), madness for Della and her kinswomen provokes a complete casting off from the community. The women's talk reveals an underlying tension, felt within themselves, between their criticism of the lines of exclusion drawn by discourses of madness and their acceptance of and complicity with those discourses. On the one hand, Della's desertion by her "people" is clearly regarded with disapproval by the women. Yet on the other, they not only understand Henry Washington's leave-taking of Della but have been expecting it as a matter of course: how could he put up with someone so "addled"? To this degree Washington is accepted by the community of women while Della Jones is not, even though Washington himself turns out to be, like both Cholly Breedlove and Soaphead Church, a molester of small girls (79). Furthermore, the women themselves cannot tolerate the presence of Aunt Julia in their midst, insisting both that she ought to "get put away" and that they would want the same for themselves in her condition. A *woman's* madness is thus construed as dangerous and potentially threatening to the community. The women Claudia overhears have accepted the imputation of a pathology rooted in the African American female.

Dominant representations of masculinity and their unquestioned acceptance by the community are also crucial in the structure of *The Bluest Eye*. The section titled "Winter," though it repeats the themes of self-contempt and internalization of white standards of beauty in the character of Maureen Peal (a popular, light-skinned African American girl), is clearly held together by representations of fathers. The section begins with a description of Claudia's father that is apparently unrelated to anything that happens subsequently. Then narrative takes over, as Claudia describes an incident in which Pecola is first teased by black boys because her "daddy sleeps nekkid," although "their own father had similarly relaxed habits" (55), and is then asked by Maureen Peal if she has ever seen a man naked. Claudia reports her memory of this conversation:

> Pecola blinked, then looked away. "No. Where would I see a naked man?"
> "I don't know. I just asked."
> "I wouldn't even look at him, even if I did see him. That's dirty. Who wants to see a naked man?" Pecola was agitated. "Nobody's father would be naked in front of his own daughter. Not unless he was dirty too."
> "I didn't say 'father.' I just said 'a naked man.' . . . How come you said 'father'?" Maureen wanted to know.
> "Who else would she see, dog tooth?" I was glad to have a chance to show anger . . . because we had seen our own father naked and didn't care to be reminded of it and feel the shame brought on by the absence of shame. (59)

On one level, of course, the nakedness of the father is actually insignificant; as Claudia points out, all the fathers including her own had "similarly relaxed habits." Yet it is impossible to ignore that this recollected scene has some particular significance for Claudia in light of what happens later to Pecola (we, as readers who know that outcome from the first pages, cannot fail to connect the two events as well), and that its significance links Pecola's father with Claudia's in some way.

A textual relation between the two fathers is underscored by the introductory (and apparently unrelated) passage in which Claudia describes hers: "My daddy's face is a study. Winter moves into it and presides there. His eyes become a cliff of snow threatening to avalanche; his eyebrows bend like black limbs of leafless trees. . . . Wolf killer turned hawk fighter, he worked night and day to keep one from the door and the other from under the windowsills. A Vulcan guarding the flames" (52). Claudia's description of her father is obviously a positive and admiring one, leading us to wonder if the passage serves as a contrast to Pecola's father. Yet the section that follows works to connect Claudia's father with Pecola's rather than to differentiate the two (they both sleep naked and have been seen naked by their daughters). Morrison, significantly, further links the two fathers by characterizing the point of view in this story as that of the "could-be victims of rape"

("Unspeakable Things" 22). Though I am not suggesting that Claudia's father is a rapist or even a potential rapist in some essential way, there is a tenuous connection here.

The source of that connection lies, perhaps, in the way that Claudia represents her father. That representation is stunningly clichéd—that is, it draws on standard images of masculinity in our society, all of which are strongly suggestive of male power. Claudia's father is "wolf killer turned hawk fighter," a "Vulcan" who will protect his family from the winter's cold. This passage stands in marked contrast to the one in which women represent one another as crazy outcasts. Both say something about the way in which potentially dangerous constructions of gender are adopted and reproduced by Claudia's community. Paternal power is certainly benign enough when it implies protection of one's children, but the rhetoric of masculine power and protectiveness can also be used to disguise and to justify quite a different form of power—a power over others which inheres in unequal gender positions.

Furthermore, the powerlessness created by racism is particularly dangerous in the hands of a man who still has a certain limited, socially sanctioned power over (female) others. When Pecola comes to Soaphead Church, we are told, he feels "anger that he was powerless to help her. . . . His outrage grew and felt like power" (137). Anger of this sort is dangerous, for it can seek power aggressively, in the form of domination. The limited exercise of power that results from Soaphead's anger—his "miracle" of turning Pecola's eyes blue—is extraordinarily destructive. Yet remarkably, Soaphead represents his "miracle" (even to himself), along with his sexual molestation of young girls—both of which are in fact warped effects of his relative powerlessness in a white society—as acts of helping, of a benevolent remembering of the children that God forgot: "You said, 'Suffer little children to come unto me, and harm them not.' . . . Did you forget about the children? Yes. . . . You let them go wanting, sit on road shoulders, crying next to their dead mothers. . . . That's why I changed the little black girl's eyes for her. . . . I did what You did not, could not, would not do: I looked at that ugly little black girl, and I loved her. I played You" (143). Although Soaphead interprets his acts in terms of protecting and loving lost children, he simultaneously recognizes the power implicit in those acts: he is playing God, the figure of the ultimate patriarch. Confronted with a racialized situation of powerlessness, Soaphead draws on a power that inheres in his position as a man; protectiveness and (fatherly) love then become guises (and excuses) for the exertion of power over those who mark the position of absolute weakness, the little girls who are not yet even women.

Cholly Breedlove's rape of his daughter, similarly, marks a complex convergence of the desire to protect (in a highly masculinized way) and the desire to wound, which is an extension of his own self-hatred. An obvious key to Cholly's character is an incident in his youth in which two white men, intruding on his lovemaking with a young girl, Darlene, force him to continue while they watch. Morrison has called this incident "Cholly's 'rape' by the whitemen" and pointed out its intimate connection to "his own of his daughter" ("Unspeakable Things" 23). Rape, that is to say, is a figure for the rendering of a person or persons powerless, and subject to abusive power, by another person or persons.

Cholly's later rape recalls his earlier "rape." Under the intruding, commanding eyes of the white men, Cholly's and Darlene's sexual act itself is turned into a rape, in which Cholly wishes to exert what highly limited power he has to harm Darlene, who signifies someone weaker than himself and to whom he can therefore transfer his self-contempt in this moment:

> With a violence born of total helplessness, he pulled her dress up, lowered his trousers and underwear. . . . Cholly, moving faster, looked at Darlene. He hated her. He almost wished he could do it—hard, long, and painfully, he hated her so much. . . . [Afterwards,] he cultivated his hatred of Darlene. Never did he once consider directing his hatred toward the hunters. Such an emotion would have destroyed him. They were big, white, armed men. He was small, black, helpless. . . . For now, he hated the one . . . who bore witness to his failure, his impotence. The one whom he had not been able to protect, to spare, to cover from the round moon glow of the flashlight. (117, 119)

Somewhere in the complex of Cholly's reactions is the desire to "protect" Darlene; but this positive impulse is inextricably tied, for him, with conceptions of gender. (It is his duty as a man to protect the "weaker sex.") Because he cannot protect her, he experiences a particularly gendered form of helplessness: he feels "impotent." That sense of impotence generates, in turn, a need to reassert some form of (masculine) power, at all costs.

Pecola's helplessness provokes in Cholly, once again, a sense of his own powerlessness to protect her from the generalized and repeated blows of racism, just as he was unable to protect Darlene from a very specific and violent form of racial hatred:

> His revulsion was a reaction to her young, helpless, hopeless presence. Her back hunched that way; her head to one side as though crouching

from a permanent and unrelieved blow. Why did she have to look so whipped? . . . The clear statement of her misery was an accusation. He wanted to break her neck—but tenderly. Guilt and impotence rose in a bilious duet. What could he do for her—ever? What give her? What say to her? What could a burned-out black man say to the hunched back of his eleven-year-old daughter? . . . How dare she love him? . . . What was he supposed to do about that? Return it? How? . . . (128)

Once again, Cholly's recognition of his own "impotence" (a gendered response to the absence of power) becomes aggression. He wants to "break [Pecola's] neck," because he knows that he is unmanned in the eyes of his daughter by his inability to protect her—that is, to be powerful in a benign and even beneficial way. Cholly reacts by needing to assert power at all costs, and his impulse takes the strange form of a protective aggression expressed in a means most calculated to prove his manhood: he feels "a tenderness, a protectiveness. . . . He wanted to fuck her—tenderly. But the tenderness would not hold." At the completion of the rape, he looks down at his daughter's limp body and feels again "the hatred mixed with tenderness. The hatred would not let him pick her up, the tenderness forced him to cover her" (128–29).

Morrison's critique in *The Bluest Eye* is thus leveled simultaneously against racist representations and practices that breed self-hatred (the ironic opposite of the name "Breedlove") in African Americans and against patriarchal representations that construct the masculine gender position as by definition one of power over women. Although this power can appear disguised in the benign forms of "protectiveness" and even "love," the social construction of, and insistence on, positions of unequal power (within or outside a family structure) are always a threat to the woman, or woman-to-be. Certainly, Morrison is quite concerned with how the reproduction of particular constructs of gender within the family function conservatively and oppressively. Nevertheless, I have been concerned in my discussion of *The Bluest Eye* to point out how Morrison's narrative, responding to and engaging with discourses of race as well as of gender, moves beyond a pinpointing of the family as locus and source of social ills which marked so much of the discourse on gender, race, and madness in the 1970s. Though Cholly's rape is a symptom of "pathology," and though that pathology takes place within the context of a family, Morrison insistently refuses to narrow the scope of her critique to the family structure. Indeed, by calling into question the use of "protectiveness" as a defense for unequal power, Morrison highlights the complicity of discourses such as Moynihan's in the pathology they claimed to study from a neutral perspective. For Moynihan, arguing fundamentally—despite his rhetorical disguises—that black men felt "unmanned" by their lack of a dominant position within the family, and that they could not "protect" their families as befitted their status as men, was participating in the construction of the very image of manhood that is revealed to be so dangerous in *The Bluest Eye*. The Breedlove family is one site among many in this novel for the practice and reproduction of unequal, gendered power relations. Furthermore, the rape is a function as much of the effects of racist representations as it is of gendered ones. These are important points to make because, as I intend to show, the family—and its extention into the community—is absolutely crucial to Morrison's envisioning of a strategy other than madness for dealing with racial (and gendered) representations within dominant culture.

As I suggested at the beginning of this chapter, a prioritizing of madness in literary criticism often goes hand in hand with a rejection of "families," seen as structures that crush the individual woman. This critical stance is particularly pervasive in scholarship on Morrison's novel *Sula*, as a brief review reveals. Cedric Bryant notes that Sula "challenges the community's collective identity [and] . . . possesses the power to destroy the community's most valuable assets—deeply rooted familial relationships" (734–35); but for Bryant this destructive capability is all to the good, challenging traditional patriarchy. Susan Willis agrees, praising the household in which Sula is raised for its "organization on a feminine principle," and contending that in all of Morrison's texts "the definition of social utopia is based on a three-woman household" (105–6). And as Deborah McDowell asserts, *Sula* "strongly suggests that one cannot belong to the community and preserve the imagination, for the orthodox vocations for women—marriage and motherhood—restrict if not preclude imaginative expression" ("Boundaries" 65). Finally, Barbara Smith detects in *Sula* a "consistently critical stance toward the heterosexual institutions of male-female relationships, marriage, and the family," and argues: "It is the fact that Sula has not been tamed or broken by the exigencies of heterosexual family life which most galls the others. . . . The town reacts to her disavowal of patriarchal values by becoming fanatically serious about their own family obligations, as if in this way they might counteract Sula's radical criticism of their lives" (175, 178). Families for these critics clearly are not the community's "most valuable asset" at all, and attending to family obligations can apparently be regarded only as a "fanatical" activity. Sula, in this view, bears a remarkable resemblance to antipsychiatry's ideal individual, liberated from the "clutches" of family and able, in good existentialist fashion, to engage in the "free assumption of identity" (Cooper, *Death* 18, 23).

This valorization of Sula as the paradigmatic figure of subversion is troubling, however, precisely for its rejection of communal responsibility, obviously a value of paramount importance for Morrison. In the matter of communal responsibility, Sula has something in common with Cholly Breedlove; both are "characters who realize total freedom and, as a result, are incapable of living in society and maintaining human relationships" (Willis 99). Cholly, we are told, "was free. Dangerously free. Free to feel whatever he felt. . . . Free to be tender or violent. . . . Abandoned in a junk heap by his mother, rejected for a crap game by his father, there was nothing more to lose. He was alone with his own perceptions and appetites, and they alone interested him" (*The Bluest Eye* 125–6). Surely we are to take the qualifier "dangerously" in this description of Cholly's freedom seriously, given the final act of rape which is an unrestrained pursuit of his own "appetites," at once "tender" and "violent." Like Cholly, whose broken family connections sever him from a larger sense of responsibility to others, Sula "lived out her days exploring her own thoughts and emotions, giving them full reign, feeling no obligation to please anybody unless their pleasure pleased her. As willing to feel pain as to give pain, to feel pleasure as to give pleasure, hers was an experimental life—ever since her mother's remarks sent her flying up those stairs, ever since her one major feeling of responsibility had been exorcised on the bank of a river with a closed place in the middle. The first experience taught her there was no other that you could count on; the second that there was no self to count on either" (*Sula* 102–3). Ashraf Rushdy has persuasively argued for the primacy of these two remembered incidents in understanding Sula: each serves as what he calls "a primal scene because it is the object of recollection, of anamnesis at critical stages in the character's life" ("Rememory" 307). Sula's "mother's remarks"—"I love Sula. I just don't like her"(49)—have the effect of severing Sula from a sense of connection to family, and by extension to community. The scene in which Sula overhears this comment is followed immediately by the second pivotal experience of her life, her accidental drowning of the boy Chicken Little, in which "her one major feeling of responsibility had been exorcised." After this event, Sula is unable to feel a sense of responsibility to anyone, including her friend Nell, and this fact is crucial to understanding her character. Sula in her freedom, like Cholly in his, "became dangerous" (*Sula* 105).

Critics who privilege Sula as a model for subversive womanhood tend to suppress another troubling aspect of this text: Sula "puts away" her grandmother Eva in a home, thus violating the strong communal ties that are central to the novel: "White people didn't fret about putting their old ones away. It took a lot for black people to let them go, and even if somebody was old and alone, others did the dropping by, the floor washing, the cooking. Only when they got crazy and unmanageable were they let go. Unless it was somebody like Sula, who put Eva away out of meanness. It was true that Eva was foolish in the head, but not so bad as to need locking up"(141). Whereas Sula's violation of other women's marriages (including Nell's) can easily be interpreted as suggesting a "disavowal of patriarchal values" and a "critical stance toward the heterosexual institutions of male-female relationships, marriage, and the family" (Smith, "Toward a Black Feminist Criticism" 178, 175), her oppression of another woman in her family—an act that is in no way related to men or patriarchal institutions—is much more difficult to appropriate to a feminist reading.

Significantly, Sula's refusal of responsibility in this instance hardly constitutes a rebellion against the community; it is, rather, perfectly in keeping with the community's own worst impulses: "Daughters who had complained bitterly about the responsibilities of taking care of their aged mothers-in-law had altered when Sula locked Eva away, and they began cleaning those old women's spittoons without a murmur. Now that Sula was dead and done with, they returned to a steeping resentment of the burdens of old people" (132). In fact, the virtual collapse of community after Sula's death merely replicates, and draws to its logical conclusion, Sula's own disdain for extended family ties.

Sula's disregard for family and community also has consequences for the more individualistic project of self-authoring in which she is engaged. "I don't want to make somebody else. I want to make myself" (80), she tells Eva; but we later learn through her recollection of the two primal incidents of her life that she has failed in this goal: "The first experience taught her there was no other that you could count on; the second that there was no self to count on either. She had no center, no speck around which to grow" (103). Sula's absence of self is intimately connected to her rejection of the notion that there are others to count on—her rejection, that is, of communal ties and communal responsibility. A notion of self, for Morrison, necessitates a notion of community; as Rushdy explains: "In Morrison's novels, understanding self and past is always a project of community" ("Rememory" 304). This is not to say that the self is the same as others, but that it can be conceived as constituted in some way other than through an opposition to (and exclusion of) others. Toni Morrison has described *Sula* as her attempt "to tell about feminine forgiveness in story form.... [T]he

point is less the thing to be forgiven than the nature and quality of forgiveness among women—which is to say friendship among women"
("Memory" 386). What Morrison is conveying here is the primacy of
connection and communal obligation, which will be (re)established by
the act of forgiveness.

The quality of forgiveness is lacking, however, in the community's
responses to Sula; the culpability of the residents of the Bottom lies in
their own refusal to envision or practice a form of connectedness that is
not based on exclusion. This flaw is crucial because it replicates on
some level the ideological operations of a hegemonic white culture
which defines itself in opposition to various Others. Sula and Nell
have both "discovered years before that they were neither white nor
male" (44), that is, that they are defined as negativity by discourses
that construct identity on the basis of exclusion. Thus Sula and Nell—
and presumably every other person who discovers that she is defined
negatively, as not what she is not—"had set about creating something
else to be" (44). But the narrative of *Sula* suggests that this project is
undermined if the "Others" of dominant discourse simply repeat a
strategy of defensive and antagonistic self-definition—that is, of constructing a self in opposition to certain Others. "White people didn't
fret about putting their old ones away," we are told, but even those residents of the Bottom who condemn Sula's putting Eva away accept
without question the appropriateness of casting those who are "crazy
and unmanageable" out of the community (141), just as the women of
The Bluest Eye do not question the necessity of putting away Della
Jones or Auntie Julia. More prominently, the residents of the Bottom
constitute themselves as a community defensively against Sula-as-
Other; their fanatical pursuit of family obligations (to paraphrase
Smith) reverses itself only after Sula's death. Cedric Bryant is absolutely right in observing that the community of the Bottom "does not
survive" because its "singular interest is in protecting—that is, 'insu-
lating'—itself from . . . the otherness that Sula represents" (741). Understanding communal obligations only as a means by which they can
exclude Sula, the residents of the Bottom feel no need to continue them
once the threat of difference is past.

Just as the community represented in *The Bluest Eye* uncritically re-
produces dominant discourses through its acceptance of the valorization of whiteness in those discourses, and its self-representation
according to those standards, so the community represented in *Sula* re-
produces dominant strategies for self-representation that are based on
opposition and exclusion. These circular, self-defeating reproductions

are, in a larger sense, the "pathology" represented in Morrison's texts—a pathology pointing to the "trauma of racism," which causes "the severe fragmentation of the self" and of the community (Morrison, "Unspeakable Things" 16). The figure for a way out in *Sula* is a "feminine forgiveness" offering the possibility of a community that is based not on exclusion but on inclusion and healing. This alternative is given a more extended articulation in *Beloved*, as I will argue, through the collecting of individual stories into a communal narrative that can challenge racist representations.

The importance of the issue of representation in *Beloved* is firmly established through schoolteacher's classroom exercise, in which he directs his students to write Sethe's "human characteristics on the left [side of the page]; her animal ones on the right" (193). The reduction of Sethe's humanity through representation becomes the fiction that justifies treatment of her as an animal—for example, when she is milked "like the cow" (200) by schoolteacher's pupils. When Stamp Paid presents Paul D with the newspaper clipping reporting Sethe's murder of her baby daughter, Paul D knows enough about dominant representations of African Americans to resist believing that the story is about Sethe, even though he cannot read a word of it: "Because there was no way in hell a black face could appear in a newspaper if the story was about something anybody wanted to hear. A whip of fear broke through the heart chambers as soon as you saw a Negro's face in a paper, since the face was not there because the person had a healthy baby, or outran a street mob. . . . It would have to be something out of the ordinary— something whitepeople would find interesting, truly different, worth a few minutes of teeth sucking if not gasps" (156). The newspapers, this passage takes pains to emphasize, represent the "interesting" (according to the judgment of a salivating white readership), not the "ordinary"; yet the sensationalized stories become a mechanism by which white society's ideas about "ordinary" blackness are both confirmed and reproduced: "Whitepeople believed that whatever the manners, under every dark skin was a jungle. Swift unnavigable waters, swinging screaming baboons, sleeping snakes, red gums ready for their sweet white blood" (198). Paul D's bitter condemnation of Sethe, "You got two feet, Sethe, not four" (165), accuses her of committing the worst possible betrayal by confirming, in the public eye, the notions of African Americans derived from newspaper representations and reproduced in schoolteacher's lesson. Sethe's repeated lament, "I made the ink. . . . He couldn't have done it if I hadn't made the ink" (271), suggests that, on some level, Sethe herself feels burdened by a sense of her complicity with dominant representations; in any case, she is unable, here, to counter the newspaper story with her own by telling Paul D about her daughter's murder. What Paul D does not understand—and what Sethe fails to explain to him—is the *share* of racist representations in eliciting her murderous impulses: "No one, nobody on this earth, would list her daughter's characteristics on the animal side of the paper" (251). Sethe chooses to kill her child rather than allow her to be subjected to racist representations like schoolteacher's. Nevertheless, unfortunately, Sethe's moment of madness traps her in the realm of dominant discourse; trying to save her daughter, she implicates herself.

This irony in *Beloved* echoes an image in *Sula* which suggests how even the most calculated efforts at resistance may participate in the reproduction of oppression. That image is Sula's attempt, as a child, to scare off four menacing white boys by cutting off the tip of her own finger with a knife. As Nell recollects later: "When fear struck [Sula], she did unbelievable things. Like that time with her finger. Whatever those hunkies did, it wouldn't have been as bad as what she did to herself. But Sula was so scared she had mutilated herself, to protect herself" (87). Dismemberment in Morrison's writing, I suggest, is actually a loaded negative image in which Morrison expands the scope of Susan Bordo's argument that "pathologies of female 'protest' . . . actually function as if in collusion with the cultural conditions that produced them" (105); Morrison's narratives represent the complexity of "protest" not just for women but for any people who occupy disempowered positions. (Escapes from language might seem a means of engaging in "untainted" forms of resistance; yet *The Bluest Eye* makes clear that such an escape simply ensures the position of absolute powerlessness constructed for a black woman by dominant discourses.)

The notion of a form of "madness" characterized by the gesture of self-defense through self-destruction has its precedent in the oral accounts of ex-slaves, to which the novel *Beloved* bears a self-conscious "family" resemblance. The story of one actual former slave, for example, tells of how her mother resisted white slave owners: "She knew what they were coming for, and she intended to meet them halfway. She swooped upon them like a hawk on chickens. I believe they were afraid of her or thought she was crazy. . . . Her body was made strong with madness. . . . Ma did not see the gun until Mr. Jennings came up. On catching sight of it, she said, 'Use your gun, use it and blow my brains out if you will' " (Cornelia 51). Certainly this is on one level an account of positive resistance: the slave woman's mother is actually physically challenging the men who claim control over her body. Nevertheless, the gesture of meeting the white slave owners halfway is not a purely resistant one; the ex-slave's words also suggest that her mother, in her desperation, was actually meeting her oppressors halfway in directing toward herself the violence to which she might be subject at their hands.

In *Beloved*, the tension between positive resistance and self-destruction is vividly recreated. Sethe's (internal) explanation of the moments before she murdered her baby daughter creates a concrete image of the experience of a slave woman's "madness," in the twin and simultaneous senses of rage and insanity: "She was squatting in the garden and when she saw them coming and recognized schoolteacher's hat, she heard wings. Little hummingbirds stuck their needle beaks right through her headcloth into her hair and beat their wings. And if she thought anything, it was No. No. Nono. Nonono. Simple. She just flew. Collected every bit of life she had made, all the parts of her that were precious and fine and beautiful" (163). The materialization of madness (in the hummingbirds which pierce Sethe's head) is accompanied by the onset of linguistic breakdown. ("Nonono" reminds us, however briefly, of the collapsing "Dick and Jane" text which signals Pecola's madness.) But just as important in the passage is the image by which Sethe visualizes her subsequent acts. That image is of a piecing together, specifically of body parts: Sethe "collected . . . all the parts of her." Yet what Sethe subsequently does belies her intent. She does not piece a body together but rather cuts the throat of her daughter in order to protect her from schoolteacher, who has come to return them all to Sweet Home and slavery. As with Sula's cutting of her finger, the image is one of dismemberment. And it can be said of Sethe, just as of Sula, that "she was so scared she had mutilated herself, to protect herself" (*Sula* 87), given that Sethe clearly understands all her children as an extension of herself: "The best thing she was, was her children" (272). Morrison has commented that *Beloved* is about how "the best thing that is in us is also the thing that makes us sabotage ourselves" (Naylor and Morrison 584–85). Sethe's act is self-sabotage; as Stamp Paid explains, "She was trying to out-hurt the hurter"—or, in the words of Cornelia, to meet him halfway.

In this sense the dramatic reenactment of the scene of Beloved's murder at the end of the novel marks a self-healing. When Sethe sees Edward Bodwin, a white man, enter her yard and thinks he is schoolteacher returned, she "directs her response to the threatening Other rather than to 'her best thing'—her children" (Henderson, "Toni Morrison's *Beloved*" 81). Her act is still somewhat problematic, as Stamp observes to Paul D afterwards:

> "I tell you something, if she had got to him, it'd be the worst thing in the world for us. You know, don't you, he's the main one kept Sethe from the gallows in the first place."
> "Yeah. Damn. That woman is crazy. Crazy."
> "Yeah, well, ain't we all?" (165)

Stamp's words highlight the continuing difficulty of recognizing the oppressor and of directing anger in the most appropriate direction for effective struggle—directing anger, that is, so that it does not "sabotage" the self. In not discerning difference between Edward Bodwin, who has helped her family, and schoolteacher, who wanted to destroy it, Sethe has once again misdirected her violence. Nevertheless, what is not acknowledged (at least overtly) by Stamp and Paul D is that Sethe has at the very least turned her fury against what she perceives as an image of the oppressor, and away from the thing she understands as a part of herself. From the ghostly Beloved's perspective at this moment, "Sethe is running away from her, running" (262)—the "reverse route," one might say, of Sethe's direction in the first tragic enactment of this event, just as, later, Paul D's "coming is the reverse route of his going" (263); changes of direction—as opposed to inward-turning circularity—are crucial to the healing process in this novel. The relative healthiness of this reversal is tacitly understood by others even while they react by calling Sethe "crazy" once again. This time her "craziness" will result not in ostracism but in inclusion: "Ain't we all [crazy]?" Stamp Paid asks, defining himself, Paul D, and Sethe within the same community through those words.

At first, given the violence that marks the mother-daughter relationship in *Beloved*, it is difficult to see just how the possibility of family is enabling to the community which Stamp and Paul D tentatively delineate. But the representation of family in Morrison's texts is complicated by slavery's historical denial of legal recognition to the slave family—and by the lingering traces of such denial in discourses that insist, ironically, that slavery's legacy is the continued debilitation of the African American family in the present. Rushdy has pointed out that "one of the recurrent tropes of the African American novel of slavery is the possible response to an institution attempting to render meaningless the mother-child relationship" ("Daughters" 576). *Beloved* is in some ways a celebration of Sethe's ties to her children, which provide her with the "courage and determination" to undertake, and to survive, the dangerous escape without her husband, Halle.[8] In the context of an institution that was legally entitled to separate slave children from their mothers, symbolically declaring in this manner the absence of any important bond between them, Sethe's attachment to her children cannot be seen simply as capitulation to the mystification of motherhood characteristic of dominant gender ideology; it in fact becomes the impetus for her absolute rebellion against a dominant race ideology, through escape from slavery. Similarly, her marriage to Halle, and her insistence on a ritual to mark that marriage, cannot be viewed simply as capitulation to heterosexual institutions, in the face of the utter lack of legal recognition for slave marriages.

Halle's sale of his "extra" labor to earn the money to buy his mother's freedom suggests the paramount role of familial obligation in the preservation of a larger history and community; it comments harshly on Sula's rejection of such obligation with regard to her grandmother, Eva. The protection of the elderly, Herbert Gutman has documented, was a priority for ex-slaves, who wished to preserve a family history and an intergenerational community at all costs and in resistance to a dominant ideology which had for so long denied the importance of slave families (210).

Baby Suggs, in a move that can certainly be described as resistant representation, repudiates the name under which she was sold and which her white owner wishes (however benevolently) to impose upon her, in favor of her "married" names:

> "Well," said Mr. Garner. . . . "if I was you I'd stick to Jenny Whitlow. Mrs. Baby Suggs ain't no name for a freed Negro."
> Maybe not, she thought, but Baby Suggs was all she had left of the "husband" she claimed. . . . He got his chance, and since she never heard otherwise she believed he made it. Now how could he find or hear tell of her if she was calling herself some bill-of-sale name? (142)

From a gender-primary perspective which fails to take into account the history of racial oppression, Baby Suggs's name—consisting of her husband's surname and the diminutive by which he called her— would be read simply as an acceptance of patriarchy's erasure of woman. But as Gutman has noted, naming practices among slaves were more complicated, serving the function of demarcating and preserving family ties in resistance to an institution that ensured their disruption: "A slave child's legal status followed its mother's legal status,

[8] In other ways, as I will discuss in Chapter 5, *Beloved* is also a critique of motherhood.

and slaveowners rarely recorded the slave fathers' names in plantation birth registers. . . . [It] is possible that children were named for fathers because fathers were more likely to be separated from their children than mothers. Naming a child for its father therefore confirmed that dyadic tie and gave it an assured historical continuity" (190). The recognition only of the " 'uterine' descent" of slaves by their owners was not some kind of victory for women; it served the ideological suppression of the social ties that bound a slave husband and wife, treating slave childbirth as a biological and economic rather than a social event. It is precisely a social tie binding her to others, however, that Baby Suggs insists upon. She names herself for her husband in order to ensure the historical continuity of her marriage, denied legitimacy by the same institution that would "render meaningless the mother-child relationship" by tearing from Baby Suggs all her children save one (139).

Morrison's texts thus constitute a counternarrative to the 1960s and 1970s radical critique of family as oppressive (and its continuation in current feminist criticism), as well as to sociological discourses which have seen the African American family purely in terms of its pathology. For Morrison, family structures and their extension into the larger community provide the basis by which oppressive discourses can be resisted, through the generation of an alternative communal story. In *The Bluest Eye*, as I have discussed, dismemberment is the operative metaphor for Claudia's ultimate inability to piece together—to re-member—the communal story which has become Pecola's. In *Beloved*, as in *The Bluest Eye*, the concrete image of a reconstituted body is linked with the act of remembering through storytelling. Sethe looks back on her race to the woodshed with her children as a moment in which she "collected . . . all the parts of her"; her vocabulary, vividly suggesting the connection of "parts" to form a single body, presents an image of (re)collecting, of (re)membering in the most literal sense. Sethe, of course, does not in this moment re-member but dismember— a point which intimates that Sethe might misunderstand the process of rememory. But Beloved, as the severed parts re-membered, will come to stand for the collective communal story.

"The idea of rememory," Rushdy writes, is intended to suggest a "collective memory" or communal history—memory "that is never only personal but always interpersonal" ("Daughters" 575–76). Sethe's explanation of rememory seems to suggest that such collective memory has a material existence: "If a house burns down, it's gone, but the place—the picture of it—stays, and not just in my rememory, but out there, in the world. . . . Someday you be walking down the road and you hear something or see something going on. So clear. And you think it's you thinking it up. A thought picture. But no. It's when you bump into a rememory that belongs to somebody else" (36). The limitations of Sethe's vision of "rememory" lie in its implicit assumption that Sethe need never tell her story to others, for they already have access to it. Yet Paul D and Sethe are both clearly ignorant of each other's stories, and so the *telling* of those stories is crucial (Ferguson 113). The critical problem faced by the characters in this novel is that they find it extremely difficult to talk about their past. Sethe has never told her daughter Denver the full story of her past life, including Sethe's murder of Denver's sister, and Denver in turn has literally refused to hear it: "Even when she did muster the courage to ask Nelson Lord's question, she could not hear Sethe's answer, nor Baby Suggs's words, nor anything at all thereafter" (103). Denver represents through her deafness all the characters of *Beloved*, who "are . . . discrete individuals prevented by various deafnesses from *hearing* the communal story to which they belong" (Rushdy, "Daughters" 591).

The function of Beloved, as a material manifestation of that story, is to move the characters to the point where they can share their stories on their own. Denver's ability to hear is returned, significantly, "by the sound of her dead sister trying to climb the stairs" (104). Beloved's subsequent embodiment forces all the characters to tell their stories and in this way to begin to see how they are linked together. She asks Denver, "Tell me how Sethe made you in the boat" (76), and Denver responds "by giving blood to the scraps her mother and grandmother had told her—and a heartbeat" (78), that is, by constituting Beloved herself. In Beloved's presence, Sethe too finds herself telling stories she had previously been reluctant to recount: "Sethe learned the profound satisfaction Beloved got from storytelling. It amazed Sethe (as much as it pleased Beloved) because every mention of her past life hurt. Everything in it was painful or lost. She and Baby Suggs had agreed without saying so that it was unspeakable; to Denver's inquiries Sethe gave short replies or rambling incomplete reveries. Even with Paul D . . . the hurt was always there" (58). But, as Amy Denver (the white girl who aids Sethe in her escape) warns while pressing her hands into Sethe's numb feet, "Can't nothing heal without pain, you know" (78). Sethe's storytelling marks the beginning of a healing process that is furthered when Denver overhears her mother tell Beloved the story she never received but so needed to know: the explanation for Sethe's murder of her child (251). Beloved's presence contributes even to Paul D's telling;

an argument between him and Sethe about Beloved segues impercepti-
bly into Paul D's narrative of what happened to Halle and himself—a
story Sethe has never known (67–68).

At the same time, and paradoxically, Beloved is a figure of madness,
of psychological disintegration mirrored in a physical disintegration:
"Inserting a thumb in her mouth along with the forefinger, [she] pulled
out a back tooth . . . and thought, This is it. Next would be her arm, her
hand, a toe. Pieces of her would drop maybe one at a time, maybe all at
once. Or on one of those mornings before Denver woke and after Sethe
left she would fly apart. It is difficult keeping her head on her neck, her
legs attached to her hips when she is by herself. Among the things she
could not remember was when she first knew that she could wake up
any day and find herself in pieces" (133). Beloved's sense of physical
fragmentation is echoed by other characters. When Paul D returns to
Sethe and offers to bathe her, she thinks, "Will he do it in sections? First
her face, then her hands, her thighs, her feet, her back? Ending with
her exhausted breasts? And if he bathes her in sections, will the parts
hold?" (272). And Paul D remembers Sixo saying of the Thirty-Mile
Woman, "She gather me, man. The pieces I am, she gather them and
give them back to me in all the right order" (272–73). Crucial to such
passages is the suggestion that bodily gathering necessitates an other;
the self cannot be "integrated" on its own, but can exist healthily only
within and through some relationship that will connect it to a larger
community. We must keep in mind that embodiment (re-
memberment), in Beloved as in The Bluest Eye, is a figure for the piecing
together of communal stories. Beloved's "madness," her hallucinated
dismemberment, posits the threat that the community's stories will not
adhere to one another—that the community will lose, or dis(re)mem-
ber, parts of its story.

Given that the story of the African American family was effaced in discourses on its pathology, exemplified by the Moynihan report, it is certainly of no small importance in Beloved that family structures lay the
groundwork for the recollection of a larger communal story. Through
her storytelling to Beloved, Denver begins to understand her mother:
"Now, watching Beloved's alert and hungry face, how she took in
every word, . . . her downright craving to know, Denver began to see
what she was saying [about her mother] and not just to hear it. . . .
Denver was seing it now and feeling it—through Beloved. Feeling how
it must have felt to her mother. Seeing how it must have looked"
(77–78). Denver is subsequently able to see the need for "protecting her
mother from Beloved" (243), a need that requires telling the story of

their situation to someone outside the family. Lady Jones, who teaches the community's children to spell, responds to Denver's story as a mother would, with the words "Oh, baby" (248). As Jean Wyatt has pointed out, "Lady Jones's maternal language indicates that Denver is a child of the community, not just of her mother" (483),[9] just as slave children's uses of the terms "aunt" and "uncle" extended kin relations to those not biologically related to them (Gutman 216–17).[10] Furthermore, even though Denver can tell her family's story only incompletely, its circulation actually constitutes community. For example, after hearing a version of the story, Ella (another woman of the community) recalls a similarity between herself and Sethe, whereas before she could see only difference: "She [Ella] had delivered, but would not nurse, a hairy white thing, fathered by 'the lowest yet. ' . . . The idea of that pup coming back to whip her too set her jaw working" (259).

Through storytelling, family ties open outward, becoming the basis for a more inclusive community. We recall that Sethe has seen an image of family in the shadows of Denver, herself, and Paul D holding hands, and has read it as "a good sign" (47); this promise is fulfilled at the novel's conclusion, when Paul D "wants to put his story next to hers" (273). Clearly this model of family, heterosexual relationship and all, offers one possible basis for community because it involves a sharing of stories, rather than an unequal sharing of power, which is precisely how community at its best comes to be constituted. Held against this possibility in Morrison's writing, however, is the persistent possibility of "pathology" posed not by "matriarchy" but by communal dismemberment.

Beloved's own ending is highly ambiguous. We are told that "some say, [she] exploded right before their eyes" (263); Beloved's fear of flying apart has been realized. But it is of course significant that she does so only in the face of a reconstituted community united in support of its former outcast, Sethe. Certainly, then, Beloved's disappearance can be read as the end of a need for Beloved as materialized rememory. Communal stories have been told and shared, establishing a network of connectedness; there is no further necessity for a memory one can just "bump into." Moreover, as we have seen, Sethe has learned to direct her rage and violence outward, toward the image of the oppressor, rather than inward, toward the self. Thus the last pages of the novel, which re-

---

[9] See also Ferguson 123.

[10] See also Orlando Patterson, *Sociology of Slavery: An Analysis of the Origins, Development, and Structure of Negro Slave Society in Jamaica* (London: MacGibbon & Kee, 1967), cited in Gutman.

count how Beloved has been "disremembered," have been read as reg-
istering the laying to rest, as it were, of destructive memories.[11]

Such a reading, however appealing, comes up against certain difficulties. One is the word "rememory" itself, which combines noun and
verb forms (memory and remember) to represent an act that is never
complete, but infinitely takes place anew. Furthermore, the notion of a
remembering that allows a "better" form of forgetting would seem to
contradict the very existence of the novel, which ensures that the story
within its pages (a story, we might recall, drawn from history) will be
remembered again and again, with each reading. The words that punc-
tuate the novel's conclusion like a chorus, "It was not a story to pass
on" (274–75), according to Mae Gwendolyn Henderson, "threaten to
contradict the motive and sense of the entire novel" ("Toni Morrison's
Beloved" 83), at least if we take them to mean that this story should not
continue to be told.

Let us examine the function of that "chorus" more closely (274–75).
The words at first seem to refer to the communal memories of Beloved.
The chorus repeats itself exactly once, then, more ambiguously, with a
difference—"This is not a story to pass on"—invoking the possibility
of some other referent in the present, perhaps the story we are reading.
The final "chorus" is another repetition with a difference which
metonymically substitutes the word "Beloved"—referring simultaneously to the ghost forgotten by all and to the novel itself—for the story
that is not to be passed on. If the "communal narrative . . . [is] Beloved
itself" (Rushdy, "Daughters" 592), it is also Beloved herself. As the communal story materialized, Beloved is a figure for the novel, for what is
a novel if not a story with a material existence? Thus we can take the
chorus at face value only if we accept that the novel itself is not a story
to pass on to others—something that we clearly cannot do. Perhaps we
must read the line for its alternative meaning, as a warning: we cannot
afford to pass by this story; we need to listen to it. In this sense, the
novel's conclusion threatens a tragic repetition of the cardinal sin of
forgetting. In the wake of Beloved's disappearance, the community
seems to revert to its old habits of silence and separation: "The girl . . .
erupts into her separate parts, to make it easy for the chewing laughter
to swallow her all away" (274). As a figure in Morrison's texts, madness finally has implications that extend far beyond one individual's
powerlessness. Madness represents the self-directed sabotage committed by all sorts of communal dis(re)membering.

[11] See, for example, Rushdy, "Daughters" 571.

5

Seeing Difference
Murdering Mothers in Morrison, Garcia, and Viramontes

In the previous chapter we saw how the 1970s attack on the family by (among others) white, middle-class feminists was not automatically embraced by women of color. Whereas white feminists, adopting for the most part the capitalist valorization of the individual, strove for personal self-actualization, historical imperatives have shaped the struggles of women of color quite differently.[1] We have also seen how the value of family can become, in the writings of women of color such as Toni Morrison, inextricably linked to the larger value of community-building; the maternal language Lady Jones uses toward Denver in *Beloved* signifies the entire community's (not just Sethe's) responsibility for Denver's well-being. This sense of family and "kinship" ties as a model for—and basis of—larger communal ties has been echoed by other women of color. The Chicana writer Helena María Viramontes, for example, has written in an autobiographical essay that "the family unit is our only source of safety. Outside our home there lies a dominant culture that . . . isolates us, and labels us illegal alien" ("Nopalitos" 293). Viramontes describes how her own "family always extended its couch or floor to whomever [sic] stopped at our house with nowhere else to go. As a result, a variety of people came to live with us" (291). In Viramontes's construction, as in Morrison's vision of family in *Beloved*, family becomes a locus of resistance, the building block for communities of people oppressed racially and otherwise.[2]

---

[1] Patricia Hill Collins has criticized the assumption that "all women enjoy the racial privilege that allows them to see themselves primarily as individuals in search of personal autonomy instead of members of racial ethnic groups struggling for power" (60). See also Thorne.

[2] The authors of an article titled "The Costs of Exclusionary Practices in Women's Studies" support Viramontes's construction of family, arguing that for marginalized cul-

Viramontes's widely anthologized short story "The Cariboo Cafe" potentially enacts this vision of family—although, as I will argue later, the vision ultimately fails. Told in shifting perspectives and parallel narrative lines, the story centers on the trope of the broken family. The first part tells of two young illegal (probably Mexican) immigrant children, Macky and Sonya, who find themselves locked out of their house one day while both parents are at work. Instilled with an omnipresent fear of the immigration officers, the children wander the city trying to find a safe hiding place. The narrative now shifts to the story of a working-class man, probably white, who operates a rundown cafe frequented by "illegals." Between bits of flashback which reveal the death of his son JoJo in Vietnam and the breakup of his marriage to his wife, Nell, he relates watching the two young children come into the cafe with another illegal, a woman. Eventually the narrative shifts again, to the story of the mysterious woman. She is, we learn, a washerwoman who has lost her five-year-old son Geraldo to a repressive Central American government; the government claimed that the child was a spy working for rebel forces. (The woman asks of the military officers who have taken her son, "Don't these men have mothers, lovers, babies, sisters?" [75], as though having such familial ties should of necessity make these men responsible to a larger community.) When the woman sees the two Mexican children, she madly believes that Macky, the boy, is her own lost son. She takes him—and, out of unthinking necessity, his sister Sonya—under her wing, feeding him at the cafe, bringing him home with her, bathing him, putting him to bed.

All three perspectives in the story are marked by a strong ambiguity of identity. We assume that the children are from Mexico, since they fear being deported to Tijuana, but the story never definitively tells us so, nor does it explicitly state the country of origin of the woman who has lost her son.[3] The cook is apparently white, given that he seems to feel a marked distance between himself and the dark-skinned immigrants. He looks at the washerwoman and sees only Otherness, foreignness, in the woman's physical differences: "Round face, burnt toast color, black hair that hangs like straight ropes. Weirdo, I've had

_____

tural or racial groups, the need "to create spheres where men, women, and children are relatively protected from racist cultural and physical assaults" takes on a special primacy (Zinn et al. 33).

[3] Yvonne Yarbro-Bejarano, who has written the introduction to Viramontes's short story collection *The Moths and Other Stories*, in which "The Cariboo Cafe" is included, identifies the washerwoman's country of origin quite firmly as El Salvador, while Nicolas Kanellos, the editor of an anthology titled *Hispanic American Literature*, which also includes "The Cariboo Cafe," identifies the country as Nicaragua based on a mention of "contras." But *contra* just means "against" in Spanish, and could refer to any rebel forces.

enough to last me a lifetime" (69). Nevertheless, he may belong to some other racial or ethnic group; the narrative never says for sure. The indeterminacy of race and of national origins is, I believe, thematically crucial, which is not to say that such identities are not important—each character's political and social subject position is a crucial part of his or her story—but simply that they are not all-determining.

In place of a community based on any one of such categories, conceived as an "essential" part of personal identity, Viramontes substitutes a vision of community that is constructed in resistance to a particular point or points of oppression—in this case, to the forms of oppression that have disrupted the family. This vision corresponds to Norma Alarcón's assertion that "in order to forge the needed solidarities against repression and oppression," diverse groups must be able to locate points of "identity-in-difference" (a term Alarcón adopts from Audre Lorde and Gayatri Spivak) among themselves, and thus to move beyond the concept of Otherness as an absolute difference from oneself which cannot be bridged (102). In "The Cariboo Cafe," it is the ruptured nuclear family at the center of each narrative line that works metaphorically as what Alarcón might call a point of identity-in-difference, opening a space for the possibility of realignments and new affiliations. In all three narrative lines, for example, family rupture is linked to both political and economic oppression. The cook and the washerwoman share the experience of having lost children who became the casualties of government policies undertaken in the name of national security, but which in fact destroyed their own citizens. Similarly, both the washerwoman and the Mexican family are the victims of a global economic situation that is the product, at least in part, of particular U.S. policies. Both parents of the two young Mexican children must work illegally, leaving the children alone after school to face potential capture by immigration officers. Analogously, the washerwoman used to be separated from her child by economic necessity: "I am a washer woman, Lord. . . . When my son wanted to hold my hand, I held soap instead. When he wanted to play, my feet were in pools of water" (74). And just as severe economic conditions are indirectly responsible for the Mexican children's vulnerability while separated from their parents, so the arrest and murder of the washerwoman's son is precipitated, the story suggests, by their poverty. The government claims that her son was selling subversive pamphlets; but as the woman points out to a government official, " 'Señor. I am a washer woman. You yourself see I cannot read or write. There is my X. Do you think my son can read?' How can I explain to this man that we are poor, that we live as best we can? 'If such a thing has happened, perhaps he wanted to make a few centavos for his mama. He's just a baby' " (73–74).

The common points of oppression among the three story lines—creating, as they do in each case, fissures in the family structure—introduce at least the possibility of imagining a community of resistance, comprising the cook, the washerwoman, and the lost children and their parents. The "power of imagination," Viramontes has written elsewhere, lies in "peeking beyond the fence of your personal reality and seeing the possibilities thereafter" ("Nopalitos," 292). The "personal reality" of each family represented in the story has the potential to expand into a larger vision of collective resistance unbounded by any single category of individual identity.

It is important to note, however, that "resistance" does not, in and of itself, imply transformation, although the terms are so often used interchangeably in feminist theory that they tend to lose all specificity. A *defensive* resistance—one that operates by attempting to protect the community from particular kinds of assaults—is suggested in Viramontes's story in the possibility of a shared ethic of care and protection against oppressive forces (such as immigration officers), a community in which protection and nurturance would spring from an extension outward of familial bonds. This potential is partially realized in the story; both the washerwoman and the cook nurture Macky because he reminds them both of their own lost sons. (I will return to this highly problematic point later in my argument.) While there is no necessary *change* of situation implied in such a vision, a more transformatory politics of resistance is also alluded to in the story, as we shall see.

The alternative understanding of the significance of family which I have outlined has, in turn, serious implications for the role of the mother. Second-wave feminism—in theory, if not in practice—tended to reject the category of the "good mother" as a role which required that women efface themselves as autonomous individual beings for the sake of the survival and well-being of their children. While certainly recognizing the dangers to children of maternal effacement, more recent writing by and about women of color tends not to theorize the role of mother as inherently conservative and constraining because of those dangers. Rather, such writing often understands "motherwork" in racial and ethnic communities as a function that "goes beyond ensuring the survival of members of one's family. . . . [It] recognizes that individual survival, empowerment, and identity require group survival, empowerment, and identity" (Collins 59). As Stanlie M. James notes, "While western conceptualizations of mothering have often been limited to the activities of females with their biological offsprings [sic], mothering within the Afro-American community and throughout the Black diaspora can be viewed as a form of cultural work"; she points to "othermothering" as the "acceptance of responsibility for the welfare of non–blood related children in [one's] community," which is a traditional cultural practice of African Americans, among others (44). In this ideal, the mother is conceived as the guardian not just of the survival of individual members of the community, but of the survival of the community as a whole, however that community may be constructed.

Paradoxically, the mother in practice is often represented as failing this ideal by becoming the mouthpiece for values of the dominant culture which would destroy the community's resistant, defensive potential. Thus Cherríe Moraga speaks of having "denied the voice of my brown mother—the brown in me" (31) as a metaphor for her rejection of Chicana identity and her attempts to "assimilate" into a white, middle-class American culture, even though she represents her mother as having, in fact, embraced and passed on America's denigration of Chicanos/Chicanas and Chicano/Chicana culture. That is, Moraga portrays her mother as having denied the brown in *herself*. This betrayal by the mother is emblematic for Moraga of how "we have taken the values of our oppressor into our hearts and turned them against ourselves and one another" (32)—the paradigmatic move represented by madness in twentieth-century women's texts, as I have argued throughout this book. The mother's *cultural* betrayal, significantly, often goes hand in hand in recent writings of women of color with a narrowed conception of her role as mother whereby she sees herself as responsible only for her biological children; this in turn leads to the mother's effacement of herself in her mothering—that is, to her internalization of the idea that the mother's worth is to be found only in her biological children. Thus she echoes and espouses the dominant culture's paradigm of the "good mother."

One of my primary interests throughout this book has been to examine the ways in which resistant potential is lost and collusion with dominant ideology is enacted, though unwittingly, to be sure. In this chapter I suggest that in the writings of women of color, internalization of the "good mother" paradigm and acceptance of its ideology represent yet again, as in white second-wave feminism, a failure of resistant potential. But for the writers I am examining here, the basis of resistance that is thwarted by this paradigm is not so much individual autonomy as communal survival and resistance.

● ● ●

The particular figure of madness that speaks to these issues is that of the murdering mother. Toni Morrison's novels *Sula* and *Beloved* both tell of female African American characters who murder their children in attempts at protection; Helena María Viramontes's short story "The Cariboo Cafe" and Cristina Garcia's novel *Dreaming in Cuban* both contain images of at least potentially murdering mothers. The image is perhaps surprising because it would seem to contradict the alternative constructions of mother as protector of culture and community that are offered by women of color. Indeed, it can easily be read as an expression of the individual woman's "rage" against dictated notions of motherhood, following Gilbert and Gubar. Marianne Hirsch, for example, argues that in *Sula*, Eva's murder of her son "signals, perhaps, the limits of what any relationship can sustain and demonstrates . . . an intense need for self-protection, a clear drawing of her own boundaries, a definitive expression of the limits of what she has to give" (181). But if we leave our reading at that, then Morrison's writing is made to resemble 1970s white feminist demands for individual autonomy; we ignore her central concern with the creation and renewal of community. Yet if we simply take at face value the murdering mother's expressed aim in killing her child—that of protecting the child she kills (or attempts to kill)—then we beg the question, how can survival of culture and community be ensured through the murder of the heirs to that culture?[4] As Judith Wilt has argued in "Black Maternity: 'A Need for Someone to Want the Black Baby to Live'" (a title that alludes to Morrison's novel *The Bluest Eye*), the "black baby" in the writings of recent African American women represents "a beleaguered race's living grasp of its future." To kill it, Wilt writes, might then suggest "a genocidal impulse" (132–33). If the murdering mother is read as a figure for cultural resistance, the "resistance" seems to me to invoke the same problems as other forms of madness I have examined: it involves, in practice, a final retreat. The dominant culture is "resisted," perhaps, but only at the cost of the symbolic annihilation of any alternative.

It might be instructive here to look at a specific form of the "murdering mother": the myth of la Llorona, "the wailing woman," in Mexican and Central American culture. While the story of la Llorona has many versions, the common thread is that of a mother whose children have been killed, and who now—gone crazy with grief—eternally wanders through the night, crying, in search of them. In some versions of the

---

[4] For examples of critics who read the murdering-mother figures I am discussing primarily as "protecting" the children at risk, see Castillo on the washerwoman and Macky in "The Cariboo Cafe" (90–91) and Thurer on Sethe in *Beloved* (299).

story she has killed the children herself. In others she is a threatening figure primarily because she seeks to replace her lost children with living ones; thus she is a sort of "bogeywomen" whom small children are taught to fear. La Llorona can be read perhaps as a preserver of culture, but certainly not in a resistant sense; she is a misogynistic image of woman who embodies a threat connected to straying from the traditional feminine role of "good mother." In other ways, she is the epitome of betrayal, rather than of preservation, of culture and community. She is connected in legend to la Malinche, the mistress of Spanish conquerer Hernán Cortés; la Malinche translated for Cortés the Aztec and Mayan languages and cultures, thus aiding in his conquest of Mexico.

La Llorona is explicitly invoked in "The Cariboo Cafe." When the washerwoman's son is taken from her by the military government, she rejects nationalism as a basis for community—"Without Geraldo, this is not my home, the earth beneath it, not my country" (75)—and imagines instead a community of those who share her particular experience of oppression: "It is the night of La Llorona. The women come up from the depths of sorrow to search for their children. I join them, frantic, desperate. . . . I hear the wailing of the women and know it to be my own" (72–73). Viramontes, I propose, is here rewriting the myth of la Llorona, the mother maddened by grief and guilt, into a symbol of resistant community based *precisely* on women's roles as mothers of lost children, reminiscent of the mothers of the Plaza de Mayo—a group of women who protested their children's (and all political prisoners') disappearance during the "dirty war" in Argentina by marching in the Plaza de Mayo in Buenos Aires.[5] Indeed, the image of "Lloronas," invoking a public rather than private "wailing" suggestive of protest, brings up for the first time in the story the possibility of a *transformative* rather than simply defensive or protective resistance based on political coalition and collective action.[6]

Although the washerwoman identifies the community of those who suffer through being robbed of their children as a community of women, in fact the cook belongs to this community as well—at least potentially. This man strikes a defensive posture in which he claims to be motivated solely by economic interests: "Like I gotta pay my bills too, I gotta eat. So like I serve anybody whose got the greens" (69). Yet what filters through his aggressive-sounding discourse is a suppressed empathy with others arising from his identity as father of a dead son.

[5] For a discussion of the Mothers of the Disappeared, see Elshtain.
[6] For another powerful re-vision of la Llorona, see Sandra Cisneros's short story "Woman Hollering Creek," in her collection by the same title.

He explains why he does not "refuse service to anyone," saying: "The streets are full of scum, but scum gotta eat too is the way I see it." The particular "scum" he is referring to here is Paulie, who is "JoJo's age if he were still alive. . . . Maybe why I let him hang out 'cause he's JoJo's age" (68). Similarly, when the washerwoman enters the cafe with the two children, the cook sees Macky and thinks, "He's a real sweetheart like JoJo. You know, my boy" (70). It is perhaps this connection that motivates him to serve burgers to all three, even though he is later "surprised" that the woman has money to pay for the food—suggesting that he did not necessarily expect payment. The cook, like the washerwoman, is thus potentially drawn into an extended community of care based on his own recollection of familial ties.

Thus far my reading suggests that the madness of the murdering mother, in the particular form of la Llorona, offers a possibility of resistance in Viramontes's text. But this reading does not explain why the story seems to end on such a bleak note. The washerwoman, betrayed by the cook, engages in a violent struggle with police over Macky, and the story suggests that she is destroyed by it: "I will fight you for my son until I have no hands left to hold a knife. . . . I am laughing, howling at their stupidity. Because they should know by now that I will never let my son go and then I hear something crunching like broken glass against my forehead and I am blinded by the liquid darkness. But I hold onto his hand. That I can feel, you see, I'll never let go. Because we are going home. My son and I" (79). At this moment the washerwoman's illusion of resistance masks the fact of absolute powerlessness. Her physical obliteration in this struggle must inevitably be followed by the end she most fears: the boy (Macky, not Geraldo) will be turned over to the government representatives (immigration officers, not military officials) after all. Indeed, given that betrayal to the immigration officers ("la Migra") and deportation is the end that Macky and his family most fear—have feared all along as the worst of all possible outcomes—the washerwoman, seen through their eyes at this moment, can only be an angel of death, a figure of ultimate destruction.

Interestingly, Debra Castillo holds the cook more responsible than the washerwoman for this unhappy ending; it is the cook who ultimately betrays the washerwoman to the law on the grounds that "children gotta be with their parents, family gotta be together" (77). Castillo suggests that the cook's mistake is that, for him, "all stories become one story, the story of JoJo and Nell," and that the cook's story "turns, thus, on misreading and misinterpretation, on the error of inserting another face, another body, into the absences left by [JoJo and Nell]. . . .

[T]he cook's story turns on the impossibility of storytelling" (84). That is, if storytelling assumes a distance that must be bridged, then the cook's misidentificafion of others with his son "ends" the possibility of storytelling because there is no need to tell the story: every story is the same. Storytelling, in other words, cannot take place under the assumption of absolute identity; this is a crucial point, which I will return to later.

But it is important to make a distinction between the cook's recognition of certain points of identity between Macky and JoJo, or Paulie and JoJo, and a collapsing of difference into identity. (The distinction is all the more apparent because, as I shall discuss, the washerwoman does literally collapse differences into identity.) The story insists on the quite different implications of simile (Macky is *like* JoJo) and metaphor (Macky *is* JoJo). The moments when the cook compares someone else to his son are marked by an optimistic empathy, and stand in sharp contrast to those jarring situations in which empathy breaks down and the cook sees only difference: "She's illegal, which explains why she looks like a weirdo" (70). It is this mentality that seems to underlie the cook's betrayal of a family of illegals who have run into his cafe seeking to hide from a raid by immigration officers at the nearby factory. As the cook explains, "I haven't seen Nell for years, and I guess that's why I pointed to the bathroom" (72). Whereas elsewhere the cook's recollections of his family seem to suggest the basis for other connections, in this moment he translates the loss of his family—that is, of his identity-in-difference with others—into an unmooring from any sort of connection or ethical obligation. He now identifies the illegals as "roaches," an image of absolute Otherness (recently employed in advertisements for the anti-immigration stances of certain political candidates), rather than as somehow connected to himself. He can turn in the family of illegals because he is indifferent to their fate in the face of his own personal tragedy. It is not that others' stories collapse into and become identical with his own, but that Others' stories become irrelevant in the face of his own. And although the cook's narrative (his version, we might say, of events) begins with a refusal of responsibility ("Don't look at me" [68]), the close of his narrative poses an internal challenge to his rejection of the accusing gaze: after betraying the family of illegals hiding from the factory raid, the cook confesses that "the older one, the one that looked silly in the handcuffs on account of she's old enough to be my grandma's grandma, *looks straight at my face*" (72; emphasis added). Notably, the sting of the cook's conscience here is represented in the language of violated familial ties. The cook subsequently tries to rectify his betrayal by turning in the washerwoman, supposedly because he is concerned to reunite the lost children, Sonya and Macky, with their parents; but even this act is represented as morally suspect, given that he really just "hopes they have disappeared" (77). By the end of the story, the cook has aligned himself, both literally and symbolically, with the oppressors of the various narrative lines.[7]

Disappearance is of obvious importance in this story, which is named for the cafe referred to as "the zero zero place" (68) because all the letters of the sign reading "Cariboo" have worn off except for the two O's, creating an image (as Castillo suggests) of doubled absence. The most obvious twin absences gestured toward in the story are the two dead children. Viramontes thus seems to be contrasting how the Central American washerwoman and the cook attempt to cope with those absences. That distinction, I submit, resides in the possibilities of imagining. Since the moment and method of death in both cases is represented as unknown and indefinite, both the cook and the washerwoman must imagine how their children died.[8] JoJo was killed in Vietnam, which has been represented again and again in our popular culture as a war against the anonymous Other. Significantly, the cook's mode for dealing with JoJo's absence finally appears to be driven by imagining Otherness as something insurmountably separated from the self. As he says when discussing the unevenly sized breasts of Paulie's girlfriend Delia—breasts that mimic the double-zero image—"You could see the difference" (69).

It is intriguing to consider the possibility that it is precisely because Geraldo's mother need not resort to obvious physical differences to imagine her son's murderers that she does not operate on the principle of Othering. Yet her desire to identify Macky *literally* with her own son, rather than analogously or metaphorically, blinds her to the reality that

[7] I thank Doreen Fowler for pointing out to me the possibilities of a psychoanalytic interpretation implied in my own reading of this portion of the story. The cook insists that he runs an "honest business" (71), where "honest" seems to be equatable with "law-abiding" (meaning that he will not harbor drugs or illegals), and he turns over both the washerwoman and the first group of illegals to the police and la Migra, representatives of the Law. Thus it might be argued that the cook becomes representative of the Lacanian Symbolic, which relies on the absolute distinction between self and other. In contrast, the washerwoman might be read as representative of the Imaginary, that realm where self is not distinguished from other (a point I will return to later in my reading) and where, consequently, language is impossible.

[8] Castillo's reading here is similar to my own, but Castillo posits the difference as one of "seeing" rather than one of imagining—that is, of what the cook has not seen (the death of his son in Vietnam) and what the washerwoman has seen ("the probable fate of her disappeared five-year-old boy" [85]). It strikes me, however, that the washerwoman has not seen the death of her son any more than the cook has seen the death of his; conversely, the cook can certainly imagine JoJo's "probable fate," just as the washerwoman can Geraldo's.

her kidnapping tears Sonya and Macky away from their own parents—who must then become the parents of lost children, like herself and the cook—and subjects them all to the immigration officers. That is to say, the washerwoman sees only identity without recognizing crucial differences. Thus it is her story, not the cook's, which revolves around the "error of inserting another face, another body, into the absences" that mark "The Cariboo Cafe." When she sees Macky and is reminded of her son Geraldo, she thinks to herself, "Why would God play such a cruel joke, if he isn't my son?" (76). The only meaning Macky's appearance can have for the washerwoman is strictly personal; she, like the cook, is ultimately unable to use her family experiences to build a larger sense of community based on ethical responsibility. Caring for and protecting Macky are possible only if he is hers. Her fierce protective instinct is thus badly misguided: just when she thinks she is most protecting Macky, she is actually exposing him to the most violence. The final passage of the story brings us back full circle to the myth of la Llorona, the mother gone mad who cries for her murdered children but who also, in at least one version of the myth, murdered the children herself. The washerwoman, crying for her lost son, fails to see how she herself might be contributing to a devastating outcome for the child she mistakes for her own. Just as children in Mexico fear being taken by la Llorona, so Macky in the United States fears (perhaps *most* fears) being "taken" by la Migra. The washerwoman becomes the agent for this dual taking.

Toni Morrison's fiction, I have already suggested, is likewise punctuated with mothers who murder their children out of the impulse to protect them. La Llorona's counterpart in African American culture, it might be argued, is the figure of the murdering slave mother. It has been widely observed—including by Morrison herself—that the character Sethe in *Beloved* is based on an actual slave mother who murdered her child rather than have it returned into slavery. In another case, a Fisk University sociologist in 1945 documented the memory of a woman, recorded only as "Cornelia," who recalled that her mother, facing sale and separation from her child, "vowed to smash [her baby's] brains out before she'd leave it" (Cornelia 52). In *Sula*, the murdering mother is embodied in Eva, the woman who burns her son to death in his bed.

Just as feminist critics, such as Susan Willis, are fond of valorizing Sula's radical individualism as a critique of patriarchy and prescribed women's roles (see Chapter 4), so do they also tend to valorize the character of Eva for heading a "three-woman household" which represents "social utopia," and for thus creating "a wholly new social collective" which is "a radical alternative to the bourgeois family model" (Willis 105–6). But I contend that Eva shares with her granddaughter Sula a primary character flaw that, contrary to Willis's assertions, impedes rather than enhances the possibility of *any* collective, radical or otherwise. The nature of Sula's flaw, as I have already suggested in Chapter 4, lies in her inability to conceive of a responsibility to others. Her friendship for Nell is no exception, since she understands it not as connectedness to another but as self-identity: "She and Nell were . . . one and the same thing" (103). This mistaken view leads Sula to surmise that she needs to account for Nell's feelings only insofar as she seeks her own experiences. But as Deborah McDowell points out, Sula and Nell are "complementary, not identical. . . . The relationship of other to self . . . throughout the narrative, must be seen as '*different but connected* rather than separate and opposed' " ("Boundaries" 62; emphasis added).[9] The ability to see self and other as "different but connected," rather than as *either* identical *or* "separate and opposed," is, I would argue, the fundamental precondition to the building of community in the texts of women of color—a precondition that the murdering mother fails to fulfill. Eva, notably, commits the same error as her granddaughter, mistaking the very important similarities between Nell and Sula for identity: "You. Sula. What's the difference?" (145). It is Eva who calls three quite different boys Dewey, erasing their differences so that "everyone . . . gradually found that [they] could not tell one from the other" (34). The Deweys, Willis notes, represent the dangers of "homogenizing society by recouping cultural difference" (85). (Willis does not deal with the implications of her statement for an understanding of Eva's character, however.) A relational model based exclusively on identity is a dangerous form of solidarity, since it will of necessity continue to exclude anything that cannot be made identical with the self. Once the Deweys have "accepted Eva's view," they (like Sula) reject any model of communal ties, "loving nothing and no one but themselves" (33).

Eva's murder of her son Plum is, arguably, another manifestation—one might say an extension—of her inability to see difference. Whereas her lack of distinction between Nell and Sula, or among the Deweys, is reminiscent of the inability of the washerwoman in "The Cariboo Cafe" to see difference between one child and another, Eva's relationship with her son is marked by an identity-without-difference of a dis-

9 Quoted passage is from Carol Gilligan, *In a Different Voice* (Cambridge: Harvard University Press, 1982), 147.

tinct sort: that between mother and child. When Plum returns home from World War I a drug addict, Eva douses him and his bed with kerosene and sets fire to him, killing him. Later, when her daughter Hannah asks why, she responds: "He wanted to crawl back in my womb and well . . . I ain't got the room no more even if he could do it. . . . I'd be laying here at night and he be downstairs in that room, but when I closed my eyes I'd see him . . . six feet tall smiling and . . . he'd be creepin' to the bed trying to spread my legs trying to get back up in my womb. . . . One night it wouldn't be no dream. It'd be true and I would have done it, would have let him if I'd've had the room. . . . I done everything I could to make him leave me and go on and live and be a man but he wouldn't and I had to keep him out so I just thought of a way" (62). Eva insists on her son's desire to merge and become one with her again, but the glimpse we get of Plum before she kills him is in fact quite different. Plum urges his mother, "Hey, Mamma, whyn't you go on back to bed? I'm all right. Didn't I tell you? I'm all right. Go on, now" (40). While Plum insists, as best he can, on his right to rise or fall independently of Eva, Eva constructs an elaborate fantasy in which his destruction through drugs is an infantilization that will render him part of her own body once again. The sexual overtones with which the fantasy is described underscore the element of desire that runs through it. Although Eva "would have let him" reenter her own body, she is also dimly aware of the danger, both to her son and to herself, of the culmination of such a fantasy. Yet the only way she can find to preserve the fragile boundaries that separate self from other is to destroy the other. Only by killing her son can Eva imagine him as a being separate from herself.

In contrast to Eva, Hannah is a mother who does not fall prey to the ideology of coextensiveness with one's children. She reveals, ironically through her devastating comment that she loves her daughter Sula but does not like her, an understanding that children are "different people" from their parents (49). Hannah comprehends that "love" does not reside in self-identity with the beloved, but is rather a recognition of ties—including family ties—that bind people with differences together, even if those differences mean that people might not "like" one another. Hannah Peace, in other words, offers the possibility of "love" that is not based exclusively on "like"-ness. Sula, who can love only that which is "one and the same" with herself, reads her mother's distinction as rejection.

In *Sula* the dangers of the murdering mother for the larger community are only implicit; it is Sula herself, rather than Eva, who becomes the figure for communal fragmentation (as I argued in Chapter 4). In

Beloved, the connections between the "selfless mother"—that is, the mother without a self, the mother whose self is others—and the threat to a larger community is brought to the foreground. Feminist critics have noted the problems created for Sethe by her understanding of her children as "her best thing," that is, her self-representation as a being of worth only insofar as she is a mother. (This is the more "typical" feminist critique of motherhood, which I discussed at the beginning of this chapter.) Jean Wyatt, in her provocative essay on *Beloved*, observes that "the maternal body [in *Beloved*] seems to lack a subjective center. During the journey [north], Sethe experiences her own existence only in relation to her children's survival. . . . [And] even after the children are weaned, her bond with them remains so strong that she continues to think of it as a nursing connection" (476).

What Wyatt describes as "the problems of Sethe's maternal subjectivity" have been pointed toward by Morrison herself. Describing the actual incident on which *Beloved* was based, Morrison explains: "A woman loved something other than herself so much. She had placed all of the value of her life in something outside herself. . . . [T]he woman who killed her children loved her children so much; they were the best part of her and she would not see them sullied. . . . [This feeling is] peculiar to women. And I thought, it's interesting because the best thing that is in us is also the thing that makes us sabotage ourselves, sabotage in the sense that our life is not as worthy, or our perception of the best part of ourselves" (Naylor and Morrison 584–85). The particular form of self-sabotage enacted by Sethe, in other words, is feminine, a product of a gender ideology that limits women's noble gestures to those of nurturing and protective motherhood. The same can be said of the washerwoman in "The Cariboo Cafe," a story that shares with *Beloved* the plot line of a mother who, driven to madness by the horrors of an oppressive system, strikes out at her own child in order to protect it. (We might call this a point of identity-in-difference between the two narratives about different ethnic or racial groups and different historical moments.) The washerwoman's great love for her son is one of the "best things" in her, the thing that might serve as a basis for a larger community of responsibility; yet it is also the thing that sabotages her by restricting her vision. Viramontes's own words on the feminine role in the family are in the same spirit as Morrison's: "Family ties are fierce. . . . But what may be seen as a nurturing, close unit, may also become suffocating, manipulative, and sadly victimizing" ("Nopalitos," 293).

While Morrison and Viramontes both acknowledge the limitations of the role of "mother" imagined exclusively with relation to a nuclear family, for both authors the critique is extended by the powerful suggestion that such a narrowly defined role prevents the mother from engaging in the cultural work of community-building. Furthermore, crucially, the work of community-building is related to the ability to narrate, to wield language. Whereas for many feminist critics the figure of the murdering mother tends to be linked to the woman writer (the child, presumably as a marker of the traditional feminine role, interferes with the woman's ability to write),[10] for Morrison, as Jean Wyatt has powerfully argued, the murdering mother is marked by her *inability* to tell her story.[11] Language, says Wyatt, referring to Lacan, depends on "the repudiation of maternal continuity" and the substitution of the absent other with the signifier that represents her; "[it] is this distance, this loss, that Sethe rejects. . . . [She] refuses to replace that baby with a signifier, to accept the irrevocability of absence by putting the child's death into words" (477).

The crisis of *Beloved* is marked by the internal monologues—"unspeakable thoughts, unspoken" (199)—of the three women of 124 Bluestone Road. Like the parallel perspectives of "The Cariboo Cafe," which Debra Castillo calls "unheard parallel monologues" (78), the monologues of 124 create "the effect of dialogue" although in fact they are "unvoiced, unheard" (Castillo 92).[12] Sethe is now willing to explain her story to Beloved ("I'll tell Beloved about that, she'll understand" [200]); but the textual representation of the unspoken "fugue" of thoughts in 124 warns of the deceptiveness of such illusory "conversations":

> You are my face; you are me. . . .
> You are mine
> You are mine
> You are mine. (217)

Like Pecola's final, mad, internal "conversation" in *The Bluest Eye*, wherein she imagines an other that is actually the same, this passage marks the collapse of difference between self and other into identity.[13]

[10] "According to [Susan] Suleiman, maternal texts are often shaped by the fantasy that the writing mother kills her child" (Hirsch 174); and Barbara Johnson speculates in "Apostrophe, Abortion, and Imitation" that "it is as though male writing were by nature procreative while female writing is somehow by nature infanticidal" (quoted in Hirsch 175).

[11] Note that it is precisely this which is suggested by Fowler's observation that the washerwoman of "The Cariboo Cafe" represents the Imaginary.

[12] Castillo is speaking here, of course, of "The Cariboo Cafe"; I make the connection to *Beloved*.

[13] In a fascinating discussion, Wyatt writes that such "speech" (if speech it is) "is motivated not by difference but by the desire to ascertain that the other is there and that the

For Sethe, talking to Beloved is really just talking to herself. Increasingly, as her narration becomes more involuted, we read that Beloved "imitated Sethe, talked the way she did, laughed her laugh and used her body the same way down to the walk, the way Sethe moved her hands, sighed through her nose, held her head. Sometimes coming upon them . . . , it was difficult for Denver to tell who was who" (241). In this respect, Sethe's self-definition as exclusively a mother robs her of the power to narrate her story to an other. And as I have argued in Chapter 4, Sethe's inability to tell her story works against the formulation of community, which depends on the telling of individual stories in the construction of a larger communal story.

Cristina Garcia's novel *Dreaming in Cuban* similarly explores the problem of "language" that does *not* spring from a recognition of otherness—of separation of the other from the self (the fundamental prerequisite of language). *Dreaming in Cuban* is marked throughout by forms of "private" language, intensely secret, that are exchanged by various pairs of characters, for example, by Luz and Milagro, the identical twin daughters of Felicia: "Luz and Milagro are always alone with one another, speaking in symbols only they understand. Luz, older by twelve minutes, usually speaks for the two of them. The sisters are double stones of a single fruit. . . . They have identical birthmarks, diminutive caramel crescents over their left eyelids, and their braids hang in duplicate ropes down their backs" (38). The unreadable symbols exchanged by Luz and Milagro are specifically equated to their almost indistinguishable identity: they are mirror images of each other.

In her relationship to her son Ivanito, Felicia reflects another version of private language. With Ivanito, Felicia talks in "colors," drawn from the symbolism of Santeria, a set of religious practices and beliefs descending from the Yoruba people and blended with Christianity in Cuba and other Latin American countries, but ripped out of their cultural-religious context in Felicia's exchanges with her son: " 'Let's speak in green,' his mother says, and they talk about everything that makes them feel green. They do the same with blues and reds and yellows" (84). At the end of the "summer of coconuts," characterized by this intensely private language, Felicia attempts to kill both herself and her son, thus demonstrating the connection Wyatt observes between the collapse of language and the inability to perceive distance and separation. For maternal filicide in contemporary popular culture is theo-

---

other is the same. It 'moves' only toward the stasis of interreflecting mirrors, ending in identical statements wherein like mirrors like" (481).

rized as a misdirected effort at suicide and is represented as intimately connected to an overdeveloped and unhealthy closeness or identification between mother and child, not to an "unmaternal" coldness and distance toward one's children, despite general expectations of the latter in such cases.[14] In attempting to kill both herself and her son, Felicia enacts this contemporary ritual of collapsed identity between mother and child, invoking yet again a critique of the ideology of the "good mother" who sees her children as the most important aspect of herself.

Once again, however, this critique is linked to the larger cultural dangers of not being able to recognize difference between self and other. Felicia's failure is represented not only as a problem of gender role (she sees her child as coextensive with herself) but also as one of racial and cultural difference. Her friend Herminia Delgado, an Afro-Cuban, recalls: "Felicia is the only person I've known who didn't see color. . . . For many years in Cuba, nobody spoke of the problem of racism between blacks and whites. It was considered too disagreeable to discuss. But my father spoke to me clearly so that I would understand what happened to his father and his uncles during the Little War of 1912. . . . The war that killed my grandfather and great-uncles and thousands of other blacks is only a footnote in our history books" (184–85). While the dominant racist ideology of Cuba results in silence about a certain portion of history, it is crucial to note that Felicia's blindness to difference results in a similar silence about the problems of racism. The antidote to the silence of history books is not Felicia's colorblindness but rather Herminia's father's oral history.

And while Felicia's colorblindness translates into an admirable lack of racism, it also reveals the serious problems created by an inability to see difference. For if one cannot see difference, one will not do the work that is necessary to bridge it. Within Felicia's relationships to her children, this danger is revealed through her inability to break out of her "private" language in order to explain to Luz and Milagro an unknown part of their own history—the history of abuse and terror to which Felicia was subjected by her husband and their father, which she eventually resisted by burning him in his bed. All that Luz and Mila-

---

[14] After Susan Smith murdered her two young sons in 1994, for example, *Newsweek* explained that child killing by a mother "can involve a form of 'boundary confusion' in which the mother 'is overly enmeshed in the lives of her children. She doesn't know where her life ends and theirs begins' " ("Why Parents Kill" 31); and *USA Today* noted that these mothers "don't emotionally distance themselves from their children" ("Why Do Mothers Kill Their Children?" 16). See also Judith Wilt's discussion of the teenager, imprisoned for killing her child, whom Meridian visits near the end of Alice Walker's novel *Meridian*. As Wilt notes, the girl's "act of murder was a kind of suicide" (135).

gro know is the burning; thus they believe their mother to be inexplicably insane and dangerous. The similarity to *Beloved*, in which Sethe never feels the necessity to explain to her living children why she killed their sister, is once again striking. Like Luz and Milagro, Denver, Howard, and Buglar can make no sense of their mother's act without having heard her story; they therefore invent "die-witch! stories" to ward off their murdering mother because they "don't know what it is" in Sethe that "makes it all right to kill her own" (205).

Sethe's sense of identity with her children is the converse of her detachment (reminiscent of Sula's) from anyone not part of herself—a detachment the community reads as "prideful." Ella remembers that Sethe "got out of jail and made no gesture toward anybody, and lived as though she were alone" (256), and Janey connects Sethe's self-imposed isolation to her madness: "This Sethe had lost her wits, finally, as Janey knew she would—trying to do it all alone with her nose in the air" (254). Denver replicates this prideful rejection of communal interdependence, refusing Lady Jones's offer of food from her church's committee "as though asking for help from strangers was worse than hunger" (248). (We recall that it is only by exchanging her family's story with those in her community that Denver can finally help her mother.) In *Dreaming in Cuban*, Felicia's obsessive identification with her son (reminiscent of Sethe's with Beloved) corresponds, likewise, to a growing isolation from all others; she "rips the telephone from the wall and locks them all in the house" (85). Thus we see that, whereas 1970s radical critiques of family, and much of the more recent work on Morrison, have generally posited community as equally coercive with the family and equally productive of madness, in both *Dreaming in Cuban* and *Beloved* it is *isolation* from a larger community that leads to madness, in a decidedly unliberating sense.

Although murdering-mother figures such as Felicia and Sethe see insurmountable differences between themselves and those in their community, and *none* between themselves and their children, they are proven as wrong about the latter idea as they are misguided about the former. It is important to note of *Dreaming in Cuban* that even the boy Ivanito is not privy to the full meanings of his mother Felicia's unique language, however much she may believe that he is: "She makes pronouncements that Ivanito doesn't understand, stays up all night hearing prophecies in her head" (85). Despite Felicia's efforts not to see difference, it is there. The question then becomes, given differences—figured in this novel by differences of language—what must be done? One possibility, of course, is translation; but some literary critics find this possibility highly suspect, if not downright imperialistic.[15] At least one character in *Dreaming in Cuban*—Pilar—seems to agree with them. Pilar insists that "painting is its own language. . . . Translations just confuse it, dilute it, like words going from Spanish to English" (59). But it is important to note that the Pilar who speaks out against that possibility is the *young* Pilar, who, in a section titled "Enough Attitude," betrays her mother's trust and humiliates her by painting a radical punk rendition of the Statue of Liberty—with a safety pin through its nose—for her mother's bakery's "Grand Opening and Fourth of July Celebration." (Pilar, by the way, is soundly punished for this by the novel's narrative.) *This* Pilar learns to grow up, and to understand and appreciate not just the possibilities but the *necessities* of translation.

Dreaming in Cuban is, in fact, a project of translation on many different levels. Most literally, both the words and thoughts of Cuban exiles in America and those of the Cubans who stayed are rendered in English; the novel's story cannot be told without this fiction of translation. Just as important to the novel is the issue of *cultural* translation and preservation. The early parts of the novel seem to suggest (supporting the young Pilar) that no translation is necessary to preserve culture, that cultural history and memory can be preserved through forms of "psychic" communication such as that which the young Pilar—just recently brought to the United States by her mother—shares with her grandmother Celia, who remains in Cuba. Celia "knows that Pilar keeps a diary in the lining of her winter coat, hidden from her mother's scouring eyes. In it, Pilar records everything. This pleases Celia. She closes her eyes and speaks to her granddaughter, imagines her words as slivers of light piercing the murky night" (7). Garcia clearly means to suggest that Pilar receives those words, for she is largely shaped by "those talks I have with Abuela Celia late at night" (63).

But cultural distance is represented metaphorically in this novel by the loss of psychic communication and the need for more mundane forms of translation. The grown Pilar feels a strong sense of cultural distance from Cuba: "We can reach it by a thirty-minute charter flight

[15] Roberto González Echevarría, for example, criticizes Julia Alvarez's novel *In the Time of the Butterflies* on the grounds that it demonstrates an apparently bewildering compulsion, "as if [Alvarez] needed to have her American self learn what it was really like in her native land, the Dominican Republic. . . . [Alvarez lacked] the realization that the *gringa dominicana* [the Dominic American] would never really be able to understand the other woman [i.e., the "real" Dominican woman on whom her novel is partly based], much less translate her"(28).

from Miami, yet never reach it all" (219). This distance interferes with her ability to communicate with her grandmother, so that when she returns to Cuba for a visit, she thinks: "I'm afraid to lose all this, to lose Abuela Celia again. But sooner or later I'd have to return to New York. I know now it's where I belong—not *instead* of here, but *more* than here. How can I tell my grandmother this?" (236). And when Celia asks Pilar, "What do all the years and the separation mean except a more significant betrayal?" Pilar's thoughts "feel like broken glass in my head. I can't understand what my grandmother tells me. All I hear is her voice, thickened with pain" (240).

Celia might believe, naively, that she no longer needs to write down her memories once Pilar is born because "she will remember everything" (245); but the section titled "The Languages Lost" insists on the naïveté of Celia's view (echoed by the youthful Pilar) that memory and history can be preserved in an undiluted form without the intervention of translation. To be remembered, it turns out, Celia's experiences must be *told*. In this sense the "Cuban situation" (the geographic, political, and cultural gulfs that separate Cubans from Cuban exiles and their children) becomes a metaphor for current attempts at "multiculturalism"—that is, at understanding across cultures, ethnicities, and other categories of identity—and of the obstacles to such understanding.

The possibility for understanding is created only by translation. Ivanito remembers his mother, Felicia, and their private language with fondness, but he does not remain confined within its circle. Rather, when Pilar comes to Cuba, he translates for her his various languages and the private experiences they represent: "I talk and talk to my cousin Pilar late at night on the beach. I tell her about Mom's devotions, about the summer of coconuts and how we'd spoken in green. I tell her about my Russian teacher, Mr. Mikoyan, and what the boys at school said, and about the time I saw my father with the black-masked whore, his sex hard with purple veins. I tell her about Mom's funeral, and how the colors all melted together like on summer days, and the radio on Abuela's doorstep addressed to me. I tell her about the Wolfman. I didn't know I had so much to say" (228). In other words, Ivanito ultimately rejects his mother's world of collapsed differences and meanings, of the unspoken and the language of pure identity. It is his narrative voice that criticizes his sisters for their failure to move beyond private language. For the twins Luz and Milagro, we might say, the possibilities of cross-cultural understanding, even in the imperfect forms created by translation, are impossible: "Pilar has tried to talk to the twins, but they answer her in monosyllables. Their world is a tight sealed box. Luz and Milagro are afraid of letting anyone inside.

They're afraid of Pilar's curiosity as if it were a stick of dynamite that could blow apart their lives" (229). At the end of the novel we learn that Ivanito's career ambition is to be a "translator for world leaders" (230), and that he leaves Cuba on the Mariel boatlift; that is, he dedicates his life to the creation of understanding across difference.

I have noted in earlier chapters that the ability to distinguish between self and other is essential to subjectivity, and that the loss of this ability often signals madness in women's texts. In this chapter I hope I have extended my point one step further, by arguing that the inability to distinguish between self and other, which characterizes the madwoman figure of the murdering mother, preempts not just individual subjectivity but the building of collective resistance as well. Such resistance depends not only on the awareness of points of similarity but also (perhaps first and foremost) on an acknowledgment of difference. Since an assumption of collective (rather than merely individual) resistance has always grounded any discussion of feminism—from 1970s visions of "sisterhood" which did indeed erase substantive differences to today's more nuanced attempts to forge coalitions across such differences—what my discussion of the madwoman in this chapter has suggested is that madness is not simply personally disabling; it is absolutely antithetical, at a fundamental level, to feminism. Furthermore, if "feminism" is ever to be reformulated so that it includes by definition a concern with multiple categories of oppression and a desire for greater cultural understanding, then perhaps its theorists must begin by discarding forever those models and metaphors that distract us from the goals of collective resistance.

Conclusion:
Toward Transformation

What—to put a new spin on an old question—do feminist scholars *want*? Surely we must be able to agree that the single factor that ties together feminists of widely disparate disciplines and conflicting approaches within disciplines—the single commitment that we (should) all share—is that we are dedicated in our work to somehow improving the lives of "real" women, however indirectly.[1] For if we cannot agree on this basic goal, then we are truly living in an ivory tower, divorced from the world we claim to care about, and talking and writing only to and for ourselves. It strikes me, then, that feminist critics who find madness in women's texts and read it, against the weight of all textual evidence to the contrary, as "empowering" are a little like the advocates of traditional feminist domesticity, such as Phyllis Schlafly, who recommend happy homemaking for other women while pursuing highly successful public careers of their own.[2] Feminist scholars writing about madness are not themselves rejecting the dominant order; they are utterly immersed in it. Every time they write another article or book about the liberatory power of madness, they demonstrate just how fully they themselves can engage in public, rational forms of discourse.

Certainly, madness can be legitimately read as a "rejection" of the social order. But when the social order leaves no alternative but madness, the next logical step is to assert that the social order must be changed.

---

[1] Recognizing that "women" are not a monolithic category, and that improving the lives of some groups of women might not affect, or might actually hurt, the lives of other women, we might clarify our goal further: to improve the lives of all *disempowered* women, proportionally to their disempowerment. This statement does not resolve contradictions and conflicts between disempowered groups, but it does serve as an ideal. *How* to do this is, of course, the subject of feminist scholarship.

[2] See Faludi 239–40.

This has always been the goal of feminism. It is true that the possibilities of doing so are historically conditioned; thus, in periods when women's powers were rigidly circumscribed, the status of madness as "resistance" was proportionally higher. The fewer the possibilities available for *transformation*, the greater the value of sheer negative *resistance*. It is surely no coincidence that "The Yellow Wallpaper" by Charlotte Perkins Gilman and *The Awakening* by Kate Chopin, appearing within less than a decade of each other at the turn of the twentieth century, both depict female protagonists who retreat from a world of insurmountable obstacles into madness and suicide, respectively, nor that, in both cases, the retreat is highly ambiguous. But if our critical practices are founded on the assumption that the world has not substantially changed for women, and as a result of the efforts of women, since 1899, then we are denying real women the claim of *agency*—of the power to act as agents on and in the world—which is so central to feminist studies today. (Ironically, we do this in the name of searching for symbolic "agency" in the texts that we read.) Instead of privileging the retreat into madness, then, let us privilege the forms of agency, and of active creative transformation in all its forms, which women engage in. And in so doing, let us open an imaginative space for women to be able to escape from madness by envisioning themselves as agents.

I close with a brief discussion of a powerful film documentary, *Dialogues with Madwomen*. This documentary contradicts its title by suggesting, like the autobiographical asylum accounts that I discussed in Chapter 1, that "dialogue" comes *after* madness, not during it—that madness itself is inimical to effective self-representation. The film is an interweaving of interviews "after the fact" with women who have been institutionalized. One striking element of the film is the persistent connection, in interview after interview, between madness and abuse. A woman who had suffered from multiple personality disorder, for example, relates how the generation of alternate personalities was a form of self-defense against the sexual abuse and neglect to which she was subjected as a child. A feminist interpretation of this woman's story from the Gilbert and Gubar school might take this information as evidence of the "resistant" powers of madness, and rightly so; through her madness, the woman "resisted" sexual abuse in the only way she could as a child. But then to *privilege* the resistance as anything but a last-ditch effort in the face of despair is to accept the abuse as inevitable and unchangeable.

As one watches the film, it is easy at first to miss its point; one is so overwhelmed by the stories of abuse, racism, and powerlessness. But the film's central message is one of hope, not despair; creation, not madness.[3] All of these women have chosen not only to tell their story but to participate as well in the creative act of its telling. Thus the women are all actors in highly artistic reenactments of the scenes of their madness, and toward the end of the film, the distance between interviewer and interviewee collapses as we realize that one of the former "madwomen" we have been watching is herself the director of the film, Allie Light, whose voice we have heard interviewing the others. The film departs from the traditional "objective" stance of the documentary, in which a situation is reported from the outside, to become a *collective self-representation*, which attempts to convey to others the highly personal experience of madness. The film traces, in other words, a movement from the personal and individual (madness) to the collective, from powerlessness to self-representation. Even as we ought to recognize the internal necessity of madness in response to particular social and historical situations, we fail as feminist critics if we fail to recognize the power and affirmation of *sanity*, and the making of the film itself as an outwardly directed, carefully crafted statement to the world.

[3] I thank Ann Russo for this insight.

Works Cited

Adams, Timothy Dow. *Telling Lies in Modern American Autobiography*. Chapel Hill: University of North Carolina Press, 1990.

Alarcón, Norma. "Chicana Feminism: In the Tracks of 'the' Native Woman." In *Understanding Others: Cultural and Cross-Cultural Studies and the Teaching of Literature*, ed. Joseph Trimmer and Tinny Warnock. Urbana, Ill.: National Council of Teachers of English, 1992.

Anzaldúa, Gloria, ed. *Making Face, Making Soul/Haciendo Caras: Creative and Critical Perspectives by Women of Color*. San Francisco: Aunt Lute, 1990.

Bart, Pauline B., and Diana H. Scully. "The Politics of Hysteria: The Case of the Wandering Womb." In *Gender and Disordered Behavior*, ed. Edith S. Gomberg and Violet Franks. New York: Brunner/Mazel, 1979.

Bassin, Donna, Margaret Honey, and Meryle Mahrer Kaplan, eds. *Representations of Motherhood*. New Haven: Yale University Press, 1994.

Baym, Nina. "The Madwoman and Her Languages: Why I Don't Do Feminist Literary Theory" (1984). Reprinted in *Feminism and American Literary History*. New Brunswick: Rutgers University Press, 1992.

Berger, James. "Ghosts of Liberalism: Morrison's *Beloved* and the Moynihan Report." *PMLA* 111.3 (May 1996): 408–20.

Bernheimer, Charles, and Claire Kahane, eds. *In Dora's Case: Freud—Hysteria—Feminism*. 2d ed. New York: Columbia University Press, 1990.

Billingsley, Andrew. *Climbing Jacob's Ladder: The Enduring Legacy of African-American Families*. New York: Simon & Schuster, 1992.

Bordo, Susan. "Anorexia Nervosa: Psychopathology as the Crystallization of Culture." In *Feminism and Foucault: Reflections on Resistance*, ed. Irene Diamond and Lee Quinby. Boston: Northeastern University Press, 1988.

——. "Feminism, Postmodernism, and Gender-Scepticism." In *Feminism/Postmodernism*, ed. Linda J. Nicholson. New York: Routledge, 1990.

Breines, Wini, and Linda Gordon. "The New Scholarship on Family Violence." *Signs: A Journal of Women in Culture and Society* 8.3 (1983): 490–531.

Brontë, Charlotte. *Jane Eyre* (1847). New York: Bantam Books, 1981.

Bryant, Cedric Gael. "The Orderliness of Disorder: Madness and Evil in Toni Morrison's *Sula*." *Black American Literature Forum* 24.3 (Fall 1990): 731–745.

Bryant, J. A., Jr. "Seeing Double in *The Golden Apples*" (1974). Reprinted in Turner and Harding.

Calisher, Hortense. "The Scream on Fifty-Seventh Street" (1962). Reprinted in *Women and Fiction*, ed. Susan Cahill. New York: New American Library, 1975.

Carlson, Eric T., and Norman Dain. "The Meaning of Moral Insanity." *Bulletin of the History of Medicine* 36.2 (March–April 1962): 130–40.

Carper, Laura. "The Negro Family and the Moynihan Report" (1966). Reprinted in Rainwater and Yancey.

Castillo, Debra. *Talking Back: Toward a Latin American Feminist Literary Criticism*. Ithaca: Cornell University Press, 1992.

Chesler, Phyllis. *Women and Madness*. Garden City, N.Y.: Doubleday, 1972.

Cisneros, Sandra. *Woman Hollering Creek and Other Stories*. New York: Random House, 1991.

Cixous, Hélène, and Catherine Clément. *The Newly Born Woman*. Trans. Betsy Wing. Minneapolis: University of Minnesota Press, 1986.

Claridge, Gordon, Ruth Pryor, and Gwen Watkins. *Sounds from the Bell Jar*. New York: St. Martin's Press, 1990.

Collins, Patricia Hill. "Shifting the Center: Race, Class, and Feminist Theorizing about Motherhood." In Bassin, Honey, and Kaplan.

Cooper, David. *The Death of the Family*. New York: Random House, 1970.

——. *Psychiatry and Anti-Psychiatry* (1967). Excerpted in *Radical Psychology*, ed. Phil Brown. New York: Harper & Row, 1973.

Cornelia. "My Mother Was the Smartest Black Woman in Eden" (1945). Reprinted in *Black Women in Nineteenth-Century American Life*, ed. Bert James Loewenberg and Ruth Bogin. University Park: Pennsylvania State University Press, 1976.

Deckard, Barbara. *The Women's Movement: Political, Socioeconomic, and Psychological Issues*. New York: Harper & Row, 1975.

de Lauretis, Teresa. *Technologies of Gender*. Bloomington: Indiana University Press, 1987.

Demmin, Julia L., and Daniel Curley. "Golden Apples and Silver Apples." In Prenshaw.

Deutsch, Albert. *The Shame of the States*. New York: Harcourt, Brace, 1948.

Dialogues with Madwomen. Directed by Allie Light. Light-Saraf Films. Videocassette. Women Make Movies, 1993.

Dunning, William V. "Post-Modernism and the Construct of the Divisible Self." *British Journal of Aesthetics* 33.2 (April 1993): 132–141.

Eagleton, Terry. *Literary Theory: An Introduction*. Minneapolis: University of Minnesota Press, 1983.

Eakin, Paul John. *Fictions in Autobiography: Studies in the Art of Self-Invention*. Princeton: Princeton University Press, 1985.

Ehrenreich, Barbara, and Deirdre English. *Complaints and Disorders: The Sexual Politics of Sickness*. Old Westbury, N.Y.: Feminist Press, 1974.

Elshtain, Jean Bethke. "The Mothers of the Disappeared: Passion and Protest in Maternal Action." In Bassin, Honey, and Kaplan.

Faludi, Susan. *Backlash: The Undeclared War against American Women*. New York: Crown, 1991.

Feder, Lillian. *Madness in Literature*. Princeton: Princeton University Press, 1980.

Ferguson, Rebecca. "History, Memory, and Language in Toni Morrison's *Beloved*." In *Feminist Criticism: Theory and Practice*, ed. Susan Sellers. New York: Harvester/Wheatsheaf, 1991.

Fishbein, Leslie. "*The Snake Pit* (1948): The Sexist Nature of Sanity." In *Hollywood as Historian: American Film in a Cultural Context*, ed. Peter C. Rollins. Lexington: University Press of Kentucky, 1983.

Foucault, Michel. *Histoire de la folie à l'âge classique* (1961). Trans. Richard Howard, as *Madness and Civilization: A History of Insanity in the Age of Reason*. New York: Vintage Books, 1965.

Friedan, Betty. *The Feminine Mystique*. New York: Dell, 1963.

Friedman, Lenemaha. *Shirley Jackson*. Boston: Twayne Publishers, 1975.

Garcia, Cristina. *Dreaming in Cuban*. New York: Ballantine Books, 1992.

Geller, Jeffrey L., and Maxine Harris, eds. *Women of the Asylum*. New York: Anchor Books, 1994.

Gilbert, Sandra M., and Susan Gubar. *The Madwoman in the Attic: The Woman Writer and the Nineteenth-Century Literary Imagination*. New Haven: Yale University Press, 1979.

Gilmore, Leigh. "The Mark of Autobiography: Postmodernism, Autobiography, and Genre." In *Autobiography and Postmodernism*, ed. Kathleen Ashley, Leigh Gilmore, and Gerald Peters. Amherst: University of Massachusetts Press, 1994.

Glass, James M. *Shattered Selves: Multiple Personality in a Postmodern World*. Ithaca: Cornell University Press, 1993.

González Echevarría, Roberto. "Sisters in Death." Review of *In the Time of the Butterflies*, by Julia Alvarez. *New York Times Book Review*, December 18, 1994, 28.

Goodman, Charlotte Margolis. *Jean Stafford: The Savage Heart*. Austin: University of Texas Press, 1990.

Gordon, Linda. "Why Nineteenth-Century Feminists Did Not Support 'Birth Control' and Twentieth-Century Feminists Do: Feminism, Reproduction, and the Family." In Thorne with Yalom.

Greenberg, Joanne [Green, Hannah, pseud.]. *I Never Promised You a Rose Garden*. New York: Signet Books, 1964.

Gutman, Herbert. *The Black Family in Slavery and Freedom, 1750–1925*. New York: Pantheon Books, 1976.

Halberstam, David. *The Fifties*. New York: Villard Books, 1993.

Hartsock, Nancy. "Foucault on Power: A Theory for Women?" In *Feminism/Postmodernism*, ed. Linda J. Nicholson. New York: Routledge, 1990.

Havemann, Ernest. "The Psychologist's Service." *Life,* January 21, 1957, 84–102.

— —. "Where Does Psychology Go from Here?" *Life,* February 4, 1957, 68–88.

Henderson, Mae Gwendolyn. "Speaking in Tongues: Dialogics, Dialectics, and the Black Woman Writer's Literary Tradition" (1991). Reprinted in *Feminists Theorize the Political*, ed. Judith Butler and Joan W. Scott. New York: Routledge, 1992.

——. "Toni Morrison's *Beloved*: Re-Membering the Body as Historical Text." In *Comparative American Identities: Race, Sex, and Nationality in the Modern Text*, ed. Hortense J. Spillers. New York: Routledge, 1991.

Henriques, Julian, et al. *Changing the Subject: Psychology, Social Regulation, and Subjectivity*. New York: Methuen, 1984.

Hill, Robert B. *Research on the African-American Family: A Holistic Perspective*. Westport, Conn. Auburn House, 1993.

Hirsch, Marianne. *The Mother/Daughter Plot: Narrative, Psychoanalysis, Feminism*. Bloomington: Indiana University Press, 1989.

hooks, bell. *Ain't I a Woman: Black Women and Feminism*. Boston: South End Press, 1981.

Hulbert, Ann. *The Interior Castle: The Art and Life of Jean Stafford*. New York: Knopf, 1992.

Jackson, Shirley. *The Bird's Nest* (1954). Reprinted in *The Magic of Shirley Jackson*, ed. Stanley Edgar Hyman. New York: Farrar, Straus and Giroux, 1965.

James, Stanlie M. "Mothering: A Possible Black Feminist Link to Social Transformation?" In *Theorizing Black Feminisms: The Visionary Pragmatism of Black Women*, ed. Stanlie M. James and Abena P. A. Busia. London: Routledge, 1994.

Jardine, Alice, and Hester Eisenstein, eds. *The Future of Difference*. Boston: G. K. Hall, 1980.

Jefferson, Lara. *These Are My Sisters* (1947). Garden City, N.Y.: Anchor Press/Doubleday, 1974.

Jones, Ann Rosalind. "Writing the Body: Toward an Understanding of *l'Écriture Féminine*." In *The New Feminist Criticism: Essays on Women, Literature, and Theory*, ed. Elaine Showalter. New York: Pantheon Books, 1985.

Kahane, Claire. "Introduction: Part Two." In Bernheimer and Kahane.

Kanellos, Nicolas, ed. *Hispanic American Literature*. New York: HarperCollins, 1995.

Kaysen, Susanna. *Girl, Interrupted*. New York: Vintage Books, 1993.

Kerr, Elizabeth M. "The World of Eudora Welty's Women." In Prenshaw.

Kesey, Ken. *One Flew over the Cuckoo's Nest*. New York: Signet, 1962.

"A Kiss in the Dark." Review of *The Three Faces of Eve* [film]. *New Yorker*, October 5, 1957, 134.

Kramer, Peter D. *Listening to Prozac*. New York: Penguin Books, 1993.

Lacan, Jacques. "The Mirror Stage as Formative of the Function of the I as Revealed in Psychoanalytic Experience." Trans. Alan Sheridan. In *Critical Theory since 1965*, ed. Hazard Adams and Leroy Searle. Tallahassee: Florida State University Press, 1986.

Laing, R. D. *The Divided Self* (1959). Baltimore: Penguin Books, 1973.

——. *The Politics of Experience* (1967). New York: Ballantine Books, 1970.

Laing, R. D., and A. Esterson. *Sanity, Madness, and the Family*. New York: Penguin Books, 1964.

Leonard, Garry M. " 'The Woman Is Perfected. Her Dead Body Wears the

Smile of Accomplishment': Sylvia Plath and *Mademoiselle Magazine.*" *College Literature* 19.2 (June 1992): 60–82.

Leonard, Linda Schierse. *Meeting the Madwoman: An Inner Challenge for Feminine Spirit.* New York: Bantam Books, 1993.

Levine, Murray. *The History and Politics of Community Mental Health.* New York: Oxford University Press, 1981.

Leys, Ruth. "The Real Miss Beauchamp: Gender and the Subject of Imitation." In *Feminists Theorize the Political,* ed. Judith Butler and Joan W. Scott. New York: Routledge, 1992.

Lizzie [film]. Review. *Time,* March 25, 1957, 106–9.

Lundberg, Ferdinand, and Marynia F. Farnham. *Modern Woman: The Lost Sex.* New York: Harper & Brothers, 1947.

Maddocks, Melvin. "A Vacuum Abhorred." *Christian Science Monitor,* April 15, 1971, 11.

Makward, Christiane. "To Be or Not to Be . . . a Feminist Speaker." In Jardine and Eisenstein.

Matthews, Glenna. *"Just a Housewife": The Rise and Fall of Domesticity in America.* New York: Oxford University Press, 1987.

Maudsley, Henry. *Body and Mind.* London: Macmillan, 1973.

McDowell, Deborah. "Boundaries: Or Distant Relations and Close Kin." In *Afro-American Literary Study in the 1990s,* ed. Houston A. Baker, Jr., and Patricia Redmond. Chicago: University of Chicago Press, 1989.

——. "Reading Family Matters." In *Changing Our Own Words: Essays on Criticism, Theory, and Writing by Black Women,* ed. Cheryl A. Wall. New Brunswick: Rutgers University Press, 1989.

McHaney, Thomas L. "Eudora Welty and the Multitudinous Golden Apples" (1973). Reprinted in Turner and Harding.

Millett, Kate. *The Loony-Bin Trip.* New York: Simon and Schuster, 1990.

Mitchell, Juliet. *Psychoanalysis and Feminism.* New York: Vintage Books, 1975.

——. *Woman's Estate* (1971). New York: Vintage Books, 1973.

Moi, Toril. "Representation of Patriarchy: Sexuality and Epistemology in Freud's Dora." In Bernheimer and Kahane.

——. *Sexual/Textual Politics: Feminist Literary Theory.* New York: Routledge, 1985.

Moraga, Cherríe. "La Güera." In *This Bridge Called My Back,* ed. Cherríe Moraga and Gloria Anzaldúa. Latham, N.Y.: Kitchen Table/Women of Color Press, 1983.

Morrison, Toni. *Beloved* (1987). New York: Plume, 1988.

——. *The Bluest Eye* (1970). New York: Pocket Books, 1972.

——. "Memory, Creation, and Writing." *Thought* 59.235 (December 1984): 385–90.

——. *Sula* (1973). New York: Bantam Books, 1975.

——. "Unspeakable Things Unspoken: The Afro-American Presence in American Literature." *Michigan Quarterly Review* 28 (Winter 1989): 1–34.

Moynihan, Daniel P. *The Negro Family: The Case for National Action* (1965). Reprinted in Rainwater and Yancey.

Mullen, Harryette. "Runaway Tongue: Resistant Orality in *Uncle Tom's Cabin, Our Nig, Incidents in the Life of a Slave Girl,* and *Beloved.*" In *The Culture of Sentiment: Race, Gender, and Sentimentality in Nineteenth-Century America,* ed. Shirley Samuels. New York: Oxford University Press, 1992.

National Women's Studies Association. "NSWA '95 Call for Papers." WMST-L (Women's Studies Listserv) electronic bulletin board posting, October 8, 1994.

Naylor, Gloria, and Toni Morrison. "A Conversation." *Southern Review* 21 (1985): 567–593.

O'Hara, J. D. "An American Dream Girl" (1971). Reprinted in Wagner.

Ohmann, Richard. "The Shaping of a Canon: U.S. Fiction, 1960–75." *Critical Inquiry* 10.1 (1983): 199–223.

O'Neill, William. *American High: The Years of Confidence, 1945–60.* New York: Macmillan, 1986.

Oppenheimer, Judy. *Private Demons: The Life of Shirley Jackson.* New York: G. P. Putnam's Sons, 1988.

Phillips, Robert L., Jr. "A Structural Approach to Myth in the Fiction of Eudora Welty." In Prenshaw.

Pitavy-Souques, Daniele. "Technique as Myth: The Structure of *The Golden Apples.*" In Prenshaw.

Plath, Sylvia. *The Bell Jar* (1963). New York: Bantam Books, 1971.

Pleck, Joseph H. "Sex Role Issues in Clinical Training." *Psychotherapy: Theory, Research and Practice* 13.1 (Spring 1976): 17–19.

Prenshaw, Peggy Whitman, ed. *Eudora Welty: Critical Essays.* Jackson: University Press of Mississippi, 1979.

Prichard, James Cowles. *A Treatise on Insanity and Other Disorders Affecting the Mind.* London: Sherwood, Gilbert, and Piper, 1835.

Prince, Morton. *The Dissociation of a Personality* (1905). New York: Johnson Reprint Corporation, 1968.

"Psychiatry and Spiritual Healing." *The Atlantic* 194 (August 1954): 39–43.

Rainwater, Lee, and William L. Yancey, eds. *The Moynihan Report and the Politics of Controversy.* Cambridge: MIT Press, 1967.

Rawick, George P. *From Sundown to Sunup: The Making of the Black Community.* Westport, Conn.: Greenwood Publishing Company, 1972.

Rhys, Jean. *Wide Sargasso Sea* (1966). New York: Norton Paperback, 1982.

Rigney, Barbara Hill. *Madness and Sexual Politics in the Feminist Novel: Studies in Brontë, Woolf, Lessing, and Atwood.* Madison: University of Wisconsin Press, 1978.

Rose, Jacqueline. *Sexuality in the Field of Vision.* London: Verso, 1986.

Rushdy, Ashraf H. A. "Daughters Signifyin(g) History: The Example of Toni Morrison's *Beloved.*" *American Literature* 64.3 (September 1992): 567–97.

———. " 'Rememory': Primal Scenes and Constructions in Toni Morrison's Novels." *Contemporary Literature* 31.3 (Fall 1990): 300–323.

Ryan, Maureen. *Innocence and Estrangement in the Fiction of Jean Stafford.* Baton Rouge: Louisiana State University Press, 1987.

Scheff, Thomas J. "Schizophrenia as Ideology" (1970). Reprinted in *Radical Psychology,* ed. Phil Brown. New York: Harper & Row, 1973.

Schmidt, Peter. *The Heart of the Story: Eudora Welty's Short Fiction*. Jackson: University Press of Mississippi, 1991.

Showalter, Elaine. *The Female Malady: Women, Madness, and English Culture, 1830–1980*. New York: Penguin Books, 1985.

Silver, James W. *Mississippi: The Closed Society*. New York: Harcourt, Brace & World, 1963.

Sizemore, Chris Costner, and Elen Sain Pittillo. *I'm Eve*. Garden City, N.Y.: Doubleday, 1977.

Skaggs, Merrill Maguire. "Morgana's Apples and Pears." In Prenshaw.

Smith, Barbara. "Toward a Black Feminist Criticism" (1977). Reprinted in *The New Feminist Criticism*, ed. Elaine Showalter. New York: Pantheon Books, 1985.

Smith, Stan. "Attitudes Counterfeiting Life: The Irony of Artifice in Sylvia Plath's *The Bell Jar*." In *Sylvia Plath: Modern Critical Views*, ed. Harold Bloom. New York: Chelsea House Publishers, 1989.

Smith-Rosenberg, Carroll. *Disorderly Conduct: Visions of Gender in Victorian America*. New York: Oxford University Press, 1986.

Snodgrass, Kathleen. *The Fiction of Hortense Calisher*. Newark: University of Delaware Press, 1993.

Stafford, Jean. "Beatrice Trueblood's Story" (1955). In *The Collected Stories*. New York: Farrar, Straus and Giroux, 1969.

Staley, Thomas F. "Jean Rhys." In *British Novelists, 1890–1929: Modernists*, ed. Thomas F. Staley. Dictionary of Literary Biography 36. Detroit: Gale, 1985.

Staples, Robert, and Leanor Boulin Johnson. *Black Families at the Crossroads: Challenges and Prospects*. San Francisco: Jossey-Bass Publishers, 1993.

Szasz, Thomas. *The Manufacture of Madness*. New York: Dell, 1970.

———. *The Myth of Mental Illness*. New York: Harper & Row, 1961.

Taylor, W. S., and Mabel F. Martin. "Multiple Personality." *Journal of Abnormal and Social Psychology* 39 (1944): 281–300.

Thigpen, Corbett H., and Hervey M. Cleckley. *The Three Faces of Eve*. New York: Popular Library, 1957.

Thorne, Barrie. "Feminism and the Family: Two Decades of Thought." In Thorne with Yalom.

Thorne, Barrie, with Marilyn Yalom, eds. *Rethinking the Family: Some Feminist Questions*. 2d ed. Boston: Northeastern University Press, 1992.

Thurer, Shari L. *The Myths of Motherhood: How Culture Reinvents the Good Mother*. Boston: Houghton Mifflin, 1994.

Torgovnick, Marianna. *Gone Primitive: Savage Intellects, Modern Lives*. Chicago: University of Chicago Press, 1990.

Turner, Darwin T. "Theme, Characterization, and Style in the Works of Toni Morrison." In *Black Women Writers (1950–1980): A Critical Evaluation*, ed. Mari Evans. Garden City, N.Y.: Anchor Press/Doubleday, 1984.

Turner, W. Craig, and Lee Emling Harding, eds. *Critical Essays on Eudora Welty*. Boston: G. K. Hall & Co., 1989.

Ussher, Jane. *Women's Madness: Misogyny or Mental Illness?* Amherst: University of Massachusetts Press, 1992.

Viramontes, Helena María. "The Cariboo Cafe." In *The Moths and Other Stories* (1985). Houston: Arte Público Press, 1995.

———. " 'Nopalitos': The Making of Fiction" (1989). Reprinted in Anzaldúa.

Wagner, Linda W., ed. *Sylvia Plath: The Critical Heritage*. New York: Routledge, 1988.

Wagner-Martin, Linda. *The Bell Jar: A Novel of the Fifties*. New York: Twayne Publishers, 1992.

Wall, Stephen. Review of *The Bell Jar* (1966). Reprinted in Wagner.

Wallace, Michelle. "Variations on Negation and the Heresy of Black Feminist Creativity." In *Reading Black, Reading Feminist: A Critical Anthology*, ed. Henry Louis Gates. New York: Meridian, 1990.

Ward, Mary Jane. *The Snake Pit*. New York: Random House, 1946.

Warren, Carol A. B. *Madwives: Schizophrenic Women in the 1950s*. New Brunswick: Rutgers University Press, 1987.

Welty, Eudora. *The Golden Apples*. New York: Harcourt, Brace and Company, 1949.

"Why Do Mothers Kill Their Children?" *USA Today (Magazine)* (December 1996): 16.

"Why Parents Kill." *Newsweek*, November 14, 1994, 31.

Wilkes, Kathleen. "Multiple Personality and Personal Identity." *British Journal for the Philosophy of Science* 32.4 (December 1981): 331–48.

Willis, Susan. *Specifying: Black Women Writing the American Experience*. Madison: University of Wisconsin Press, 1987.

Wilt, Judith. "Black Maternity: 'A Need for Someone to Want the Black Baby to Live.' " In *Abortion, Choice, and Contemporary Fiction: The Armageddon of the Maternal Instinct*. Chicago: University of Chicago Press, 1990.

Wolfe, Ellen. *Aftershock: The Story of a Psychotic Episode*. New York: G. P. Putnam's Sons, 1969.

W[olff], G[eoffrey]. "*The Bell Jar*." Review (1971). Reprinted in Wagner.

Wong, Sau-ling Cynthia. "Autobiography as Guided Chinatown Tour? Maxine Hong Kingston's *The Woman Warrior* and the Chinese American Autobiographical Controversy." In *Multicultural Autobiography: American Lives*, ed. James Robert Payne. Knoxville: University of Tennessee Press, 1992.

Wurtzel, Elizabeth. *Prozac Nation: Young and Depressed in America*. Boston: Houghton Mifflin, 1994.

Wyatt, Jean. "Giving Body to the Word: The Maternal Symbolic in Toni Morrison's *Beloved*." *PMLA* 108.3 (May 1993): 476.

Yaeger, Patricia. *Honey-Mad Women: Emancipatory Strategies in Women's Writing*. New York: Columbia University Press, 1988.

Yalom, Marilyn. *Maternity, Mortality, and the Literature of Madness*. University Park: Pennsylvania State University Press, 1985.

Yarbro-Bejarano, Yvonne. "Introduction." In Viramontes, *The Moths and Other Stories*.

Zinn, Maxine Baca, et al. "The Costs of Exclusionary Practices in Women's Studies" (1986). Reprinted in Anzaldúa.

Index

Aboulia, 118
Aftershock (Wolfe), 10, 19
Agency: multiple personality in terms of, 119–23
Alarcón, Norma, 161
Anorexia nervosa, 3
Antipsychiatry movement, 8–9, 22, 53, 82–83, 126
Artist, the, in Welty's fiction, 64–65
Awakening, The (Chopin), 181

Bart, Pauline, 70
"Beatrice Trueblood's Story" (Stafford), 10, 54, 68, 72–82
Bell Jar, The (Plath): as autobiographical novel, 19–20; experience with electroshock treatment, 22–23, 29; inability to read or write, 42–43; metaphor of the bell jar in, 47, 50; portrayal of madness, 46–47; protagonist's subjective experience, 40; treatment of lesbianism in, 28–29
Beloved (Morrison): Beloved as figure of madness, 155–58; Denver's deafness, 155; depiction of family in, 131, 156–58; embodiment in, 156; mother as murderer in, 169, 176; portrayal of madness in, 11; remembering through storytelling, 154–57; Sethe's self-imposed isolation, 176; slavery as subject in, 131–32, 150–53
Billingsley, Andrew, 130
Bird's Nest, The (Jackson), 10, 96; moral dichotomy in, 106, 108–9, 121; naming and namelessness in, 120–25. See also Multiple personality

Bluest Eye, The (Morrison): Cholly's self-hatred and powerlessness, 143–44; Claudia's representation of her father, 141–42; depiction of family pathology in, 134–35, 138–45; dismemberment as metaphor, 154; embodiment in, 156; Pauline's obsession for ordering in, 136–37; Pecola's pregnancy and madness in, 132, 135, 138–39; portrayal of madness in, 11; racism in, 139–45; representations of masculinity in, 140–43; representations of pathology in, 135; self-hatred in, 137; Soaphead's representation of power, 142–43
Bordo, Susan, 3, 117, 124
Brontë, Charlotte, 1, 3–5, 12–17. See also *Jane Eyre*
Bryant, Cedric Gael, 135–37, 145, 148

Calisher, Hortense, 10, 54–55. See also "Scream on Fifty-Seventh Street, The"
"Cariboo Cafe, The" (Viramontes): community of sufferers in, 165–66; family disruption and oppression in, 160–62, 172; la Llorona in, 165–66, 169; mother's attempt to kill child, 11
Carper, Laura, 131
Castillo, Debra, 166–67, 173
Chesler, Phyllis, 21, 33–34. See also *Women and Madness*
Chopin, Kate, 181. See also *Awakening, The*
Cixous, Hélène, 1–3, 12, 71, 78
Cleckley, Hervey M., 10, 96, 98, 101, 106–13, 116. See also *Three Faces of Eve, The*
Clément, Catherine, 3, 71, 78

Community: in *The Bluest Eye*, 135;
community of sufferers in "The Cariboo
Cafe," 165–66; created by madness in
"The Scream ...," 90–93; defined in "The
Scream ...," 83–90; in "June Recital" and
The Golden Apples, 57–68; perceptions
of in *The Bluest Eye*, 140–41;
production of madness by, 93; role in
"Beatrice Trueblood's Story," 72–82;
Sethe's isolation from in *Beloved* , 149;
storytelling as communal history or
collective memory (Morrison), 154–56;
Sula's challenge to, 145–49; women
silenced by, 93
Cooper, David, 126
Cultural distance: representation in
Dreaming in Cuban, 177–78

Deckard, Barbara, 8–9
de Lauretis, Teresa, 4, 10, 11, 57–58, 72,
102–3, 109, 137
Deutsch, Albert, 5, 21, 53. *See also Shame
of the States, The*
Dialogues with Madwomen, 181–82
Dichotomy, moral: in *The Bird's Nest*,
106, 108–9, 121; in *The Three Faces of
Eve*, 106–8
Differences, as reason for exclusion in *The
Golden Apples*, 63
Disappearance, in "The Cariboo Cafe,"
168
Dismemberment: in *Beloved*, 150–51,
156; in *The Bluest Eye*, 134–35,
154
Dissociation of a Personality, The (Prince),
101, 103, 113–18
Divided Self, The (Laing), 89, 93
Dreaming in Cuban (Garcia): Felicia's
identification with her son, 176; levels
of translation in, 177; mother's attempt
to kill her child, 11, 175–76; private
language in, 174–78

Eagleton, Terry, 125
Electroshock treatment: in *The Bell Jar*,
29–31; experiences of women writers,
22–23; in *The Female Malady*, 29–30;
feminist criticism of, 29–30

Family: African Americans under slavery,
127; in "The Cariboo Cafe," 160–62;
depicted in *Beloved*, 131, 156–58;
depicted in *Sula*, 145–49; depiction of
pathology in *The Bluest Eye*, 134–35,
138–45; nuclear family in feminist
thinking, 126; pathology described in

Moynihan report, 128–31, 156;
perception in second-wave feminism,
127; revised conception in feminist
thinking, 126; Viramontes's
construction of, 159–62
Farnham, Marynia, 53–54, 58. *See also
Modern Woman: The Lost Sex*
Female Malady, The (Showalter), 29–30
Feminine Mystique, The (Friedan), 52–53
Femininity: association of madness with,
11; in "Beatrice Trueblood's Story,"
72–82; hysteria connected to, 69; of Miss
Eckhart in *The Golden Apples*, 63–66;
in multiple personality, 103, 109–10;
rhetoric of moral dichotomy in postwar
construction of, 106
Feminism: different perceptions of family,
126–27; forms of treatment of mentally
ill in theories of, 32; lesbianism as, 28
Feminism, second-wave: conception of
family in, 127–28; conception of mother
in, 162
Ferguson, Rebecca, 133
Foucault, Michel, 22; analysis of modern
madness by, 52; on self-regulation,
84–85. *See also Madness and
Civilization*
Friedan, Betty, 21, 52–53. *See also
Feminine Mystique, The*

Garcia, Cristina, 11, 174–78. *See also
Dreaming in Cuban*
Geller, Jeffrey L., 21. *See also Women of
the Asylum*
Gender: construction and destruction in
"Beatrice Trueblood's Story," 72–82;
criteria of normalcy based on ideology
of, 114; madness as technology of, 114;
postwar rearrangement of roles, 96,
98–99
Gilbert, Sandra, 1, 2, 5. *See also
Madwoman in the Attic, The*
Gilman, Charlotte Perkins, 4, 181. *See also
"Yellow Wallpaper, The"*
Girl, Interrupted (Kaysen), 10, 19–20;
asylum treatment described in, 36–37;
author's personal perspective, 27–28;
failure in communication, 40; model of
madness in, 40
Glass, James, 98, 100
Golden Apples, The (Welty): functions of
myth in, 55–63; portrait of Miss Eckhart
in, 58–65; violence to women in stories
of, 62–63
Gordon, Linda, 126
Greenberg, Joanne, 19–20, 31, 37–38,

49–50. *See also I Never Promised You a Rose Garden*
Gubar, Susan, 1, 2, 5. *See also Madwoman in the Attic, The*
Gutman, Herbert, 127–28, 153, 156–57

Harris, Maxine, 21. *See also Women of the Asylum*
Hartsock, Nancy, 100
Havemann, Ernest, 6
Henderson, Mae Gwendolyn, 2, 133, 158
HERmione (H.D.), 4
Hill, Robert B., 130
Hirsch, Marianne, 164
hooks, bell, 129
Hysteria: characteristics of hysterical patients, 71; connected to femininity, 69–70; as female protest, 3; feminist argument, 71; Freud's interpretation of women's, 70–72; link to stereotypical feminine image, 70; Stafford's representation in "Beatrice Trueblood's Story," 69, 72–82

Identity: in "The Cariboo Cafe," 160–61, 167–70; to have a sense of, 117; perception of multiple personality of, 119; questioned by widow in "The Scream," 83–96; as viewed by person with multiple personality, 98–101; in *Wide Sargasso Sea*, 14–15. *See also* Naming; Self; Subjectivity
I Never Promised You a Rose Garden (Greenberg): as autobiographical novel, 19–20, 31; differentiation between greater and lesser sanity, 37–38; madness portrayed in, 49–50
Institutionalization, forced (Millett), 43–46
Interaction, social: breakdown in "The Scream ...," 83–93

Jackson, Shirley, 10, 96. *See also Bird's Nest, The*
James, Stanlie M., 162–63
Jane Eyre (Brontë), 1, 3–5, 12–17
Jefferson, Lara, 10, 19, 31–32. *See also These Are My Sisters*
Johnson, Leanor B., 130
"June Recital" (Welty), 10, 11, 54, 56–68

Kahane, Claire, 71
Kaysen, Susanna, 10, 19–20, 35, 37, 40, 50. *See also Girl, Interrupted*

Kesey, Ken, 31. *See also One Flew Over the Cuckoo's Nest*
Kramer, Peter, 32–33, 38, 48. *See also Listening to Prozac*
Kristeva, Julia, 2, 133

Labeling theory, 8
Laing, R. D.: on developing a sense of identity, 89–90; on madness, 8; model of mental illness, 85, 92–93. *See also Divided Self, The; Politics of Experience, The*
Lesbianism: equated with feminism, 28; labeled as madness, 28
Levine, Murray, 5, 6
Leys, Ruth, 100–103, 118, 125
Linguistic failure. *See* Speech
Listening to Prozac (Kramer), 32–33, 38–39
Llorona, la, 165–66, 169
Loony-Bin Trip, The (Millett), 10, 20; asylum narrative in, 23–24; author's personal encounter with madness and depression, 43–45; lesbianism labeled as mental illness in, 28–29
Lundberg, Ferdinand, 53–54, 58. *See also Modern Woman: The Lost Sex*

Maddocks, Melvin, 46
Madness: alternative solution to in Welty's symbolism, 93–94; American narratives of, 17; antipsychiatry view of, 128; association with femininity, 11; of Bertha in *Jane Eyre*, 1, 3–4, 16–17; connected to race and ethnicity, 10–11; connected with manlessness, 54–55; depicted in *Beloved*, 151; evaluation in *The Snake Pit*, 40–43; explanations in postwar climate, 53; Foucault's analysis of modern, 52, 84–85; Laing's analysis in social context, 82–83; lesbianism seen as, 28; as metaphor, 2; Millett's definition of, 43–46; of Miss Eckhart in *The Golden Apples*, 65–66; model of in *Girl, Interrupted*, 40; Morrison's depiction in *The Bluest Eye*, 132–35, 138; Morrison's depiction in *Sula*, 135–36; in Morrison's fiction, 11, 132, 135–37; 1960s theories of, 8; portayal in *I Never Promised You a Rose Garden*, 49–50; portrayal in *The Bell Jar*, 46–50; purposes served by representations of, 52; seen by women writers as final surrender, 11–12; in Stafford's fiction, 68–69; as technology of gender, 114; in "The Scream on Fifty-Seventh Street,"

Madness (*continued*)
83–93; treatment by feminist theorists
and critics, 1–4; wandering as in *The
Golden Apples,* 56–57; in *Wide
Sargasso Sea,* 16–17
Madness and Civilization (Foucault), 22
Madwoman in the Attic, The (Gilbert and
Gubar), 1, 2, 5
Makward, Christiane, 2
Manliness: defined in "Beatrice
Trueblood's Story," 75, 77; depicted in
The Bird's Nest, 104–5
Matthews, Glenna, 96
Maudsley, Henry, 5
McDowell, Deborah, 130, 145, 170
Mental health reform movement, 5–8, 21
Mental illness: accounts in late twentieth
century of, 20–21; labeling theory on
diagnosis of, 8; Laing's search for
causes of, 82–83; models of Laing and
Esterson, 85, 92–93; in postwar
American culture, 95–96; post–World
War II issues of, 5–9, 95; women's
responsibility for (Lundberg and
Farnham), 53–54. *See also* Madness;
Multiple personality
Millett, Kate, 10, 20, 23–24, 43–46. *See also
Loony-Bin Trip, The*
Mirror stage, Lacanian, 119
Mitchell, Juliet, 127
Mitchell, S. Weir, 69
Modern Woman: The Lost Sex (Lundberg
and Farnham), 53–54
Moi, Toril, 66, 71, 122–23
Moraga, Cherríe, 163
Moral dilemma: of psychiatrist in *The
Bird's Nest,* 11, 104–6, 108–14; of
psychiatrist in *The Three Faces of Eve,*
106–8
Morrison, Toni, 11, 131–32, 135–45,
154–58, 164, 169–71, 176. *See also
Beloved; Bluest Eye, The; Sula*
Mother: within African American
community, 162–63; in "The Cariboo
Cafe," 171; as murderer in *Sula* and
Beloved, 164–66, 171–72; role in second-
wave feminist thought, 162–63
Moynihan, Daniel Patrick, 128–31, 137–38.
See also Negro Family, The
Mullen, Harryette, 2, 132–33
Multiple personality: in *The Bird's Nest,*
103–6, 116–25; constructed by
psychiatric discourse, 109; as failure of
identity, 101; Morton's text on, 101;
postmodern perspective, 98, 100;
postwar representations of, 96–99;

Prince's explanation of, 113–14; as
subject of fiction, film, and case study,
95; in *The Three Faces of Eve,* 96, 98,
106–13
Myths: in *The Golden Apples,* 55–63,
67–68; of King MacLain in *The Golden
Apples,* 55–58; of Miss Eckhart in *The
Golden Apples,* 58–63, 67–68

Namelessness, in multiple personality,
120
Naming, in *The Bird's Nest,* 120–25
Negro Family, The (Moynihan), 128–31,
137–38

O'Hara, J. D., 46
Ohmann, Richard, 20–21
One Flew Over the Cuckoo's Nest
(Kesey), 31

Patterson, Orlando, 127–28
Plath, Sylvia, 19, 22–23. *See also Bell Jar,
The*
Politics of Experience, The (Laing), 8,
33
Prince, Morton, 101, 103, 113–18, 125. *See
also Dissociation of a Personality, The*
Prozac Nation (Wurtzel), 10, 19–20
Psychiatrist: depicted in *The Bell Jar,* 40;
depicted in *The Snake Pit,* 24–25, 39–40;
in *I Never Promised You a Rose
Garden,* 37–38, 49–50; moral dilemma
in *The Bird's Nest,* 104–6, 108–14; moral
dilemma in *The Three Faces of Eve,*
106–8

Racism: in *The Bluest Eye,* 142–44; in *The
Golden Apples,* 62–63; powerlessness of
(Morrison), 142–44; trauma of
(Morrison), 139
Rawick, George, 131
Representations: in *Beloved,* 149; of
hysteria in "Beatrice Trueblood's
Story," 72–82; Morrison's challenge to
dominant, 135, 137–38
Rhys, Jean, 12–17. *See also Wide Sargasso
Sea*
Rose, Jacqueline, 100–101
Rushdy, Ashraf, 146, 147, 152, 154–55
Ryan, Maureen, 68–69

Schmidt, Peter, 55, 59, 64
"Scream on Fifty-Seventh Street, The"
(Calisher), 10, 54, 83–93
Scully, Diana, 70
Self: misrecognition of in multiple

personality, 117–23; in Morrison's novels, 147–49; self-destruction in *Beloved*, 151; self-hatred in *The Bluest Eye*, 137; self-monitoring in "The Scream on Fifty-Seventh Street," 84–88; substitution of for another, 117, 119
Sexuality: in *The Bird's Nest*, 104–5; in "June Recital," 58–60; in *The Three Faces ...*, 107–8. *See also* Lesbianism
Sexual Politics (Millett), 44
Sexual/Textual Politics (Moi), 122–23
Shame of the States, The (Deutsch), 5, 21
Showalter, Elaine, 3, 22, 23, 28–30, 34n7, 42, 71. *See also Female Malady, The*
"Shower of Gold" (Welty), 61
Sizemore, Chris Costner, 108, 116, 125
Slavery: African American family under, 127–28; Moynihan's idea of pathology related to, 129–31; Rochester's rejection of in *Jane Eyre*, 15–16; as subject in *Beloved*, 131–32, 150–54
Smith, Barbara, 145
Smith-Rosenberg, Carroll, 3, 69
Snake Pit, The (Ward), 10; ability to grasp meaning, 41–42; asylum treatment described in, 35–36, 38; as autobiographical novel, 19–22; concern with asylum reform, 21–22; erroneous judgments of protagonist, 38–41; madness narrative in, 24–26; patient's memory, 38; purpose of film entitled, 21
Speech: disintegration of in multiple personality, 119–23; linguistic failure of mentally ill patients, 41–42, 48; problems of multiple personality with, 117–19; slavery as means to silence, 132; as social act in "The Scream ...," 91–92; speaking subject, 122–23
Stafford, Jean, 10, 54–55. *See also* "Beatrice Trueblood's Story"
Staples, Robert, 130
Subjectivity: in *The Bird's Nest*, 117–23; in *Girl, Interrupted*, 27–28; limited nature of, 124; in *Wide Sargasso Sea*, 14–15
Sula (Morrison): dismemberment in, 150; mothers as murderers in, 164, 169–71; Shadrack's madness in, 11, 135–36; Sula's challenge to community, 145–49
Szasz, Thomas, 53

These Are My Sisters (Jefferson), 10, 19, 31; author's description of her mad self, 38; imaginings of illness, 41; signs of return to health, 42
Thigpen, Corbett H., 10, 96, 98, 101,

106–13, 116. *See also Three Faces of Eve, The*
Thorne, Barrie, 126, 128
Three Faces of Eve, The (Thigpen and Cleckley), 10, 96, 98, 101, 106–13, 116
Torgovnick, Marianna, 139

Ussher, Jane, 60

Violence to women, in *The Golden Apples*, 62, 67
Viramontes, Helena María, 11. *See also* "Cariboo Cafe, The"

Wagner-Martin, Linda, 26
Wallace, Michele, 135, 138
"Wanderers, The" (Welty), 57, 66
Ward, Mary Jane, 19–26, 35–36, 38–43. *See also Snake Pit, The*
Welty, Eudora, 10, 11, 54–55; *The Golden Apples*, 55–68; wanderers in fiction of, 56–57, 65–67
Wide Sargasso Sea (Rhys), 12, 13–16
Widowhood, in "The Scream on Fifty-Seventh Street," 83–93
Wilkes, Kathleen, 115n3
Will, in multiple personality, 118
Willis, Susan, 145–46, 169–70
Wilt, Judith, 164
Wolfe, Ellen, 10, 19, 23, 47
Wolff, Geoffrey, 46
Women: African American women as source of family pathology, 128–30, 139–40; challenge to silencing of speech of African American, 133; depicted in cases of multiple personality, 95–100; hysteria as mode of expression, 69–70; reconfiguration of postwar roles, 96, 98–99; responsibility for their mental illness (Lundberg and Farnham), 53–54; silenced by the community, 93; unmarried woman depicted in *The Golden Apples*, 56–68. *See also* Violence to women
Women and Madness (Chesler), 21, 29, 33–34
Women of the Asylum (Geller and Harris), 21
Wurtzel, Elizabeth, 10, 19–20, 47, 48–49. *See also Prozac Nation*
Wyatt, Jean, 156, 172, 173

Yalom, Marilyn, 21

"Yellow Wallpaper, The" (Gilman), 4, 181

Reading Women Writing

A SERIES EDITED BY

Shari Benstock
Celeste Schenck

Tainted Souls and Painted Faces: The Rhetoric of Fallenness in Victorian Culture
by Amanda Anderson
Greatness Engendered: George Eliot and Virginia Woolf
by Alison Booth
Talking Back: Toward a Latin American Feminist Literary Criticism
by Debra A. Castillo
Articulate Silences: Hisaye Yamamoto, Maxine Hong Kingston, and Joy Kogawa
by King-Kok Cheung
H.D.'s Freudian Poetics: Psychoanalysis in Translation
by Dianne Chisholm
From Mastery to Analysis: Theories of Gender in Psychoanalytic Feminism
by Patricia Elliot
Feminist Theory, Women's Writing
by Laurie A. Finke
Colette and the Fantom Subject of Autobiography
by Jerry Aline Flieger
Autobiographics: A Feminist Theory of Women's Self-Representation
by Leigh Gilmore
Going Public: Women and Publishing in Early Modern France
edited by Elizabeth C. Goldsmith and Dena Goodman
Cartesian Women: Versions and Subversions of Rational Discourse in the Old Regime
by Erica Harth
Borderwork: Feminist Engagements with Comparative Literature
edited by Margaret R. Higonnet
*Narrative Transvestism: Rhetoric and Gender in
the Eighteenth-Century English Novel*
by Madeleine Kahn
The Unspeakable Mother: Forbidden Discourse in Jean Rhys and H.D.
by Deborah Kelly Kloepfer
*Recasting Autobiography: Women's Counterfictions in
Contemporary German Literature and Film*
by Barbara Kosta
Women and Romance: The Consolations of Gender in the English Novel
by Laurie Langbauer
Nobody's Angels: Middle-Class Women and Domestic Ideology in Victorian Culture
by Elizabeth Langland

Penelope Voyages: Women and Travel in the British Literary Traditions
by Karen R. Lawrence
Autobiographical Voices: Race, Gender, Self-Portraiture
by Françoise Lionnet
Postcolonial Representations: Women, Literature, Identity
by Françoise Lionnet
Woman and Modernity: The (Life)styles of Lou Andreas-Salomé
by Biddy Martin
In the Name of Love: Women, Masochism, and the Gothic
by Michelle A. Massé
Imperialism at Home: Race and Victorian Women's Fiction
by Susan Meyer
*Outside the Pale: Cultural Exclusion, Gender Difference, and
the Victorian Woman Writer*
by Elsie B. Michie
Dwelling in Possibility: Women Poets and Critics on Poetry
edited by Yopie Prins and Maeera Shreiber
Reading Gertrude Stein: Body, Text, Gnosis
by Lisa Ruddick
Conceived by Liberty: Maternal Figures and Nineteenth-Century American Literature
by Stephanie A. Smith
Kassandra and the Censors: Greek Poetry since 1967
by Karen Van Dyck
Beyond Consolation: Death, Sexuality, and the Changing Shapes of Elegy
by Melissa F. Zeiger
Feminist Conversations: Fuller, Emerson, and the Play of Reading
by Christina Zwarg

Caminero-Santangelo, Marta, 1966–
   The madwoman can't speak: or why insanity is not subversive /
Marta Caminero-Santangelo.
      p.   cm. — (Reading women writing series)
   Includes index.
   ISBN 0-8014-3514-5 (cloth : alk. paper). — ISBN 0-8014-8514-2
(paper : alk. paper)
      1. American fiction—Women authors—History and criticism.
2. Literature and mental illness—United States—History—20th century.
3. Feminism and literature—United States—History—20th century.   4. Women
and literature—United States—History—20th century.   5. American fiction—20th
century—History and criticism.   6. Mentally ill women in literature.   7. Social
norms in literature.   I. Title.   II. Series: Reading women writing.
PS374.M44C36   1998
813'.5409353—dc21

                                                                    98-4027

"*The Madwoman Can't Speak* is one of the most interesting works I've read in some time. It boldly takes on a number of tropes and beliefs that have marked the history of feminist criticism for decades. The notion that madness is subversive and a route to power is rightfully challenged with in-depth readings of key texts."
—Linda Wagner-Martin, University of North Carolina, Chapel Hill

She's out of the attic.

In this provocative work, the subversive madwoman so privileged by feminist theorists and critics emerges from her confinement into the world of real social power. How, Marta Caminero-Santangelo asks, can such a figure be subversive if she's effectively imprisoned, silent and unseen? Taking issue with a prominent strand of current feminist literary criticism, Caminero-Santangelo identifies a counternarrative in writing by women in the last half-century, one that rejects madness, even as a symbolic resolution.

Caminero-Santangelo considers such writers as Toni Morrison, Eudora Welty, Sylvia Plath, Cristina Garcia, Kate Millett, Helena Maria Viramontes, and Shirley Jackson, locating their narratives of female madness within the context of popularized Freudianism, sociology of "the" African American family, images in the mass media, and other elements of culture to which their writings respond. Their works, Caminero-Santangelo maintains, appropriate images linking madness to feminine aberrance, but do so to expose the regulatory functions that such images serve. These writings reveal how the silent protest emblematized by the madwoman, and celebrated in feminist critical practice, simply serves to lock women into stereotypes long used to oppress them.

The Madwoman Can't Speak offers an alternative explanation for the compelling nature of the figure of the madwoman, allowing a critical move away from the dangerous, ultimately disempowering notions of the subversive potential of madness.

MARTA CAMINERO-SANTANGELO is Assistant Professor of English at the University of Kansas.

Reading
WOMEN
Writing

Cornell Paperbacks
Cornell University Press

ISBN 0-8014-8514-2

90000

9 780801 485145